C000015846

Intimate Politics

Contemporary Political Communication

Robert M. Entman, *Scandal and Silence*

Max McCombs, R. Lance Holbert, Spiro Kiousis and Wayne Wanta, *The News and Public Opinion*

Craig Allen Smith, *Presidential Campaign Communication*

James Stanyer, *Intimate Politics*

Intimate Politics

Publicity, Privacy and the Personal Lives of Politicians in Media-Saturated Democracies

James Stanyer

polity

Copyright © James Stanyer 2013

The right of James Stanyer to be identified as Author of this Work has been asserted in accordance with the UK Copyright, Designs and Patents Act 1988.

First published in 2013 by Polity Press

Polity Press
65 Bridge Street
Cambridge CB2 1UR, UK

Polity Press
350 Main Street
Malden, MA 02148, USA

All rights reserved. Except for the quotation of short passages for the purpose of criticism and review, no part of this publication may be reproduced, stored in a retrieval system, or transmitted, in any form or by any means, electronic, mechanical, photocopying, recording or otherwise, without the prior permission of the publisher.

ISBN-13: 978-0-7456-4476-9
ISBN-13: 978-0-7456-4477-6 (pb)

A catalogue record for this book is available from the British Library.

Typeset in 11 on 13 pt Sabon
by Servis Filmsetting Ltd, Stockport, Cheshire
Printed and bound in Great Britain by the MPG Books Group Limited

The publisher has used its best endeavours to ensure that the URLs for external websites referred to in this book are correct and active at the time of going to press. However, the publisher has no responsibility for the websites and can make no guarantee that a site will remain live or that the content is or will remain appropriate.

Every effort has been made to trace all copyright holders, but if any have been inadvertently overlooked the publisher will be pleased to include any necessary credits in any subsequent reprint or edition.

For further information on Polity, visit our website: www.politybooks.com

Contents

Figures and tables   vi

Acknowledgements   x

Introduction: Politicians' Personal Lives in the Media
Spotlight   1

1 Soft Focus: Leaders' Personal Lives Close-up   32

2 Digging for Dirt: Publicizing Politicians' Sex Lives   73

3 Changing Exposure: Critical Moments and the
   Uncovering of Politicians' Infidelity   101

4 Transnational Revelations: Flows, Access and Control
   in a Global News Environment   130

5 Drawing Conclusions: Intimization and Democratic
   Politics   152

Appendix: Research Notes   171

Notes   189

References   191

Index   213

Figures and tables

Figures
0.1   Political persona and spheres of action   13
0.2   The personal sphere   15
1.1   The appearance of national leaders on television
      entertainment talk shows while in office:
      1990–2009   54
1.2   Yearly average visibility of French Presidents'
      personal lives based on four indicators over their
      period in office   59
1.3   Yearly average visibility of US Presidents' personal
      lives based on four indicators over their period in
      office   60
1.4   Yearly average visibility of UK Prime Ministers'
      personal lives based on four indicators over their
      period in office   61
1.5   Yearly average visibility of Australian Prime Ministers'
      personal lives based on four indicators over their
      period in office   62
1.6   Yearly average visibility of Spanish Prime Ministers'
      personal lives based on four indicators over their
      period in office   63
1.7   Yearly average visibility of Italian Prime Ministers'
      personal lives based on four indicators over their
      period in office   64

Figures and tables

1.8   Yearly average visibility of German Chancellors' personal lives based on four indicators over their period in office   65

3.1   Publicized cases of politicians' infidelity over time: 1970–2009   103

4.1   The number of news items mentioning politicians' infidelity in Australia, the UK and US in *Le Monde*: 1992–2009   134

4.2   The number of news items mentioning politicians' infidelity in Australia, the UK and US in *Taz – die Tageszeitung*: 1992–2009   135

4.3   The number of news items mentioning politicians' infidelity in Australia, the UK and US in *La Stampa*: 1992–2009   136

4.4   The number of news items mentioning politicians' infidelity in Australia, the UK and US in *El País*: 1996–2009   137

5.1   Cluster map showing levels of intimization across seven democracies   153

Tables

0.1   Personal information/imagery typology   16

1.1   Yearly average number of news items mentioning the national leader's spouse on his or her own over a 15-year period: 1995–2009   36

1.2   Yearly average number of news items mentioning the national leader's children over a 15-year period: 1995–2009   37

1.3   Yearly average number of news items mentioning the national leader's holidays over a 15-year period: 1995–2009   41

1.4   Appearance of elected politicians on *Australian Story*   43

1.5   Yearly average number of news items mentioning the national leader's birthdays over a 15-year period: 1995–2009   47

1.6   Yearly average number of news items mentioning
       the national leader's spouse's birthdays over a
       15-year period: 1995–2009   48
1.7   Yearly average number of books focusing on
       national leaders' personal lives while in office:
       1992–2009   55
1.8   Yearly average visibility of national leaders' personal
       lives based on four indicators: 1995–2009   56
1.9   Yearly average visibility of national leaders' personal
       lives based on four indicators by leader   58
1.10   Causal recipes for the visibility of national leaders'
       personal lives   68
1.11   Causal recipes for the lack of visibility of national
       leaders' personal lives – the negation   69
2.1   The number of cases of publicized infidelity
       2000–2009   75
2.2   Causal recipes explaining high levels of publicized
       infidelity   92
2.3   Causal recipes explaining the absence of high levels
       of publicized infidelity – the negation   93
2.4   The number of cases of 'outing' 2000–2009   94
2.5   Causal recipes explaining high levels of outing   98
2.6   Causal recipes explaining the absence of outing –
       the negation   98
3.1   The actual and annual average number of cases of
       publicized infidelity per decade 1970–2009   103
3.2   The use of private investigators by British
       newspapers (top five users of private investigators)   127
4.1   The number of cases of politicians' infidelity in
       Australia, the UK and US reported in French,German,
       Italian and Spanish newspapers (1992–2009)   132
4.2   The number of newspaper news items mentioning
       the rumours of Nicolas Sarkozy and Carla Bruni-
       Sarkozy's extra-marital affairs, in six countries   140
4.3   The number of newspaper news items mentioning
       the Italian Prime Minister Silvio Berlusconi's extra-
       marital trysts, in six countries   140

4.4   Coverage by country of the *Mail on Sunday*
      reporting of Gerhard Schroeder's extra-marital affair
      and of *El País*'s publishing of paparazzi photographs
      of Silvio Berlusconi at the Villa Certosa (number of
      news items mentioning the event)   144
4.5   The number of posts mentioning Noemi Letizia on
      Italian blogs and blogs in other languages   147
4.6   The number of posts mentioning Mara Carfagna on
      Italian blogs and blogs in other languages   149
5.1   Causal recipes explaining the visibility of national
      leaders' personal lives   156
5.2   Causal recipes explaining the levels of publicized
      infidelity   157
6.1   Causal conditions for membership of fuzzy set
      'leaders with highly visible personal lives'   183
6.2   Causal conditions for membership of fuzzy set
      *'democracies with high levels of publicized infidelity
      2000–2009'*   187
6.3   Causal conditions for membership of the fuzzy set
      'democracies with high levels of outing 2000–2009'   188

Acknowledgements

This book would not have been possible without the help of numerous people and institutions. I would like to thank Loughborough University for a series of small grants to undertake some of the necessary research and for providing a semester's leave to work on the book.

A special thank you goes to the team at Polity Press, especially Andrea Drugan for being patient and understanding in the preparation of this manuscript. I would also like to thank my colleagues in the School of Social, Political and Geographical Sciences, the anonymous reviewers of the original book proposal and the finished manuscript, and those who provided comments at conferences and seminars where findings from the book were presented.

I am also indebted to the following people who have all contributed to this book in various ways and to different extents: Freddie Attenborough, Rafaella Bianchi, Hélène Bilger-Street, Jay Blumler, Andrea Burmester, Donatella Campus, María José Canel, Cristopher Cepernich, Andrew Chadwick, John Corner, Jamil Dakhlia, David Deacon, Claes De Vreese, John Downey, Frank Esser, Mike Gane, Peter Golding, Murray Goot, Emily Harmer, Richard Heffernan, Frank Henseler, Michael Higgins, Christina Holtz-Bacha, Oliver James, Bengt Johansson, Emily Keightley, Raymond Kuhn, Ana Langer, Guido Legnante, Philippe Maarek, Paolo Mancini, Gianpetro Mazzolini, Susanne Merkle, Sabina Mihelj, Andreas Muellerleile, Graham Murdock, Ralph Negrine, Rui Novais, Henrik Örnebring, Heather Owen, Barbara Pfetsch,

Acknowledgements

Mike Pickering, Carsten Reinemann, Andy Ruddock, Karen Sanders, Paula Saukko, Tamir Sheafer, Liz Stokoe, John Street, Jesper Strömbäck, Mick Temple, Peter Van Aelst, Liesbet Van Zoonen, Silvio Waisbord, Dominic Wring, Reimar Zeh.

I owe a special debt of gratitude to Fleur for her constant support throughout the time spent writing this book. Any errors are, of course, my own.

Introduction

Politicians' Personal Lives in the Media Spotlight

If you are applying for the presidency of the United States of America, then by definition you have given up your privacy; people are going to want to know what you have done in your life and what you stand for.' (Barack Obama, on the stump in Oregon, the 2008 US presidential campaign, *BBC World at One*, 19 May 2008)

I think people have a right to know a bit about you and your life and your family, what makes you tick, and what informs your thinking. (David Cameron, ITN interview, cited in Winnett & Prince, 2008)

It is often remarked that the personal lives of politicians, like those of sports, film and television stars and hosts of other celebrities, have become a familiar part of the public's daily media consumption. The public, it might be said, know more detail about politicians' personal lives than their policy stance or voting records. Like celebrities in other fields, they have willingly surrendered their privacy, or have been unable to defend it from a celebrity-obsessed media.

Across democracies, academics have observed the increasingly personal nature of political communication (see, for example, Stanyer & Wring, 2004; Van Zoonen, 2005). In many democracies, studies show that politicians are increasingly prepared to disclose aspects of their personal lives. Research by Dakhlia (2010) has documented the 'peopolisation' or celebritization of French politics in the 2000s, a key aspect of which has been personalized self-disclosure. Leading French politicians make regular carefully choreographed appearances on television talk shows and in glossy celebrity magazines (see Chenu, 2008; Dakhlia, 2008, 2010; Neveu, 2005). For example, Errera (2006) found that leading politicians' relationships, personal health, their home and family life, personal financial issues and their past life were very much to the fore in magazine coverage in the 1990s. In the run-up to the 2007 presidential election the Socialist candidate, Ségolène Royal, appeared in her bikini in *Voici*, *Closer* and *VSD* (Dakhlia, 2008). The former President Nicolas Sarkozy exploited his private life for political purposes, openly using his family to bolster his presidential ambitions (Kuhn, 2010, 2011). Indeed, Kuhn notes, the extent to which he exploited his spouse and family was considered groundbreaking in a French context (Kuhn, 2010). His subsequent very public divorce from his second wife, Cécilia, and courtship of and marriage to supermodel and singer Carla Bruni, were conducted very much in the media spotlight. Photo opportunities of the new lovers were staged for the media, and intimate interviews given (Chrisafis, 2007; Kirby, 2010). In the UK, Deacon (2004) observes that Prime Ministers have been quick to use their personal lives as a resource. Tony Blair has frequently disclosed aspects of his private life to the public and might be accused of over-sharing some of the more intimate aspects. For example, in an interview with Tony and Cherie in the *Sun* during the 2005 general election campaign, Tony confessed he was 'up for it' at least five times a night, a point corroborated by Cherie, who, when asked if he was 'up to it', said he always was (Marrin, 2005). There is some evidence of a broader trend; research by Langer shows that coverage of UK Prime Ministers' private lives increased in *The Times* over the post-World War Two period, rising from around 1 per cent of leaders' coverage in 1945 to 8 per cent during Tony Blair's tenure in office, a trend David Cameron has continued (Langer, 2007, 2012).

In the US, personal self-disclosure has become normalized on the presidential campaign trail; indeed, politicians feel that they have to reveal aspects of their personal lives or will be greeted with suspicion. Perloff observes that, 100 years ago, presidential candidates hardly spoke in public; now they 'trip over each other to disclose psychologically correct tidbits from their personal lives' (Perloff, 1998, p. 279). Intimate moments from candidates' personal lives are shared with an audience of unknown others; for example, during the 1992 race for the White House, Al Gore discussed the near-death of his son, while Bill Clinton shared stories of his brother's battles with drug addiction (Perloff, 1998; see also Gamson, 2001; Hart, 1999). In 2004, both candidates for the presidency, and their wives, talked about their families and a range of family-related matters on the *Dr Phil Show*; George W. Bush and Laura Bush were asked openly if they had spanked their children (see Van Zoonen et al., 2007).

In Italy, numerous authors have remarked on the personalized nature of political communication since 1994 and the formation of the Second Republic (Allum & Cilento, 2001; Campus, 2010a; Mancini, 2008, 2011; Paolucci, 2002). Silvio Berlusconi is the most high-profile politician to have used his private life to promote himself to the Italian people. During the 2001 general election campaign, he distributed a *Hello*-style glossy brochure to millions of households; entitled 'An Italian Story' (Una Storia Italiana), the publication featured his family and life story (Campus, 2002). During the 2006 Italian general election campaign, his main rival, Romano Prodi, and his wife released their autobiography. Both Berlusconi and Prodi appeared on a variety of entertainment talk shows where they discussed aspects of their private lives and other matters (Campus, 2006).

Research shows that in Germany, government ministers' personal relationships are more visible than ever before (Holtz-Bacha, 2004). For example, in 2000, the then Defence Minister, Rudolf Scharping, and his new lover granted the popular magazine *Bunte* an exclusive interview in which they spoke openly about their love for each other. The following year they appeared again in *Bunte*, this time on holiday in Majorca (Holtz-Bacha, 2004). In the Netherlands, leading politicians share personal moments and intimate aspects of their lives with the celebrity media, and the demand for such intimate details has increased. Such coverage often focuses on their family life and the tensions that emerge between career and the family (Van Zoonen, 2005). Studies in

Australia show politicians, like celebrities, are increasingly keen to parade their personal lives in the media. They have been quick to use their family lives to enhance their electoral appeal. As a new leader of the Australian Labor Party, Mark Latham used his family to project a family-friendly image to the electorate in 2004 (Muir, 2005b). Australian politicians are also increasingly aware of the importance of non-traditional media in connecting with voters. Shows such as *Australian Story* regularly feature prominent politicians. In 2001, the show went behind the scenes to provide an intimate look at the home life of John Howard, then Prime Minister, and leader of the opposition, Kim Beazley (Bonner & McKay, 2007). Popular celebrity magazines provide another outlet for politicians to parade their personal lives before the voter. Federal Senator Natasha Stott Despoja underwent a fashion makeover for magazine *Cleo* and, during the 1998 general election, Australian Labor Party MP Cheryl Kernot used an appearance in a woman's weekly magazine to pose in a variety of gowns and talk as much about 'her family life' as her 'public prominence' (Turner et al., 2000, p. 135; see also Muir, 2005a).

In some democracies the literature points at the increased proclivity of certain media to intrude into the private lives of politicians (Sabato et al., 2000; Tumber & Waisbord, 2004a, b). The peccadilloes of leading politicians find their way into the press. Bill Clinton's presidency was dogged by a series of allegations and revelations concerning his fidelity. In 1992, while campaigning for office, the supermarket tabloid the *Star* disclosed that he had been unfaithful to his wife (Gronbeck, 1997). After he was elected, there was an almost constant stream of rumours concerning spurned lovers and children out of wedlock, much publicized in the tabloid media. In 1998, sexual revelations, drip-fed through gossip-based websites, published in the press and the *Starr Report*, provided an extremely intimate insight into his extra-marital affair with Monica Lewinsky (Maltese, 2000; West & Orman, 2003). The media digging for and publishing dirt on politicians is now a permanent feature of US politics at all levels, not just the presidency (see Neiwert, 1998; Sabato et al., 2000; Splichal &

Garrison, 2000). For example, court divorce records are now a newsworthy source of personal information that news outlets have been keen to exploit. In 2004, divorcé Jack Ryan withdrew from the contest for the Republican nomination for an Illinois Senate seat after a Californian judge was persuaded by Chicago news outlets to unseal his divorce files, revealing intimate details about his split from actress Jeri Ryan (Chase & Ford, 2004).

In the UK in the 1990s, the Major government was subject to a raft of media revelations about marital infidelity of government ministers and MPs (Parris & Maguire, 2005). One of the most colourful concerned the then Heritage Minister, David Mellor, whose sexual antics in his Chelsea FC football strip and penchant for sucking toes received wide coverage in the tabloid press (Tunstall, 1996). Research by Bob Franklin found that, between 1990 and 1994, sex scandals and misconduct involving politicians were the third most popular subject in press coverage, with almost 10 per cent of the 820 news items examined focusing on it (Franklin, 1997, p. 236). Indeed, the sexual exploits of Tory politicians were even fictionalized, in the 1995 Channel Four-produced *The Politician's Wife*, a drama based loosely on actual events. Since the 1990s, tabloid press intrusion into the private lives of politicians has become normalized (Deacon, 2004). Within a year of winning office, three UK ministers in the coalition government – William Hague, Chris Huhne and David Laws – have been forced to issue public statements about their sex lives when confronted by revelations and rumours in the media.

In democracies where the private lives of politicians have been very much legally protected, certain media outlets seem increasingly eager to publish gossip about public figures, and to challenge existing privacy norms and the ability to control access to their private lives. For example in Finland, in 2006, Finnish Prime Minister Matti Vanhanen's former girl friend Susan Kuronen appeared semi-naked in a gossip magazine, where she suggested that Vanhanen was a boring lover. The following year, she then went on to write the country's first kiss-and-tell memoir, *The PM's Bride*, based on her relationship with Vanhanen, revealing the most intimate details about their relationship (Laine, 2010). The ensuing coverage of the book and attempts to quash its publication dominated the media for months (Juntunen & Valiverronen, 2010; Karvonen, 2009). Other Scandinavian countries, despite strict laws designed to protect the privacy of public figures, have also seen a growth in the media exposure of politicians' private lives (see Allern et al., 2012). In France, Kuhn (2011) notes, that despite strict privacy laws there has been a 'striking' decline in the control politicians exercise over the press in the last decade, especially regarding the Internet. Dakhlia (2010) observes that, over the last decade, celebrity magazines have not shied away from publishing paparazzi pictures of leading politicians in their swim suits, something that would have been unheard of before. Often, recourse to privacy laws does not prevent exposure in an increasingly transnational news environment. For example, in January 2003, lawyers acting for the then German Chancellor, Gerhard Schroeder, tried to stop the British tabloid, *Mail on Sunday*, publishing the rumours about his supposed marital difficulties. The original *Mail on Sunday* allegations were then reprinted in German newspapers, which cited the *Mail on Sunday* as their source (Holtz-Bacha, 2004). In March 2010, rumours emerged on Twitter that Nicolas Sarkozy, then President of France, and his wife, Carla Bruni, were having affairs (Kirby, 2010). While the French press at first hesitated to cover the allegations, the global news interest meant that the story could not be ignored as the President wished, and it was eventually reported in the French media.

These different nationally focused examples, I would argue, cannot be ignored; they point to a potentially significant development in democratic political communications, namely the growing focus on the personal lives of politicians. They suggest that across a range of advanced industrial democracies the personal lives of politicians are no longer a purely private matter but are instead an increasingly ubiquitous feature of the mediated public sphere. The zone of privacy which once surrounded politicians and those in public life seems to be slowly disappearing with and without politicians' consent. These documented incursions of the personal into the public sphere are an indication for some of a public realm that 'no longer has anything to do with civic commitment' and is increasingly colonized by the trivial and inane (Rössler, 2005, p. 170). In other words, the growing flow of personal information about those who govern us has important consequences for the nature of information citizens receive in advanced industrial democracies.

However, while the above examples provide a tantalizing glimpse of recent developments, they are far from conclusive; it is hard to determine whether there is a trend across advanced industrial democracies and difficult to identify the consequences of such developments – in short, more evidence is needed. This book sets out to examine the personalized nature of mediated political communication across a range of advanced industrial democracies. It seeks to tease out developments, drawing on a wide range of primary and secondary sources, assessing the extent to which the personal lives of politicians have become a prominent feature of political communications. The book seeks to comprehend the shifting boundaries between the public and private and whether these developments are indeed universal. This introductory chapter sets the scene for the rest of the book, starting with existing attempts to conceptualize developments and comprehend the wider processes involved.

Conceptualizing developments: personalization or intimization?

While concepts are of primary importance to social science research (see Goertz, 2005; Sartori, 1970), the robustness with which concepts are defined varies. It is sometimes the case that the same concept is defined differently by different authors – in other words, there is a lack of conceptual agreement (see Sartori, 1984). This is particularly the case with the concept of personalization, increasingly used in political science and political communication research (see Van Aelst et al., 2012). For example, one might instinctively think that what the above examples show is evidence of the personalization of politics; after all, they document growing media coverage of politicians' personal lives in different countries.

However, the way the term 'personalization' has often been applied, especially in political communication research, means that matters are not so straightforward. The majority of studies conducted on personalization do not deal with the flows of information and imagery about politicians' private lives (for synoptic accounts, see Adam & Maier, 2010; Karvonen, 2010). Rather, most focus on the visibility of individual politicians, especially party leaders and candidates, compared to political parties or institutions; indeed, Plasser and Lengauer (2008) define it as 'an increasing focus on candidates at the expense of their parties or even policy issues' (2008, p. 257; see also Dalton & Wattenberg, 2000; Kriesi, 2010; Mughan, 2000; Reinemann & Wilke, 2007). Rahat and Sheafer (2007) observe that, in the personalization literature, personalization does not mean the growing disclosure of information about politicians' private lives; in fact, the 'personization' of politics would perhaps be a more accurate description of how the concept is defined. The growing visibility of politicians compared to parties, however important, is only part of the story. The personalization literature, with noted exceptions (see Langer, 2012), overlooks the flow of personal information and imagery. With the concept being operationalized in such a way by numerous studies, the utility of redefining it for the purposes of this book is limited.

If the use of the term 'personalization' is problematic, what other concepts might be used? Several authors make a distinction between personalization (meaning the visibility of politicians) and what they term 'privatization': 'a media focus on the personal characteristics and personal life of individual candidates' (Rahat & Sheafer, 2007, p. 68; see also Holtz-Bacha, 2004, pp. 48–9). While 'privatization' captures the process by which information and imagery about politicians' personal lives enters into the public domain, it is problematic for several reasons. First, it is a word most commonly associated with the sale of state-owned assets to the private sector, which distracts from its explanatory potential. Second, the word in that context has a different meaning: it does not mean making the private public, but the reverse, privatizing of something that is public – the opposite of what is meant in Rahat and Sheafer's or Holtz-Bacha's definition (see Benn & Gaus, 1983, and Weintraub & Kumar, 1997, for a discussion of the term). Third, it has little to say about questions of intrusion and control: for example, on the extent to which the focus on the personal characteristics and personal life of individual candidates is the product of intrusion. While not explicitly acknowledged, the research overwhelmingly focuses on examples which are benign, or at least could not be described as damaging, although we do know from the examination of sex scandals that politicians are not always in control of such flows (see Adut, 2008; Thompson, 2000).

The developments described earlier might be better understood by drawing upon the varied literature that has examined the changing nature of intimacy in contemporary societies. Take for example Sennett's seminal work *The Fall of Public Man*, whose central concern is the emergence of what he terms the 'intimate society' and its consequences. This is a society where the display of personality comes to dominate the public realm and group (class) interests become subordinate to the belief in the innate abilities of the individual. Sennett's concern is how such an ideology emerged in capitalist societies in the nineteenth century and how the public have been seduced by it and have come to accept it and the withering of an impersonal public realm. While his concern is not primarily with changing political communication, he is clear what role the media plays in promoting personality, especially in the political sphere. He argues that television shows a 'compulsive' interest in personality, arousing amongst audiences an interest in the personality of the politicians they see before them (Sennett, 2002[1974], p. 285). Television is crucial to the promotion of personality politics that deflects public interest away from effective public action to questions of personal character; for Sennett, politics becomes something more akin to the Hollywood star system, its function to routinize the selection of charismatic leaders (2002).

Other studies have approached questions of intimacy and communication technology more directly, examining television's ability to create a new form of intimacy. The notion of tele-mediated/

non-reciprocal intimacy gained much attention in the 1950s; as Lang and Lang note, this is not intimacy in the proper sense – there are 'no two way responses and exchange of feelings' – but rather it is illusory: the viewers believe they know what public figures are really like, based on tele-mediated experience (Lang & Lang, 1956, p. 110). Horton and Wohl, in their now-classic 1956 study, observe that the audience comes to see the person on television as directly addressing them. Like the Langs, they note television gives the 'illusion of a face-to-face relationship with the performer'; the audience enjoy what they call a 'para-social relationship' with the person they see before them (Horton & Wohl, 1956, p. 215). They go on to suggest that television enables them to 'know such a persona in the same way they know their chosen friends: through direct observation and interpretation of his appearance, his gestures and voice, his conversation and conduct in a variety of situations' (1956, p. 216). Joshua Meyrowitz, several decades later, in his account of how television has undermined traditional political leadership, observes that television 'brings the politician close for the people's inspection . . . [and] brings a rich range of expressive information to the audience'; it can show politicians perspiring, their facial gestures, intonations and mispronunciations (Meyrowitz, 1985, p. 272). Schickel, similarly, in his 1990s examination of celebrity, observes that 'thanks to television and the rest of the media we know [celebrities]. To a greater or lesser degree we have internalised them, unconsciously made them a part of our consciousness, just as if they were, in fact, friends' (Schickel, 2000, p. 4). They are no longer seen 'from the alienating distance of the stage or the lecture hall, which is where we were forced to view them in the pre-electronic age' (p. 10). He notes 'we are able, over months and years . . . , to learn these faces as we learn those of our best friends and relatives'; we come to know 'their tics, blinks and glances' (p. 11; see also Perloff, 1998). One could even, perhaps, go back further in time to the mechanical reproduction of photographs in the mass-circulation press in the 1880s, which meant that the public would see not only the name and face but also realistic images of political actors, in the course of the daily consumption of media output (Gamson, 1994; Murdock, 2010).

However, any understanding that relates purely to an individual's non-reciprocal, tele-mediated relationships with distant others, thanks to whatever technology, overlooks the nature of the information and imagery to which an audience is exposed. The nature of the information and imagery is important in relation to what audience members know about the actors they see.[1] Take the example of the spouses of national leaders. The high level of mediated visibility of the US First Lady is not recent. Since the early twentieth century, with the rise of photography, mass-circulation media and the moving image, the US First Lady has been visible to the US population at large (Ponder, 1999), a point that could also be made for the wife of the UK Prime Minister (Seymour-Ure, 2003). However, today, partners in the US and UK are not just visible, there is also a lot of personal information about them in the media; for example, we know about their taste in clothes, their relationship, their family histories, etc. (Stanyer, 2007). In other words, not only are public figures and leading politicians more visible and familiar as faces, but more information about their personal life circulates in the mediated public sphere. This latter point has been picked up by other studies: see, for example, Lowenthal's classic study of American celebrity (1961) and Ponce de Leon's (2003). Van Zoonen (1991) develops the concept of 'intimization' in relation to content of television news. She defines it as a process whereby 'values from the private sphere are transferred to the public sphere' (1991, p. 223). Hirdman et al.'s study of changes in Swedish journalism from the 1880s to the present defines intimization as a process which sees increased journalistic attention on the family, sexuality and the private – what they term the 'intimate sphere' as opposed to the public sphere (Hirdman et al., 2005, p. 109).

Intimization in the context of this book relates primarily to media content formation and dissemination and should not be conflated with non-reciprocal or tele-mediated intimacy (see Horton & Wohl, 1956; Thompson, 1995). That said, it should be noted such a concern with media content does not negate audience relations to it but merely emphasizes the importance of the nature of information and images which audiences consume. Further, it is not a technologically centred process; the driving force of change is not assumed to be new communication technology but a combination of economic, political and social factors – as will be illustrated later. Implicit in the notion of intimization is that it is a temporal process, if you like: that the indicators of intimization become more visible, more pervasive in national mediated public spheres over time; this can also be seen in Hirdman et al.'s study of Swedish media. Of course, intimization might be connected with other temporal processes, for example, the rise of the personalization of politics, as classically defined, or the celebritization of politics (see Dakhlia, 2010; Gamson, 1994; Ruddock, 2010; Street, 2004). As politicians become more visible, or political celebrities emerge, their personal lives may become more discussed but it might well be possible to have the greater visibility of politicians without an increased flow of information about their personal lives; Rahat and Sheafer (2007) clearly show this is the case. This is not say that the way intimization has currently been understood is problem-free, but I think it has significant potential in helping make sense of current developments in the political communication environment highlighted at the start of this chapter. The next section seeks to flesh out a fuller definition of intimization.

Defining intimization

A good starting point in defining intimization is Corner's model of the spheres or arenas in which politicians operate. Corner (2003) observes that elected officials operate in three different but overlapping spheres. The first is the sphere of 'political institutions and processes': this is the world of party organizations, legislatures and government. Second is the 'private sphere': this includes all private aspects of a politician's life from biography to familial relations. The final sphere is the 'sphere of the public and popular': it is the mediated space in which politics takes place and politicians perform; it is, in his words, 'the stage where, for instance, politicians develop reputations, draw varying levels of support, are judged as good or bad, undergo meteoric or steady advance-

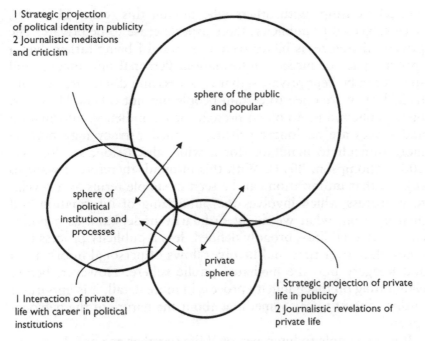

1 Strategic projection
of political identity in publicity
2 Journalistic mediations
and criticism

sphere of the public
and popular

sphere of
political
institutions and
processes

private
sphere

1 Interaction of private
life with career in political
institutions

1 Strategic projection of private
life in publicity
2 Journalistic revelations of
private life

Figure 0.1 Political persona and spheres of action

Source: Corner, 2003. Reprinted by permission of SAGE publications, London,
Los Angeles, New Delhi and Singapore.

ment, decline, resign or are sacked' (Corner, 2003, p. 74). Corner identifies a range of flows of information from the institutional and private spheres into the sphere of the public and the popular (see figure 0.1). Information continually circulates between these spheres. In this context, intimization refers specifically to the flow of information and imagery between the private sphere and the mediated public sphere.

However, caution needs to be exercised in how the term 'private' is used. What Corner defines as the private sphere (see also Bauman, 2011, 'private realm'; Thompson, 1995, 'private domain'), I would argue, is better comprehended as the personal sphere. The personal sphere can be understood to be all aspects of a politician's personal life, including information about the politician as an individual, his or her living spaces and domestic life and relationships with others who inhabit this realm. However, once subjected to publicity, these aspects cease to be private. The private, therefore, is better seen as a state of being rather than a specific space or piece of information. Personal information and spaces can be kept private – that is, access and disclosure are controlled, they are open to certain people but not others. However, once publicized to a non-co-present media audience, information and spaces are no longer private, or their privacy may become more difficult to maintain (for a wider discussion, see Rössler, 2005; Thompson, 2011). With this in mind, therefore, I want to suggest that intimization can be seen in simple terms as a revelatory process which involves the publicizing of information and imagery from what we might ordinarily understand as a politician's personal life – broadly defined. It is a publicity process that takes place over time and involves flows of personal information and imagery into the mediated public sphere. However, before elaborating on this publicity process in more detail, it is important in this context to say something about the nature of the personal sphere.

It is too simple to lump personal life together as one – I want to develop a more nuanced understanding of the personal sphere. The personal sphere is not simply a back region as defined by Goffman (1971[1959]): it consists of three overlapping parts or domains (others have suggested two; see Rawlins, 1998, and Van Zoonen, 1998). The *first* domain concerns what I term the inner life of a politician. This includes, for example, his or her health, well being, sexuality, personal finances, deeds, misdeeds, key milestones (such as birthdays), life experiences and achievements, but also choices about the way an individual wants to live his or her life: for example, life-style choices, ways of behaving, choice of religion or questions of taste. The *second* domain concerns significant others in a politician's personal life and his or her relationship with these actors. This includes relationships with partners, other immediate and extended family members, friends and extra-marital lovers. The *third* domain concerns an individual's life space: this includes his or her home but it also includes happenings in locations outside the home where the individual is not performing a public

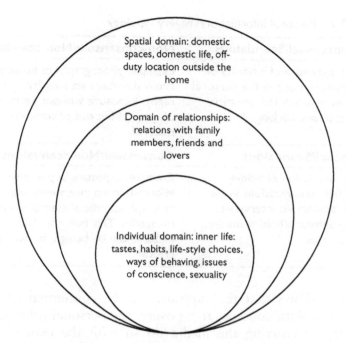

Figure 0.2 The personal sphere

function and might want privacy, such as on family holidays (see figure 0.2). I want to suggest that intimization consists of the publicizing of information and imagery from these three domains: in other words, exposure of information and imagery about the politician as a person; the public scrutiny of personal relationships and family life; and the opening up of personal living spaces or spaces a politician might reasonably expect to be private from the public gaze. Of course such personal exposure is not limited to politicians but can be seen in relation to other public figures, including celebrities and royalty.

The nature of information and imagery and its publicity

It is important at this point to say something about the nature of the information on, and imagery of, politicians' personal lives that flows into the mediated public sphere and how it is publicized.

Table 0.1   Personal information/imagery typology

Non-consensual/Scandalous	Non-consensual/Non-scandalous
Example: exposure of infidelity or other transgressions in the personal domain via kiss-and-tell; unofficial memoirs; phone hacking.	Example: photographs of holidays and family members via long-lens photography. Exposure without permission of actor(s) but not of scandalous material.
Consensual/Scandalous	**Consensual/Non-scandalous**
Example: admission of infidelity or other transgressions in the personal domain via interviews; autobiographies; official memoirs; documentaries.	Example: exposure of personal information via interviews; (auto) biographies; official memoirs; documentaries. This non-scandalous material can be benign, laudatory or critical.

Table 0.1 shows that the exposure can be consensual or non-consensual. With consensual exposure, the personal information and imagery entering the media do so with the expressed or implied consent of those they feature. An example might be an act of self-disclosure on a talk show or in an autobiography which is then recycled in the media. It is the exposure of the personal life that politicians might expect as part of being in the public eye, but is not the product of unwarranted intrusion into areas of the personal domain. With non-consensual exposure, personal information and imagery enter the media *without* expressed or implied consent. Examples might include paparazzi photographs of politicians backstage or off-duty, taken without the subject's permission, phone hacking, a kiss-and-tell exclusive or some other breach of confidentiality. Non-consensual exposure is an unwarranted intrusion into areas of the personal domain that politicians want to remain private.

Table 0.1 also shows that information and imagery disclosed can either be scandalous in nature (it reveals a transgression of societal norms in a politician's personal life) or non-scandalous. While the former includes information that might have the potential to damage a politician's reputation, career or personal relations, the latter includes all information and imagery from a politician's personal life that can largely be considered benign, although they may sometimes be critical or laudatory. This does not mean that such information and imagery are of a single type – they can relate to any of the domains of the personal sphere as highlighted in figure 0.2.

Intimization can involve, for example, both the flows of non-scandalous personal information and imagery consensually co-disclosed in the media, and scandalous information and imagery gathered and publicized in the public realm without a politician's consent. However, in different democracies, such flows might be weighted towards the former or the latter due to numerous factors.

What drives intimization?

While it is important to document the nature of the information on politicians' personal lives, it is crucial to identify the factors enabling or inhibiting the intimization process. Intimization is not the result of one factor, such as communication technology, but the outcome of a complex interplay of a range of factors. One of the shortcomings of both Meyrowitz (1985) and Schickel (2000) is that these studies place too much emphasis on the power of television. To imply that this alone is responsible for intimization of political communication is to ignore the other variables that might contribute. When thinking about causes of intimization, we need to consider the numerous factors that potentially might contribute to publicizing the personal lives of politicians. These include a mix of macro and micro variables which may work in combination to produce an outcome (see Adam & Maier, 2010). At a micro level, we need to take account of the various political actors in any political communication system. Perhaps most obviously there are the politicians themselves, who routinely self-disclose, or might be expected to self-disclose, aspects of their personal lives or seek to expose elements of their opponents' personal lives that might damage their chance of being elected or re-elected. Politicians, therefore, selectively disclose information in order to ensure non-co-present others form an appropriate positive or negative impression (see Stanyer, 2008). In addition, information and imagery may originate from actors who know the politician personally – for example, family members or significant others, such as, for example, a jilted lover. Finally, there are actors in the public sphere who might take an interest in a politician's personal life: the police, investigatory magistrates and other judicial and quasi-judicial actors, and journalists and media actors. These agents together ask questions, package and disseminate information and imagery, and recycle them.

In media-saturated democracies, this information and imagery come to public attention through a myriad of media outlets and via different media genres. The presence and/or absence of different outlets and genres might be influential in determining the nature of information and imagery that reach the mediated public sphere. Media interviews are now a well-established means through which politicians talk about themselves; in many democracies, interviews on entertainment talk shows or in glossy magazines have become a routine part of a campaign (Just et al., 1996; Van Zoonen, 1998). In addition, politicians' personal lives feature in documentaries and books, which in turn often receive coverage in the wider news media, and also via media investigations; the tabloid or boulevard press is often at the forefront of coverage of the personal lives of public figures. In other words, a media system which sees a flourishing of such outlets and genres might well provide greater opportunities for personal disclosure.

Acts of self-disclosure may also reflect politicians' needs to ensure electoral support in a political environment where they can no longer rely on the loyalties of voters, and voters often make electoral choices based on personal factors (Clarke et al., 2004; Corner & Pels, 2003). In such situations, politicians need to develop new ways of building and maintaining support. Developing a personal connection with the electorate might be one of several means open to them. Further, the nature of the political system might well incentivize personal disclosure. In presidential democracies where the national leader is directly elected, candidates for high office may need to make personal disclosures to a greater extent than in a parliamentary system, where voters choose a party or parties to govern.

The normative environment governing what it is acceptable or permissible for politicians to reveal about themselves may also play a role. Politicians, like other public figures, are embedded in a culture where talking about their personal lives, however intensely intimate, is no longer seen as inappropriate but, rather, is normalized, even expected, in some countries (Adut, 2008; Solove, 2007). If we take Calvert's thesis, politicians are embedded in a culture that is increasingly voyeuristic, a culture which is dominated by 'the consumption of revealing images of and information about others' (Calvert, 2000, p. 2). People's personal space and private lives are laid bare through an endless series of highly popular programmes, articles and websites (2000). Reality TV shows, such as *Big Brother*, talk shows, docu-soaps, in addition to tabloid newspapers/magazines and Internet sites such as YouTube, provide a constant stream of personal imagery and information that allows the public to gaze upon the lives of their fellow citizens as well as a cast of celebrities. Robin Anderson, commenting on the US, notes: 'almost no boundaries exist between what can and cannot be said in public, no revelation, confession, or disclosure is so personal that it cannot be exposed'. He continues, 'In this atmosphere of total exposure, no secrets are allowed' (cited in Calvert, 2000, p. 82). For Furedi, politicians inhabit a world where strong pressures exist on the individual to display emotions in public, and distrust is expressed towards to those who want to keep their feelings private, especially those in public life. Furedi notes that, implicit in the value system of this 'therapeutic culture', is a disapproval of the right to privacy (2004). It is a culture which applauds the 'open display of emotions' at the same time as ridiculing self-control as 'a dishonest attempt to cover up pathologies' (Furedi, 2004, p. 66; see also Nolan, 1998). For Parry-Giles and Parry-Giles (2002), politicians, subject to the gaze of the citizen, manufacture an 'illusory intimacy' which maintains viewer attention (p. 25). The politicians are compelled to open up any personal space as they seek to 'maximize their intimacy with the voter' (p. 25). The weight of expectations might mean that politicians, especially leading political actors, have to reveal a lot about their personal lives, and not to do so, as Adut suggests, might be interpreted as being 'stuck-up or suspicious' (Adut, 2008, p. 209; see also Hart, 1999). Politicians as public figures cannot escape these cultural forces, even if they might wish to. They have to appeal to a public using the grammar and style of a 'voyeur culture' or a 'therapeutic culture', but also be subject to others' investigations and claims. They seek to assert control over what is disclosed but their ability to control is aided or hindered by a range of factors. A key aspect of the intimization process is the ability of politicians to manage disclosure in the face of changing societal normative expectations and intrusion, and the extent to which politicians are able to control intrusion or are victims of it.

Non-consensual exposure may also be incentivized by different elements in the political and media systems. In the US, for example, personal morality has been placed on the political agenda by the Christian right, mainly in the Republican Party (Williams, 2010). This in turn has led opponents in the press and politics to expose those that espouse such a moral position in public but fail to live up to those high standards in their personal lives. In some countries the moral behaviour of politicians is becoming increasingly part of the competitive struggle for power (Davis, 2006; Lowi, 2004).

Tabloid press, in many democracies locked in a circulation battle, might seek to expose the peccadilloes of a leading politician to boost their circulation temporarily as well as damage the political prospects of that politician, if they are opposed to him or her. Indeed, the exposure may need to be seen against the background of a media industry which, in part, financially incentivizes exposure, in some cases by paying for 'kiss-and-tell' exclusives or illicitly taken photographs, or turning a blind eye to questionable practices by journalists making covert use of surveillance technologies such as concealed tape recorders and cameras (Phillips et al., 2009). There is also a growing global secondary-media industry, which is financially dependent on exposing the private lives of public figures, including politicians (Kurtz, 2009;

Thompson, 2000). The changing media environment might reflect a wider change in the conventions on privacy. Thomas Nagel (2002), reflecting on the Clinton–Lewinsky affair, notes that there has been a change in the conventions on reticence and privacy in American society. He observes that the 'sexual taboos of a generation ago . . . had the salutary effect of protecting persons in the public eye from invasions of privacy by the mainstream media' (p. 3). These taboos, which 'meant that the sex lives of politicians were rightly treated as irrelevant', no longer have any force (p. 3). Today, the media and the public, he continues, feel 'entitled to know the most intimate details of the life of any public figure, as if it is part of the price of fame' (p. 3). In other words, the invasions of privacy are a side effect of vanishing taboos surrounding public discussion about sex (Nagel, 2002).

However, those factors that incentivize non-consensual exposure need to be weighed against potential brakes on its development. Politicians, like others in public life, seek to guard those elements of their personal life they are not prepared to disclose. Their ability to do so is shaped by numerous factors, not least the law. Many European states provide legal protection for public figures' privacy; there may also be a widespread tacit respect amongst media professionals for such boundaries, and this might find its way into professional codes of conduct. It is intrusion into parts of the personal sphere that a politician wants to remain private which has the greatest potential to generate conflict. Such intrusion might be due to misunderstandings between actors, second parties may unwittingly reveal information, but it might be deliberate and it is these incursions that generate most conflict. Such intrusion maybe justified on a number of grounds, including public interest, but this may have no impact on the conflict that emerges. The length to which politicians are prepared to go to defend their privacy also differs and may vary from verbal criticism to full-blown legal action. Many complain about intrusion: in the UK, Tony Blair, when Prime Minister, regularly complained to the Press Complaints Commission about press coverage of his children; some politicians make use of libel laws. Of course, as this book will explore further, intrusion is perhaps more likely in countries where boundaries have no legal recognition and exposure is incentivized politically or economically.

The presence or absence of the publicizing of personal lives therefore is the result of a complex chain of enabling and retarding factors. Although far from exhaustive, this section has identified some of those micro and macro variables and how they potentially might work together and what the consequences might be.

Critical events

While identifying the underlying causal conditions is crucial, we should not overlook the importance of major incidents or crises in explaining change. Major events can have a dramatic impact on media and political systems, bringing about significant change in their wake. There is a growing interest in the social sciences in the idea of critical junctures (see Mahoney, 2001). Critical junctures in simple terms can be seen as 'trigger events that set processes of institutional or policy change in motion' (Hogan & Doyle, 2007, p. 885). Critical junctures are often seen as crises leading up to the point of change (2007). When thinking about causes of intimization, we need to consider not only the mix of macro and micro variables which work in combination to produce an outcome but also possible critical junctures within the historical timeline of any democracy. For example, several studies point to events that altered journalistic attitudes to politicians' infidelity destroying a 'gentleman's agreement' that marked political reporting in the US (Splichal & Garrison, 2000). Ross argues that reticence in reporting extra-marital sex lives of politicians came to an end in the US in 1969 when Ted Kennedy drove his Oldsmobile off Dike Bridge at Chappaquiddick, leaving his passenger, Mary Jo Kopechne, to drown. This, Ross argues, triggered a re-examination of the extra-marital sex lives of the other Kennedy brothers (1988, p. 193). Summers suggests that the reticence of US journalists finally ended with the Clinton–Lewinsky scandal. He observes that, for a good deal of the twentieth century there was reluctance to expose personal malfeasance, this reticence has now vanished and the muckraking and mudslinging which characterized early

US politics have emerged once more (2007[2000]). Splichal and Garrison point to several events, arguing that the death of journalistic reticence began with revelations about the Kennedy brothers' extra-marital antics, became more contentious with Vietnam and finally broke down with the Gary Hart exposé (see also Schudson, 1995). While there is no consensus as to which incidents mark the point of change, there is agreement that events in themselves might mark a point of change.

Intimization in cross-national context

Based on the examples from different countries highlighted at the start of this chapter, one might be persuaded to conclude that intimization now occurs to the same extent across democracies, and that all politicians are equally willing to invite the cameras into their homes, or media outlets in different countries equally willing to intrude into the private lives of politicians. However, despite these examples, national differences persist, sometimes significantly so. In many advanced industrial democracies there is still a reticence amongst journalists about exposing the private lives of politicians or publishing unsubstantiated allegations or paparazzi photographs (see national studies by Chalaby, 2004; Esser & Hartung, 2004; Rahat & Sheafer, 2007; Sanders & Canel, 2004). This rectitude is often underpinned by privacy laws and norms in the wider society. The therapeutic culture highlighted by Furedi is by no means universal. Based on the secondary literature, it might be assumed that there is a 'cluster of countries' (see Castles & Obinger, 2008) where the boundaries between public and private are more fluid and a cluster of countries where the boundaries are less so, but assumptions require empirical underpinning.

Of course, such a state of affairs is not static, as mentioned at the start; studies suggest that the zone of privacy around politicians is also shrinking in democracies where they have traditionally enjoyed greater privacy protection (Dakhlia, 2010). There are laws and other constraining factors which, if not preventing its appearance, may limit the way a therapeutic culture develops.

For example, one could argue that the increasingly global nature of media markets and technology may conspire to place limits on the national constraints of privacy laws, but what these limits are is unknown. It could be argued, with some evidence, that, while privacy legislation makes some difference, these differences may be made irrelevant by the spread of a tabloid journalistic culture, a competitive media industry, the global flow and ubiquity of information and images and their easy access over the Internet, but we do not know the extent of these processes.

National political fields are not sealed from global mediated news and, increasingly, politicians and their activities are filtered through it. Politicians, while protected at home, may be exposed to the full glare of the media elsewhere. As noted, the London-based *Mail on Sunday* reported Chancellor Schroeder's marital difficulties before the German press felt able to do so (Deacon, 2004). The Internet has eroded the control once exercised by political elites over the dissemination of information. Private indiscretions by public figures can, and are, being publicized online: news of President Clinton's affair with Monica Lewinsky first appeared on maverick journalist Matt Drudge's website (Hayden, 2002; Shepard, 1998).

What emerges, therefore, is a complex picture. Intimization might well be an uneven process that reveals tensions and is transnational in scope, one that ebbs and flows over time. What is required is a cross-national longitudinal study of developments that explores the flow of benign and potentially embarrassing or damaging personal information and imagery. It is a process that needs to be identified and mapped across democracies to determine what trends there are (for a discussion of the importance of comparative research see Davis, 2010; Gurevitch & Blumler, 2004; Norris, 2009).

Capturing intimization in comparative context: challenges and responses

This book follows in the long tradition of so-called 'small-N' comparative research. One of the key benefits of small-N comparative research is that it enables a greater in-depth exploration of each country, one that is more sensitive to the historical, cultural and political nuances of each case, all of which are important for developing a 'fine-grained contextually sensitive analysis' (Brady et al., 2010, p. 22). Increasing the N, so to speak, might be desirable for some scholars, but in addition to logistical problems it risks an untenable level of generality and loss of contextual knowledge (see Brady et al., 2010 for a discussion). This book examines seven countries – an ideal number given the need for fine-grained contextually sensitive analysis and the time-scale and available budget. Several factors shaped the selection of cases. The first factor was my expectations of the level of intimization derived from the existing secondary literature. Based on this one might expect, for instance, that the exposure of politicians' personal lives would be highest in the US and lower in other democracies – after all, the connection between politics and the world of celebrity has a longer history there than in other democracies (see Gronbeck, 1997; Ponder, 1999; West & Orman, 2003). However, intimization might be a feature of presidential democracies generally and absent elsewhere. For example, Adam and Maier suggest, personalization might be more evident in countries where the national leader is a directly elected, visible figurehead, compared to where he or she shares power with cabinet colleagues (Adam & Maier, 2010). In France, as noted, President Sarkozy flagrantly used his personal life to bolster his presidential ambitions. That said, intimization may also be found in other countries where there is a strong two-party system that places the focus on party leaders, rather than in multiparty systems where media focus is more diffused (2010). The UK witnessed growing levels of personalization especially with the election of Tony Blair (Langer, 2012). One might also suppose that the exposure of politicians' personal lives is more evident in countries that have witnessed a greater weakening of party affiliation and increase of personal voting than in countries where such trends are less evident (Dalton & Wattenberg, 2000). That said, one might also assume that intimization might be more of a feature in countries where there is a strong celebrity tabloid media – for instance, the US and the UK

– rather than in democracies where it is absent. However, it might be that the attitudes of journalists towards exposing politicians' personal lives is significant due to other factors. The secondary literature suggests possible differences between countries that are part of a so-called 'North Atlantic' or liberal media cluster that share common freedom-of-expression norms, levels of regulation and professional cultures and those that are part of a polarized pluralist or democratic corporatist cluster that have different regulatory and cultural traits (Donsbach & Klett, 1993; Hallin & Mancini, 2004).

The second factor shaping country selection was language. Languages often pose a major stumbling block to effective comparative research, curtailing sampling ambitions. This study was also constrained by the need to find research assistants fluent in a large number of world languages and able to conduct content-based research. The study had access to assistants who spoke French, German, Italian and Spanish and could be trained in analysing media content. After consideration, the following democracies were selected: Australia, France, Germany, Italy, Spain, the UK and the US.

Having decided on which countries to include in the study, a series of further challenges remained. First, which political actors should the research focus on? Should the research concentrate on the national leader, leaders of the main political parties or a broad range of politicians? Most studies on personalization focus on national leaders; a very few look at a top-two or, more broadly, a top-ten of politicians in a country (see Kriesi, 2010). If focusing on national leaders only, how representative are claims for all politicians? If focusing on a range of politicians, what number might be most representative? Further, should the focus be on all politicians, or all politicians in a national legislature? What about their families – should they be included? Of course, any selection needs to be weighed against issues of feasibility, especially resources and time-scale. A study of all elected politicians in a country might be desirable but is not necessarily feasible. This study focused both on national leaders and on ordinary politicians. When examining the flow of consensual/non-scandalous personal information and imagery, the study focused on national leaders. The reason for such a focus was logistical and resource-based (see appendix). To compensate, the examination of scandalous revelations looked at all elected politicians, not just leaders.

The second challenge concerned the sampling period. Most studies on personalization focus on election periods (see, for example, Kriesi, 2010; Rahat & Sheafer, 2007), and fewer look outside this period (for an exception, see Langer, 2007). While the attraction of focusing on election campaigns is obvious, such constraints would inevitably be limiting for an examination of the exposure of politicians' personal lives. This study focused on a broad period over which disclosure and exposure might take place – namely, the term the person was in office.

The third challenge concerned the size of the mediated public sphere in advanced industrial democracies. Within time and resource constraints, it is not possible to examine all media. Most studies of personalization have used newspapers as a proxy for wider media coverage (see, for example, Langer 2007); while this has advantages, it means that trends in other media might be missed, especially the non-news media. For example, in order to gauge the flow of consensual/non-scandalous private information and imagery, the study used several measures, national press coverage of leaders and their families and indicators based on non-news content, namely the books dealing with the leader's personal life and the appearance of national leaders on entertainment talk shows.

The final challenge concerned the indicators selected in respect to consensual and non-consensual, scandalous and non-scandalous personal information and imagery. A range of variables have been used by existing studies to measure the mediated exposure of politicians' private lives (see Errera, 2006; Langer, 2007). Elements of exposure that seem common, such as family and early life, appear in these studies (see Rawlins, 1998, p. 370). However, it should be noted that such variables do not capture the invasive aspects of disclosure. The content analysis for the current study used a combination of indicators to measure consensual intimization in different countries: newspaper coverage of the birthdays of national leaders and their spouses; coverage of national leaders' family holidays; coverage of national leaders' families (see appendix). In addition, as noted, the study documented the number of books focusing on the personal lives of national leaders published while they were in office and their appearance on entertainment talk shows. These indicators were designed to capture the flow of consensual/non-scandalous information and imagery and ensure that all domains of the personal sphere were captured. For indicators of scandalous revelations, the study identified every publicized case of marital infidelity by politicians over a forty-year period, 1970 to 2009, in each selected country (see appendix). In addition, the study documented all publicized cases of the 'outing' of gay politicians. Together, these indicators act as an index of intimization.

Explaining intimization

Any study needs not only to demonstrate systematically the intimization of political communication in different democracies but also to try and explain why this might occur. As Tilly and Goodin observe, social research is like puzzle solving (2006). Why might intimization be more developed in some democracies than in others? What variables advance or retard the process? Such questions remind us that research is about not just measuring developments but understanding why they may or may not occur in different countries – the issue of causation is central to research. In national case studies, causal explanations often take the form of a descriptive narrative; while illuminating, such stories are not always satisfactory in explaining developments. The multivariate statistical techniques used in large-N comparative work are not appropriate for small-N or medium-N studies (for a discussion, see Collier et al., 2010). To elucidate the causes underlying intimization, this book employs two case-oriented methods: a within-case historical analysis of the paths taken by specific cases under investigation (Bennett, 2010; George & Bennett, 2005) and a cross-case analysis in the form of fuzzy set qualitative comparative analysis, fsQCA (Ragin, 2000, 2008).

FsQCA is a set-theoretic approach that enables both an effective classification of findings and attribution of causation across cases. It is unlikely that intimization will be developed to the same extent in each country; some democracies will be more intimized and others less so. So, unlike most similar systems design (MSSD) and most different systems design (MDSD) which require variables to be crisp, that is present or not present, fsQCA takes account of variance; it allows researchers to calibrate membership of sets on a variety of possible scales. Countries can be full members, partial members or full non-members of any particular set. In addition, fsQCA provides an alternative way of thinking about causation that recognizes the complexity of the social world. Instead of a set of discrete causal variables, it sees variables, or causal conditions, working together to produce an outcome. Further, it acknowledges that different combinations of conditions or recipes may produce the same outcome and that the presence or absence of an outcome may be explained by different recipes. So, for example, when thinking about why the intimization process might be more advanced in some democracies than in others, the answer may lie not in the net effect of individual variables but in a number of different combinations or recipes. Finally, fsQCA explicitly uses counterfactual analysis, including logically possible combinations that have no empirical instances, to simplify causal recipes and produce more focused comparisons. Comparative research would be more straightforward if social scientists were faced with a social world with cases showing all possible recipes, so cases that only differed by one single causal condition could be matched and more focused comparisons produced (see Ragin, 2000, 2008, and Mahoney, 2007, for a wider discussion of Mill's methods of agreement and disagreement). However, as Ragin notes, this is not possible, as naturally occurring social data are limited in their diversity (2008). While the limited diversity of the social world may be thought to hinder any simplification of causal recipes, the inclusion of counterfactuals allows such a simplification of recipes; conditions that make no difference to the generation of an outcome can be identified and removed, producing a more parsimonious recipe of causal conditions that can explain the development of intimization.

Structure of the book

This book explores the extent to which political communication is becoming intimized in a range of advanced industrial democracies. It examines the level of exposure of politicians' personal lives occurring across countries and over time. The book's structure in part reflects the divide identified earlier in this chapter between consensual and non-consensual exposure of scandalous and non-scandalous personal information and imagery. Chapter 1 is devoted to examining the consensual exposure of politicians' personal lives in each of the seven democracies. It looks at the routine publicity given to non-scandalous information and imagery from the different domains of national leaders' personal lives. It examines the coverage of significant events in their personal life, such as birthdays, coverage of their domestic realm and family life and their life stories. It then ascertains the extent to which exposure has changed over time. The chapter finally seeks to understand what factors may be responsible for producing particular outcomes and, using fsQCA, how they work together to produce that outcome.

Chapters 2 and 3 explore the non-consensual exposure of personal information and images in the media. Chapter 2 looks at evidence of publicized cases of infidelity across the seven countries and at the outing of gay politicians. It seeks to explain the findings considering a range of causal factors and how they work in combination, once more utilizing fsQCA. Chapter 3 places non-consensual revelations in a comparative historical context, examining trends in the exposure of politicians' infidelity between 1970 and 2009. Chapter 4 explores the global flow of news and information on politicians' transgressions of marital norms. It examines the way in which the transnational news environment challenges politicians' ability to protect their privacy, especially in countries with high levels of privacy protection, and how it is opening up potentially new spaces for publicizing scandalous personal information.

The book seeks to ascertain whether there is a discernible trend towards more intimate political communications across numerous countries, whether distinct differences remain between countries, or whether there are clusters of countries witnessing similar developments and why this might be. The book finishes with a conclusion reprising the main issues and arguments, looking at the consequences and extrapolating bigger themes.

1

Soft Focus: Leaders' Personal Lives Close-up

A lot of the publicity that politicians' personal lives receive does not involve any intrusion by the media, and what is revealed is not considered scandalous in any sense. This information and imagery are often the product of cooperation between media professionals and political advocates, and are used with the express or tacit consent of the political actors in question. The information and imagery touch on a range of different dimensions of leading politicians' personal lives, from incidents in their life stories and concerns about their personal well being to their relationships with family members and their domestic space (see figure 0.2). While existing nationally focused studies suggest such information and imagery increasingly permeate contemporary political communication in some democracies (see the introduction), there is no comparative data on the degree to which this aspect of politicians' personal lives receives publicity, nor any attempt to explain coherently why this might be.

This chapter looks at the mediated visibility of the different domains of national leaders' personal lives in a consensual non-scandalous context (see table 0.1). It examines the publicity given to each domain of the personal sphere, both cross-nationally and over time, in order to get a sense of whether and how coverage might have evolved in different countries. It starts by examining the publicity given to national leaders' domestic realm and to those they have close relationships with (the second and third domains outlined in the introduction). It then examines the publicity given to national leaders' inner lives (the first domain outlined in the introduction). It documents the coverage of significant events in the personal lives of national leaders and coverage of their life stories and incidents from those stories. Finally, it explores the possible causes underlying the findings.

Family life and the domestic realm

Research suggests that leading politicians' family members, family life and domestic spaces are increasingly subject to media coverage (Chenu, 2008; Cockerell, 1989; Schroeder, 2004). Growing evidence points to the fact that the spouses and children of national leaders are in some democracies now subject to greater media exposure than ever before and are becoming public figures in their own right (Ponder, 1999). Similarly, in some countries, family events such as weddings, christenings and the annual family vacation attract coverage. Research also suggests that some leading politicians have been quick to invite cameras into their homes, to capture informal downtime with their families. This section examines press coverage of national leaders' spouses and children, their family holidays and their home in order to get a sense of the extent to which their family life and domestic realm receive exposure.

Leaders' families in the media

Perhaps the most striking findings in regard to the growing visibility of the spouses and children of national leaders comes from studies of the US First Lady and the so-called 'first family'. Although the US First Lady does not 'operate under a constitutional directive', or receive 'a policy portfolio', studies show her mediated visibility has grown dramatically over the course of the twentieth century (Winfield & Friedman, 2003, p. 549). For most of the nineteenth and early twentieth century, the First Lady's visibility was largely confined to official photographs. Florence Harding was the first to assume a limited public role in the 1920s, appearing with her husband during official photo opportunities; this trend continued with Grace Coolidge, who, in addition, made frequent appearances in newsreels of the day and women's fashion magazines (Ponder, 1999). Eleanor Roosevelt was the first presidential spouse to attain a media presence independent of her husband, meeting regularly with journalists (see Bystrom, 2004; Caroli, 2003). However, according to some, it was not until the advent of television and Jacqueline Kennedy, who was dubbed the first 'First Lady of the television age', that the President's wife obtained widespread global visibility (Schroeder, 2004; Watson, 2000). The subsequent First Ladies have all been more visible than their early- and mid-twentieth-century predecessors (Caroli, 2003). Hillary Clinton gained particular media prominence. According to one estimate, over a three-month period early in the Clinton presidency, Hillary gained more coverage than Vice President Al Gore. She appeared for a total of 52 minutes on three network evening news bulletins, compared to Gore's 4 minutes (Diamond & Silverman, 1997). Laura Bush maintained a high public profile and Michelle Obama has continued attracting widespread media coverage in a variety of roles, and recently appeared in *Vogue*.

The President's children have, historically, largely been invisible, well shielded from the prying media eyes. Of course there have been exceptions. Alice, the daughter of President Teddy Roosevelt, was the subject of much press coverage. Interest in the 'often outspoken debutante and party goer' did not subside until she married in 1906 (Ponder, 1999, p. 32). Studies suggest that the President's children, especially from the latter part of the twentieth century, have gained an increasing amount of attention in the media compared to their predecessors, and their names are now widely known (see Quinn-Musgrove & Kanter, 1995; Wead, 2003).

Outside the US, the picture is less clear; it is not known whether the partners and children of leaders of other democracies receive a similar level of media attention. In the UK, various authors have pointed to the high media profile Cherie Blair achieved. Heffernan and Webb observe that Cherie Blair enjoyed such a profile during the 1997 electoral campaign in a way that was not true for the partners of previous party leaders, even Prime Ministerial ones (2004, p. 53; see also Page, 2003). Seymour-Ure (2003) has likened her profile during her husband's time in office to that of the US First Lady. For example, in June 2007, the BBC screened *The Real Cherie Blair*, a fly-on-the-wall documentary with unprecedented access to Cherie's private life over a six-month period. Sarah Brown, the wife of the former British Prime Minister Gordon Brown, although she did not enjoy the high media profile of Cherie Blair, did not shy away from the limelight and played a public role, speaking at set-piece events such as the annual party conference, guest-editing the *News of the World*'s supplement magazine in July 2009, and playing a prominent role in the 2010 general election campaign (see also Smith, 2008). There is some evidence of the Prime Minister's children receiving attention. The escapades of Mark Thatcher and the love life of James Major gained coverage, as did the drunken antics of Euan Blair, his choice of university, even his mother's attempt to buy him a flat in Bristol.

Studies of the visibility of leaders' spouses and children in other democracies are also few and far between. The high profile of the former French presidential First Lady, and former model, Carla Bruni, has excited much comment. Her whirlwind romance and marriage to Nicolas Sarkozy attracted global attention. She subsequently released an album and appeared on the cover of a range of magazines, in and outside France. In Spain, the 2002 marriage of the daughter of then Spanish Prime Minister José María Aznar became a major media event, with numerous glossy magazine spreads and television coverage (Sanders & Canel, 2004). Sanders and Canel note that Spanish politicians have regularly appeared with their families in magazines. Popular magazines such as *Diez Minutos* and *Semana* have regularly featured government ministers and heads of regional government and their families (2004, p. 205). This may hint at a transformation of politics, but there is no sense of whether partners and children of other national leaders attract the same levels of visibility as the US first family.

Table 1.1 Yearly average number of news items mentioning the national leader's spouse on his or her own over a 15-year period: 1995–2009

Country	Mean
UK	53
US	30
France	29
Spain*	16
Italy	8
Germany	7
Australia	6
Mean	21

* Spain 1996 onwards. All numbers rounded.

Source: compiled by author. Measure: one newspaper, excludes tabloid newspapers.

Table 1.1 shows the average number of news items on leaders' spouses (on their own, without the leaders) over a 15-year period in one serious or quality newspaper.

The table reveals that national leaders' spouses in the UK, the US and France have been the subject of the greatest number of news items over the period, followed by those in Spain, Italy, Germany and Australia, whose leaders' families received less attention. Although not shown in the table, the data revealed that coverage was concentrated on the spouses of certain leaders, namely Michelle Obama and Hillary Clinton in the US, Cherie Blair in the UK and Carla Bruni in France.

Table 1.2 shows the coverage of national leaders' children (still living at home and dependent on their parents). The table reveals that national leaders' children are most visible in the US, the UK and Italy, and less visible in Australia, France, Spain and Germany. Again coverage was not spread evenly but concentrated on the children of particular leaders, namely Chelsea Clinton in the US, Euan Blair in the UK and Barbara Berlusconi in Italy. It should be noted the children and the spouses with the highest coverage are also mainly those that secondary literature suggested had the highest profiles.

Table 1.2 Yearly average number of news items mentioning the national leader's children over a 15-year period: 1995-2009

Country	Mean
US	12
UK	9
Italy	6
Australia	1
France	0
Spain*	0
Germany	0
Mean	4

* Spain 1996 onwards. All numbers rounded.

Source: compiled by author. Measure: one newspaper, excludes tabloid newspapers. Up to 2 children still living at home and dependent on their parents. Where the leader has more than 2 children, the additional children were not counted. Children not dependent on their parents were also discounted. For exclusions, see appendix.

Leaders and family holidays

All leaders and their families take regular vacations throughout their time in office. Although they occur outside the domestic realm, they cannot be considered, I would argue, public events but, rather, a time when leaders are off-duty, relaxing with members of their family and friends even though they may receive publicity. While it is not clear from existing secondary sources how much publicity leaders' vacations attract across countries, these sources do provide some insight into their vacationing habits. Leaders seem to opt either for up-market destinations, at home or abroad, or choose to stay somewhere less glamorous, including home. In the US, Bill Clinton and his family opted for the former, holidaying in a variety of desirable destinations while in office, including Martha's Vineyard; Hilton Head Island, South Carolina; the Virgin Islands; and Jackson Hole, Wyoming – to name a few. In the US, the Clintons' holidays were often taken strategically. For example, ahead of the 1996 election, Dick Morris conducted a series of focus groups to find the best place to vacation; the answer, a hunting holiday in Arkansas – a trip which the Clintons then took, on the basis of the focus group findings (Wilby, 2005). In 1999, the family holiday fitted around Hillary Clinton's campaign to become a senator for New York: the family holidayed in Long Island and then the Finger Lakes, both in New York State. Their travels around the US stand in contrast to those of other US Presidents: Ronald Reagan regularly took holidays at Rancho del Cielo, his southern Californian ranch; George Bush Senior vacationed at the family home in Kennebunkport, Maine; and George W. Bush stayed almost exclusively at his ranch in Crawford, Texas. The younger Bush, said to have taken the longest holidays of any President, spent part of his vacation time working, meeting visiting heads of state, interspersed with clearing brush from the 16,000-acre estate. Indeed, he termed these long holidays working vacations – his 2005 vacation lasted five weeks. President Obama and his family seem more in the Clinton mould: in his first term as a new President, they took trips to Hawaii and Martha's Vineyard.

In the UK, the Prime Minister's annual holiday has evolved from a quiet getaway to a long-haul trip to sunny climes. Prime Ministers Harold Macmillan and Alex Douglas Home spent their holidays shooting grouse on family or friends' estates; Jim Callaghan retreated to his farm in Sussex, while Edward Heath spent his vacation sailing his yacht (White, 2008). It is said that Margaret Thatcher did not take holidays – not true, she took breaks in Cornwall and Austria – while John Major took some of his summer holidays in Spain (White, 2007). The Blairs only holidayed in the UK once while Blair was Prime Minister, with the Prime Minister preferring Tuscany, the south of France, the Algarve, Sharm el-Sheikh, the Seychelles or the Caribbean. The August after winning the 1997 election, the whole Blair family went on a two-destination holiday: stop one, the Tuscan villa of millionaire Labour MP, Geoffrey Robinson; stop two, a chateau south of Toulouse. The Blair family was back in Tuscany over the next three summers. Blair's sole summer holiday in the UK was in the wake of the foot-and-mouth crisis after the 2001 election campaign, but this was a short break followed by a longer stay in Gascony, France. In contrast, Gordon Brown, as Prime Minister, opted to stay in the UK: a cottage in Dorset in 2007; one in Southwold, Suffolk in 2008; and in the Lake District in 2009. In 2007, there was much emphasis on the 'modesty' of his choice compared to that of Tony Blair and his family, and on the fact he cut short his holiday to deal with an outbreak of foot-and-mouth disease in Surrey. Gordon Brown deliberately sought to communicate that he holidayed in the same places as the average UK family – a UK seaside holiday: 'I have been holidaying in parts of Britain for the past four years and this is the best place in the world to be' was his patriotic tone (Walker, 2007). David Cameron has continued the trend of holidaying in the UK, spending two weeks with his family in Cornwall in 2010.

In Australia, for most of his premiership, John Howard chose to spend his holidays at his official residence, Kirribilli House. This was, in part, a response to the media intruding on his family vacation at Hawks Nest, their traditional holiday haunt in northern New South Wales. In early 1998 the *Newcastle Herald* had printed directions to their Hawks Nest holiday home on its front page, with the suggestion that the public take any complaints straight to him. While Howard's holiday delight was being wrapped up in a book, other Prime Ministers have been comparatively more adventurous. Kevin Rudd spent his first vacation as PM in 2009 on a walking holiday with family in Tasmania, and Paul Keating, when premier, opted for sailing holidays on board the America's Cup yacht *Cambria*.

In Spain, José María Aznar spent most summer holidays, as leader, at Les Platgetes de Bellver de Oropesa on the Mediterranean coast, the highlight of which was his participation in the local beach tennis tournament, although towards the end of his term in office he had given up the beach tennis and taken up golf. In contrast, José Zapatero and his family holidayed at a variety of destinations in Spain, including the Asturias (northern Spain), the Canary Islands, the Doñana National Park and Menorca. Further, these vacations were often focused on his favourite activities: 'fishing, cycling and reading' ('pesca, bicicleta y lectura'). In Germany, Helmut Kohl's summer holidays were, by and large, uneventful stays in a villa by Lake Wolfgang near Salzburg, Austria. In comparison, both Chancellors Merkel and Schroeder have chosen a wide variety of destinations – Schroeder: Pesaro (Italy), Positano (Italy), Marbella (Spain), Majorca (Spain), in addition to holidays taken in Germany; Merkel: Ischia (Italy), South Tyrol (Italy), La Gomera (Spain), and regular visits to the Richard Wagner Festival at Bayreuth with her husband. In both 2006 and 2008, Merkel went hiking in the South Tyrol with the mountaineer Reinhold Messner.

In France, Presidents have tended to vacation in their official residence in the south of France. Jacques Chirac spent his holidays in French overseas departments, including La Réunion and winter vacations in Morocco. President Sarkozy broke with tradition in 2007, holidaying in the US at Wolfeboro, Maine. Subsequently he has also taken very visible holidays with Carla Bruni. In Italy, Silvio Berlusconi spent his summer holidays at his private villa near Porto Rotondo in Sardinia; his predecessor Massimo D'Alema, a keen sailor, spent his holidays on board his custom-designed yacht *Ikarus* cruising the Mediterranean; Romano Prodi often spent family holidays at the so-called 'Castle Bebbio' in Emilia-Romagna but the family also holidayed in destinations all over Italy, including the Pantelleria Islands and Castiglione delle Pescaia in Tuscany.

Table 1.3 provides the first systematic picture of the publicity that national leaders' holidays gained. It shows the news items on leaders' holidays in three quality or serious newspapers during two one-month periods over a fifteen-year timespan.[1] Based on this evidence, it seems that there are important national variations in the extent to which this aspect of family life has gained publicity. The table shows a significant difference between the UK, Spain and the US, on the one hand, and France, Italy, Australia and Germany, on the other. The leaders' holidays in the former countries received generally high coverage over a fifteen-year period, while holidays of leaders in the latter received much less attention. It should be noted that coverage also focused on some leaders' vacations more than others, namely those of José Zapatero in Spain, Bill Clinton, George W. Bush and Barack Obama in the US, and Tony Blair in

Table 1.3 Yearly average number of news items mentioning the national leader's holidays over a 15-year period: 1995–2009

Country	Mean
UK	46
Spain*	25
US	21
France	16
Italy	7
Australia	7
Germany	3
Mean	18

* Spain 1996 onwards. All numbers rounded.

Source: Compiled by author. Measure over two one-month periods. Measure: three newspapers, excludes tabloid newspapers.

the UK. The reasons for this are explored in more detail later in the chapter.

Leaders and their families at home

In an ordered way, Presidents and Prime Ministers have let the media go behind the scenes, revealing the spaces where they and their families retreat from public view. One area of notable exposure has been the national leader's official residence. For example, President Clinton, in his last month in office in 2000, gave a personal tour of the White House for the Fox TV show *The First Family's Holiday Gift to America* (Schroeder, 2004). He was following a tradition in the US that stretched back to Harry Truman's time but, perhaps, was most famously carried out by Jacqueline Kennedy in 1962, with her Valentine's Day tour of the newly redecorated White House (Tebbel & Watts, 1985). Nixon invited cameras into the White House for a CBS Christmas Eve special in 1971, which included an interview, with his family clearly visible in the background putting up Christmas decorations (Schroeder, 2004). In the UK, the media has been invited into the Prime Minister's official residence in Downing Street. BBC

Radio was asked inside Number 10, Downing Street in 1977 to talk to Audrey Callaghan about life in the house (Stanyer, 2007). Margaret Thatcher let a film crew into Number 10 to film part of a series entitled *The English Woman's Wardrobe*, in which she talked openly about her taste in clothes and where she bought her underwear (Cockerell, 1989). Tony Blair, while PM, granted unprecedented access behind the scenes in Downing Street to a range of programme makers: for example, in 2004, he starred in a fly-on-the-wall documentary on Channel 4 entitled *Tony and June*, in which youth-TV presenter June Sarpong spent 24 hours living with the Prime Minister.

In France, *Paris Match* has a long history of providing coverage of life in the Élysée Palace. In 1954, *Paris Match* presented a photo spread of newly elected President René Coty and his family there (Kuhn, 2007). The photographs included his wife engaged in a variety of household chores, and the President and his daughter posing in their swimming costumes. Through the 1970s, *Paris Match* continued to be granted access to the Élysée. For example, in a May 1976 edition, Mme Giscard d'Estaing was pictured gardening in the palace grounds under the caption 'Her third Spring at the Élysée Palace' (Chenu, 2008). Her husband the President was pictured, with his pet Labrador, at his desk.

In Australia, *Australian Story* is a half-hour evening programme, a hybrid between documentary and current affairs. It has been running on the Australian Broadcast Corporation (ABC), Australia's public-service channel, since 1996, and regularly gains audiences of 1 million (Bonner & McKay, 2007). The show's subjects range from prominent public figures to ordinary Australians who, often, have had extraordinary experiences (2007). The aim of the show is provide a personal insight into its subject matter. It has gained a reputation for providing a safe space where public figures such as politicians can talk freely about their personal lives; as its executive producer commented in 2001, it enables 'people to talk about themselves' (2007, p. 641). Bonner and McKay note that the show seeks to mix informality with serious topics but does not try to catch its subjects off-guard, revealing something they would rather not have disclosed. The audience sees the home, the family

Table 1.4 Appearance of elected politicians on *Australian Story*

Date of appearance	Name	Post
June 1997	Natasha Stott Despoja	Federal Senator
October 2001	John Howard	Prime Minister
November 2001	Kim Beazley	Labor Party Leader
September 2002	Philip Ruddock	Immigration Minister
June 2003	Simon Crean	Labor Party Leader
May 2006	Barnaby Joyce	Federal Senator
March 2006	Julia Gillard	Federal MP
April 2007	Alexander Downer	Foreign Minister
September 2007	Belinda Neal	Federal MP
August 2009	Malcolm Turnbull	Liberal Party Leader

Source: compiled by author from *Australian Story* archive.

and learns about the private life of the guests, which they can identify and feel comfortable with (2007). They note: 'it is a favoured site, especially for those already in the public gaze, for the revelation of matters which could be considered private but which have been chosen by the subjects themselves to be made public' (p. 645). They observe: 'families use the chance the programme provides to comment on foibles or mild character weakness or to talk about the stress of politics, but, while candid, the comments [are] not controversial or substantively critical' (p. 646). Rather like a celebrity magazine such as *Hello*, *Australian Story* is produced with the full cooperation of the guest. Over the fourteen years the show has run, there have been nineteen shows on political actors, including elected politicians, those seeking elected office, appointed officials, those closely associated with them and activists; as a total, this represents around 4 per cent of shows. Table 1.4 shows the ten programmes that focused on elected politicians.

Based on an examination of show descriptions and transcripts of the shows available on the ABC website, what is striking is the personal nature of the content. Nearly all the shows involve family members, are set mainly in the home of the politician, and involve often candid and frank discussions. In the show focusing on John Howard, ABC were given access to the PM's official Sydney residence, Kirribilli House, and, in 2001, the leader of the opposition, Kim Beazley, gave access to his home in Perth. Both shows featured members of the respective politicians' families talking about family life and the character of the politician in question.

In sum, when it comes to mediated visibility of family life and the domestic realm, the examination of newspaper coverage shows a divide between countries. Taking two measures, coverage of family members and family holidays, UK Prime Ministers and US Presidents seem most visible. This is followed by the leaders in France, Spain and, to a slightly lesser extent, Australia and Italy. In these democracies family members and family holidays are visible, if not quite to the same level as in the US and the UK. Finally, in Germany, the national leader's family life receives the least attention.

Significant events in national leaders' personal lives

As noted, one of the key domains of the personal spheres of politicians concerns their inner life. This inner life, like that of all individuals, is marked by significant events. These include important one-off occurrences such as a marriage, a divorce, the birth of a child or grandchild, the death of a family member, and repeated noteworthy happenings such as wedding anniversaries and birthdays. These are significant events that concern the person and maybe those that know him or her, but are not formal public events, although they may gain publicity.

A systematic comparison of the extent to which significant events in leading politicians' personal lives attract regular attention requires the selection of an event which all politicians and their families experience on a regular basis. A birthday is a clearly significant moment in the life of an individual and their immediate family and friends; it is not a formal public event, at least not for national leaders in the countries examined here, but, rather, a personal one that a leader or spouse and friends may choose to celebrate publicly or not. However, the evidence on how much publicity birthdays attract is, at best, patchy.

Secondary sources from the US perhaps provide the clearest

evidence of national leaders' birthdays attracting widespread attention. In the US there is a history of Presidents using their birthdays for publicity purposes. Although not covered by this research, both Franklin D. Roosevelt and John F. Kennedy turned their birthdays into media events, partly to boost their profile as a sitting Presidents, but also to raise campaign funds (West & Orman, 2003). According to Schroeder (2004), Roosevelt was the first President to celebrate his birthday openly in an overtly public manner. Roosevelt invited Hollywood stars, along with the great and good of Washington (and the newsreel cameras), to a formal ball in 1934, an event that continued annually till his death in 1944 (2004). These celebrations gained widespread attention in the media: Schroeder notes that by 1940 his birthday had become a firm fixture in national life (2004). The idea of the public birthday extravaganza was rekindled by John F. Kennedy. In May 1962, Madison Square Garden, New York was the venue for President Kennedy's 45th birthday celebration. The event was a star-studded affair with famous names from Hollywood and show business, including Harry Belafonte, Peggy Lee, Ella Fitzgerald and, perhaps most memorably, Marilyn Monroe, who sang her famous rendition of 'Happy Birthday' (Schroeder, 2004). Nancy Reagan made regular efforts to celebrate Ronald Reagan's birthday publicly: in 1988, for example, Nancy threw the President a surprise birthday party at the White House with over seventy guests, including Cabinet members and close family friends. The highlights included a huge two-tiered birthday cake and singer Donna Marie Elio, accompanied by an eight-piece Marine band, singing 'He's Our Man: the Ronald Reagan March', composed especially by Marvin Hamlisch. Bill Clinton resurrected the birthday spectacular in 1996 when he hired Radio City Music Hall, New York, for his 50th birthday fundraiser. The event featured stars from Hollywood and the world of music, including Jon Bon Jovi, Aretha Franklin, Smokey Robinson and Shania Twain, who sang songs from each of the decades of the President's life (2004). However, not every President has sought to celebrate their birthday in such a manner. George W. Bush kept his birthday celebrations confined to family and close friends. Barack Obama's birthdays have been fairly low-key affairs too. In 2010, he celebrated his 49th birthday at a Chicago restaurant with friends and figures from the world of show business, including Oprah Winfrey.

In the other democracies there does not seem to be the same history of national leaders turning their birthdays into media events, although this does not mean they receive no coverage. While most celebrations tend to be low-key, there are one-off, sometimes high-profile celebrations of significant milestone birthdays that attract media attention. In Australia, for example, Bob Hawke celebrated his 60th birthday in 1989 with a large event at the Lodge in Canberra (the Prime Minister's official residence) with friends from the worlds of business and entertainment and sport, including golfer Greg Norman. In the UK, while John Major celebrated his 50th with a small dinner, Tony Blair's 50th birthday was a more high-profile affair. Held in the wake of the invasion of Iraq in 2003, Cilla Black sang 'Happy Birthday' to him on BBC2, and several newspapers carried photo-montages of how he had aged while in office. In Germany, Chancellors Kohl, Schroeder and Merkel have avoided making their birthday a major event, or at least initiating public celebrations. This, though, has not stopped others celebrating. For example, there have been celebrations of Chancellor Angela Merkel's birthday: in 2008 she was serenaded by a choir in Algeria on an official visit and, in 2009, party members wished her a happy birthday at the CSU Party congress. Her predecessor Gerhard Schroeder held a major celebration for his 60th birthday for friends and family while on holiday in Tuscany. In France, Presidents' birthdays have been modest affairs, but there are signs, perhaps, that things are changing. In her first year in the Élysée Palace, Carla Bruni threw a surprise party for her new husband Nicolas Sarkozy, which gained widespread publicity.

Evidence from the US also suggests that national leaders' spouses' birthdays can attract publicity as well. Hillary Clinton publicly celebrated her birthday on several occasions while First Lady. Her 50th birthday in 1997 was a two-day celebration which included a gathering at the Chicago Cultural Center and an appearance on *The Oprah Winfrey Show*. In 1999 there was a gala event at the Ford Center for Performing Arts, Chicago,

Table 1.5 Yearly average number of news items mentioning the national leader's birthdays over a 15-year period: 1995–2009

Country	Mean
UK	10
Australia	10
US	8
France	3
Germany	3
Italy	2
Spain*	0
Mean	5

* Spain 1996 onwards. All numbers rounded.

Source: compiled by author. Measured over three days over the birthday. Measure: three newspapers, excludes tabloid newspapers.

hosted by talk-show host Rosie O'Donnell and featuring stars from a range of Broadway shows. The event culminated in Hillary blowing out candles on a red, white and blue birthday cake. The following year the Miramax boss Harvey Weinstein hosted a birthday event in New York's Roseland Ballroom compèred by Chevy Chase, featuring stars such as Cameron Diaz and Ben Affleck and songs by Cher and Barbra Streisand. Amongst recent First Ladies, she seems to have been an exception: Nancy Reagan's celebrations were low-key, as were Barbara Bush's. Laura Bush's birthdays were also modest, with most attention paid to the gifts lavished on her by George W., including a diamond necklace and a Scottish terrier. Similarly, Michelle Obama's birthdays have not been major events attracting attention. For example, in January 2010, Barack Obama threw a surprise birthday party for Michelle at an organic restaurant in Washington, DC. Again, in the other democracies, there is evidence that birthdays of some national leaders' spouses also gain media attention. In the UK, for instance, Sarah Brown's surprise birthday party in 2007 received coverage, but this seems to have been an exception.

Table 1.5 provides a quantitative measure of the extent to which birthdays have received media attention across countries. It shows

Table 1.6 Yearly average number of news items mentioning the national leader's spouse's birthdays over a 15-year period: 1995–2009

Country	Mean
US	5
UK	1
Australia	1
France	0
Germany	0
Italy	0
Spain*	0
Mean	1

* Spain 1996 onwards. All numbers rounded.

Source: compiled by author. Measured over three days over the birthday. Measure: three newspapers, excludes tabloid newspapers.

the average number of news items mentioning the national leader's birthday over a three-day period every year while in office, in three quality or serious newspapers over a 15-year period, 1995 to 2009 (see appendix for more details). The table reveals that the national leader's birthday gets greater-than-average annual coverage in the UK, Australia and the US, and more than in continental European countries. In France, Germany and Italy, the average yearly number of news items is a fifth to a quarter that of the UK, and in Spain coverage in the press was almost non-existent. Coverage in the UK, Australia and the US, however, was not spread uniformly but focused on certain leaders' birthdays, namely those of John Howard in Australia; Bill Clinton and Barack Obama in the US; and Tony Blair in the UK. This reinforces the secondary evidence raised earlier that some leaders' birthdays attract more attention, for a variety of reasons, compared to others. Table 1.6 shows media attention paid to the birthdays of national leaders' spouses. The table shows that the First Lady's birthday in the US received the greatest press attention by some margin, compared to the rest. While there was, on average, a story per year in the UK, the number of news items on spouses' birthdays in all the other democracies averaged less than a story per year. Again coverage was focused on one or two spouses' birthdays: in the US, those of Michelle Obama, Laura Bush and Hillary Clinton, and in the UK those of Cherie Blair and, to a lesser extent, Sarah Brown.

Overall, based on this evidence, it would seem there are important national variations in the extent to which significant personal events, like birthdays, gain publicity. The birthdays of national leaders and their partners in the UK, the US and Australia are seen as more important news events than in other democracies. That said, there are variations between the leaders and between their partners in these countries, with some gaining more attention than others. Finally, in France, Germany, Italy and Spain, the birthdays of leaders and their spouses gain little if any publicity, they are not shared and are only covered sparsely by the media.

Life stories and the self

There are now a growing number of media spaces where leading politicians can talk about aspects of their inner life. Entertainment interviews, documentaries and magazines all provide an insight into the life history of politicians, their health, relationships and psychological state of being, and it has been observed that leading politicians have taken the opportunity to talk openly about their formative years, their tastes, families and relationships through these outlets (Van Zoonen, 1998). This section explores the extent to which national leaders' biographies receive publicity. It looks at two media forums where aspects of national leaders' life stories are discussed – entertainment talk-show interviews and books about political leaders.

Entertainment talk-show interviews

As mentioned, the growth of non-politically focused outlets such as celebrity magazines and entertainment talk shows has provided national leaders (and leading politicians) with new spaces for sharing their personal lives. Politicians using these new spaces are aware of their expectations. Those that appear have to 'play the game', so to speak; they have to be prepared to share, although they are unlikely to face hostile questioning as they would in the conventional political media. Such interviews are not risk-free; over-sharing always generates the possibility of embarrassing headlines recycled in the media. One often-cited example concerns Jimmy Carter's interview with *Playboy* magazine in 1976 (see Bauer, 2008). Carter, Democrat presidential candidate at the time, admitted in the interview to having 'looked at women with lust' and that he had 'committed adultery [in his] heart many times' (p. 98). These few lines, in what was a long series of interviews, were picked up by the news media and further publicized. A few decades later in the UK, in 2008, Liberal Democrat leader, Nick Clegg, in an interview in *GQ* magazine, talked openly about how many women he had slept with prior to his marriage; when asked 'How many are we talking about? 10, 20, 30?' he responded 'Not more than 30. . .'. He also then went on to rate his own sexual performance as 'not particularly brilliant or particularly bad' (Jones, 2008). These claims were also publicized by different media outlets and online, earning Clegg the nickname 'Cleggover' in one newspaper.

On television, across democracies, there has been an increase in the number of entertainment-oriented talk shows (for the US, see Timberg & Erler, 2002). Research conducted in different countries reveals that politicians are regular guests on this type of talk show, especially, although not exclusively, during election campaigns (see Bastien, 2008; Baum, 2005; Campus, 2006; Clayman & Heritage, 2002; Ericson, 2010; Neveu, 2005). In Germany, talk shows on commercial channels have proved an important additional platform for leading politicians in the last week of the campaign, providing an opportunity for last-minute appeals (Van Zoonen & Holtz-Bacha, 2000). In Italy, entertainment talk shows are now a destination for party leaders during election campaigns (Campus, 2006). The structure of these shows provides the politicians with a platform to talk about themselves. The shows are informal; in France, Neveu notes, there is common 'use of the pronoun "tu" instead of the formal "vous"' (2005, p. 326). Such shows have sometimes been described as a soft venue for appearance (Maarek,

2011; Stanyer, 2007). Guests usually appear one-to-one with the host in front of an audience. Discussions between host and guest tend to avoid substantive political issues and focus on personal matters (see Bastien, 2008; Baum, 2005; Ericson, 2010; Holtz-Bacha, 2004; Just et al., 1996; Maarek, 2011; Van Zoonen & Holtz-Bacha, 2000). Research by Holtz-Bacha (2004) found that in Germany about half of the topics discussed on entertainment talk shows focused on private matters. Bastien (2008) found that 60 per cent of the content of Canadian shows was devoted to personality and private-life matters.

The first appearance of a politician on an entertainment talk show came in the US in 1960 when both John F. Kennedy and Richard Nixon were guests on *The Tonight Show* with Jack Paar (Cogan & Kelso, 2009; Schroeder, 2004). However, it was not until the 1992 presidential contest that entertainment talk shows became an established stop on the campaign trail (Just et al., 1996). Shows like *Larry King Live*, *The Arsenio Hall Show*, *The Oprah Winfrey Show* and *Tavis Smiley* all featured presidential hopefuls as guests. Clinton perhaps most famously appeared on *The Arsenio Hall Show* in June 1992, where he not only talked about himself but also played the saxophone. Clinton's Republican rival, George Bush Senior, appeared on *Larry King Live* and *MTV*, and Ross Perot, the other candidate that year, appeared on a similar range of talk shows (Cogan & Kelso, 2009; Hayden, 2002). In subsequent campaigns, entertainment talk shows have been a permanent fixture on the presidential campaign trail. During the 2000 presidential race in the US, both Al Gore and George W. Bush were guests on *The Oprah Winfrey Show*, while the other candidate that year, Ralph Nader, appeared on *The Tonight Show* with Jay Leno. In 2004, both candidates for the presidency and their wives appeared on *The Dr Phil Show* presented by Phil McGraw. The show puts guests in the therapeutic hot seat, so to speak. The candidates and their wives talked about their families and a range of family-related matters: for example, George W. Bush and Laura Bush were asked if they had spanked their children (see Holbert, 2005; Van Zoonen, et al., 2007). Barack Obama was a guest on a number of entertainment talk shows during the 2008 campaign and, as President, has continued to appear. In 2009, he and his family appeared on an *Oprah Winfrey* White House Christmas special. In this first appearance on an entertainment talk show since taking office, Obama talked about a range of family matters.

In the UK, Margaret Thatcher was the first serving British Prime Minister to appear on an entertainment talk show in 1984. During her term in office she was a guest on *Aspel and Company*, the *John Dunn Show* and *Wogan*, as well as appearing five times on *The Jimmy Young Show* (Stanyer, 2007). Tony Blair, as Prime Minister, made more appearances on chat shows than any of his predecessors. During his first term in office, he was a guest on *The Jimmy Young Show*, *The Frank Skinner Show* and *Des O'Connor Tonight* (Foley, 2000). In a 1998 appearance on the *Des O'Connor show*, he talked about his life before politics, his time spent as a waiter in France, his student days at Oxford playing in a band called Ugly Rumours, and his family and his passion for football (Street, 2011). In 2006, he appeared on ITV's *Parkinson Show* where he talked about his heart operation, God and joked about gaffes he had made. Until his appearance on *Piers Morgan's Life Stories,* Gordon Brown, the UK Prime Minister, had been reluctant to talk about many aspects of his personal life; in an interview with the BBC's *Today* programme, he noted, 'I'm as honest and open as possible . . . I don't parade my private life around the place and I certainly don't want my family brought into situations' (30.09.09, *Today*, BBC Radio 4). However, his reluctance to talk about his personal life had become an issue, especially when his predecessor Tony Blair and rival David Cameron readily talked about their own. The interview for Piers Morgan was the first time Brown fully opened up about his personal life. The interview largely focused on Brown's private life: he talked about his relationship with Sarah, how they first met, and how he proposed, how many girl friends he had had. He went on to talk about coming to terms with the loss of his baby daughter Jennifer (he was in tears when talking about Jennifer's death), the illness of his second son Fraser (diagnosed with cystic fibrosis), his loss of sight in one eye and insults about being blind, his life as a student, drinking, whether he had ever used drugs. The interview content was widely trailed in advance by Downing Street and received widespread attention.

In France, Neveu observes most shows encourage their political guests to talk about 'what they like and love' and to refrain from discussing politics (2005, p. 327; see also Kuhn, 2011). The usual topics include biographies and hobbies and interests (Neveu, 2005). In Spain, leading politicians have not shied away from appearing on talk shows. Government ministers have been regular guests on shows such as *Fuentes y cia* (Sanders & Canel, 2004). In Italy, in the 2006 election campaign, Silvio Berlusconi and his main rival Romano Prodi appeared on a range of political and e-talk shows. Berlusconi's appearances included a show entirely devoted to football, *Il Processo di Biscardi*; the leading e-talk show *Il senso della vita* (The Meaning of Life) on Channel 5 (his own network), where he spoke about his 'youth, family and passion for music and soccer'; and a series of radio and TV shows where he sang and talked about his musical tastes (Campus, 2006, p. 520). His rival, Romano Prodi, not to be outdone, appeared on one TV show, *Che tempo che fa* (What Time Does) on RAI 3, where he answered questions about his life and his family, and spoke about his new book (2006). Berlusconi had turned down the offer of appearing on a show that was not on one of his networks. In Australia, while John Howard and other leaders have shunned such shows, Kevin Rudd appeared on the evening talk show *Rove Live*, both as leader of the opposition and as Prime Minister (Wilson, 2011). True to the nature of the show, questions during both appearances were highly suggestive: in 2007, one memorable question Rove asked was who he would turn gay for – Rudd replied, oddly, his wife; and, in 2008, he was asked how many times he 'shook the sauce bottle' (a veiled reference to masturbation); he replied, 'not enough'.

Figure 1.1 shows the number of appearances on entertainment-oriented talk shows (evening talk shows as opposed to soft-news shows) while in office. These are programmes where discussions between host and guest tend to focus on personal matters not substantive political issues, as mentioned earlier. The graph shows some national differences. There is a clear distinction between the

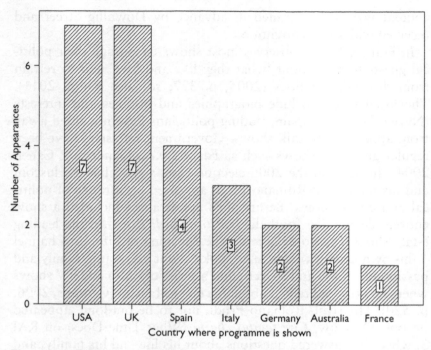

Figure 1.1 The appearance of national leaders on television entertainment talk shows while in office: 1990–2009

Source: compiled by author from MDB and other sources

US, the UK and the other countries. Leaders in the US and the UK seem to appear on entertainment talk shows more regularly. The figures also show that certain leaders seem keener to appear on these shows than others. These data do not provide a comprehensive picture but reveal that opportunities to talk about the self are not used by all leaders, although some use them repeatedly.

Books on personal lives

Books about politicians are a major source of personal information. In addition to biographies and autobiographies there has been a growth of new genres: books which examine national leaders' relationships, health, religion, even psychological profile.

Table 1.7 Yearly average number of books focusing on national leaders' personal lives while in office: 1992–2009

	Yearly average number of books that focus on personal life	Yearly average number of books on leaders
US	5	13
France	2	6
Germany	1	3
UK	1	3
Italy	1	2
Australia	1	2
Spain	1	1
Mean	2	4

Source: compiled by author: see appendix. All numbers rounded.

In any book shop, there is often an array of titles examining a variety of dimensions of politicians' personal lives. The number of political titles published in the US has grown in recent years and there has been an expansion in other countries too (Gibran, 2006). The publishing industry in many countries is often prepared to pay large advances to publish leading politicians' political memoirs and there is often stiff competition for rights to publish and to serialize memoirs; Bill Clinton's advance for his memoir was said to be between $10 million and $12 million, George W. Bush's advance around $7 million, and Tony Blair's £4.6 million (Glover, 2008). Very little time, if any, elapses between leaving office and producing an autobiography. A growing cast of prominent political actors is approached in-office to pen or cooperate in the production of a book.

This research sought to establish what proportion of books focus on the personal lives of national leaders compared to their public lives. Given the sheer number of books, the study focused on all those published about national leaders while they were in office (see appendix for more details). Table 1.7 shows the number of books published on national leaders' personal lives as a yearly average between 1992 and 2009. On average, the greatest number of books on leaders' personal lives were about the US President,

Table 1.8 Yearly average visibility of national leaders' personal lives based on four indicators: 1995–2009

Country	Yearly average based on 4 indicators
UK	109.7
US	64.1
France	49.9
Spain	42.1
Australia	23.4
Italy	17.7
Germany	13.4
Total	45.8

Source: compiled by author from previous tables. The four indicators are: birthdays, holidays, spouses and personal books (from 1992 onwards). These were added together to gain an overall score. All numbers rounded.

followed by the national leaders of France, Germany and the UK, with Italy, Australia and Spain seeing far fewer books published over the period. It should be noted that books focused on the personal lives of some leaders more than others – namely, Barack Obama and Bill Clinton in the US; Nicolas Sarkozy in France; Angela Merkel and Gerhard Schroeder in Germany; Tony Blair in the UK; and Silvio Berlusconi in Italy.

In sum, there is certain variation between countries in the levels of publicity given to each domain of a leader's personal life. In the UK and US, all three domains of the personal attract high levels of attention. In France and Spain, one of the domains of the personal sphere gains attention while the others less so. For the other democracies, the attention given to the various domains is generally lower. Table 1.8 combines some of the individual indicators into an overall measure of consensual exposure of non-scandalous content by country. Four of the indicators were selected: the average number of news items on leaders' birthdays, on leaders' holidays and on leaders' spouses, and the average number of books on personal lives of leaders. These were chosen as they were the most universal of the indicators presented in this chapter. The scores for each country were added together to produce an overall measure of exposure.

Table 1.8 shows that exposure, as measured by these four indicators, is most prevalent in the UK, but this is only one of three countries where output was greater than the group mean. The US and France show above-average exposure, but with lower levels than the UK. Finally are Spain, Australia, Italy and Germany, where yearly average exposure of leaders' personal lives is lowest. Before exploring the reasons for this outcome, it is worth examining in more detail which leaders' personal lives gained the most attention.

Personal difference

The tables so far provide a snapshot of average yearly exposure of leaders' personal lives by country, a useful comparative indicator but, as this chapter has indicated, the national picture disguises variation between leaders which needs to be explained in more detail (see also Langer, 2010). This study compared the publicity given to a number of leaders across four indicators: the average mentions of birthdays, holidays and the family, and the average number of books on personal lives. In order to show which leaders' personal lives gained the most attention, Table 1.9 ranks twenty-seven national leaders according to the index of personal coverage. The data were sampled over a longer time period for some countries to ensure the inclusion of a greater number of leaders.

When placed in order from most to least coverage, we can see there is a clear difference between leaders. There is a top five with scores of 200 or more, three from the US and two from other countries: Blair and Sarkozy. The next six still above the mean include George W. Bush, José María Aznar, Kevin Rudd, Gordon Brown, Jacques Chirac and Ronald Reagan. There are no leaders from Italy or Germany in the top half of the table. The bottom half of the table seems dominated by leaders from earlier periods.

The exact difference between leaders of countries over time can be seen clearly in figures 1.2–1.8 (pages 59–64). The seven figures show variations in publicity by the leader in order of when they were elected. They show that in all but one country the publicity surrounding leaders' personal lives has increased over time. The

Table 1.9 Yearly average visibility of national leaders' personal lives based on four indicators by leader

Politician's name	Overall yearly average
Barack Obama	368.5
Nicolas Sarkozy	261.8
Bill Clinton	259.4
George Bush Snr	230.4
Tony Blair	219.3
George W. Bush	167.3
José María Aznar	158.5
Kevin Rudd	155.3
Gordon Brown	142.4
Jacques Chirac	140.9
Ronald Reagan	123.9
José L. R. Zapatero	86.1
Silvio Berlusconi	57.8
John Major	52.7
John Howard	51.1
Helmut Kohl	38.4
Paul Keating	34.0
Gerhard Schroeder	32.5
Felipe González	26.0
Massimo D'Alema	23.4
Bob Hawke	21.7
Romano Prodi	19.6
Angela Merkel	14.9
Lamberto Dini	14.0
Giuliano Amato	11.8
Margaret Thatcher	11.6
François Mitterrand	6.7
Mean	101.07

Source: author compiled. All numbers rounded. Line indicates cross-over point for fuzzy set membership.

most dramatic increase in personal coverage has been in France. There is a dramatic difference in the publicity that the personal life of Nicolas Sarkozy gained compared to those of past French Presidents, especially François Mitterrand. Figure 1.2 clearly shows

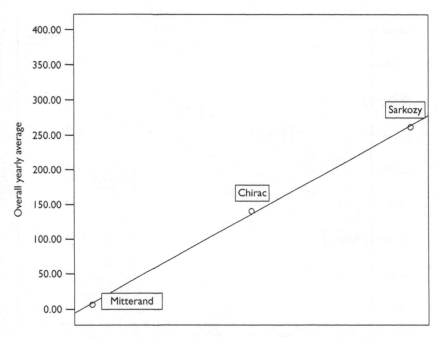

Figure 1.2 Yearly average visibility of French Presidents' personal lives based on four indicators over their period in office

the extent to which Sarkozy's personal life became a media spectacle, compared to those of his predecessors. There are also steep rises in the US and the UK. In the US there is a clear Obama surge, reflecting the intense media interest in Obama's personal life, amplified by his status as the first African-American President of the United States. In the UK, Blair and Brown have attracted more personalized coverage than previous Prime Ministers. There have been less dramatic rises in Australia, Spain and Italy. In Australia, Kevin Rudd gained slightly more exposure than his predecessors, as have Prime Ministers Aznar and Zapatero in Spain, though Zapatero's personal life was less visible than Aznar's. In Italy, there is very little upward movement, and certainly not a major Berlusconi effect. It could be that, although Berlusconi has placed himself at the centre of campaigning, intimate details about his personal and family life have been largely absent, ignored by the

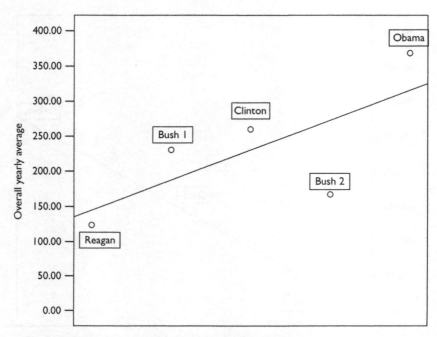

Figure 1.3 Yearly average visibility of US Presidents' personal lives based on four indicators over their period in office

press – at least over the period the data were gathered. That said, it should be noted that Berlusconi's personal life gained marginally more attention than those of his rivals. Only in Germany has the publicity of leaders' personal lives fallen, if only slightly. This reflects both each Chancellor's avoidance of personal publicity, especially Angela Merkel's, and media reticence about publishing on leaders' personal lives (Esser & Hartung, 2004). While Germany is the only country with a decline over time, the increase has not been especially dramatic in others – see, for example, Australia and Italy. That said, across democracies, taking this four-part measure as an indicator, the trend line indicates that there has been an increase in the attention paid to the personal lives of national leaders, although obviously varying in degree. Consensual exposure of non-scandalous content seems to have increased over time, if not at the same rate or to the same extent in each democracy.

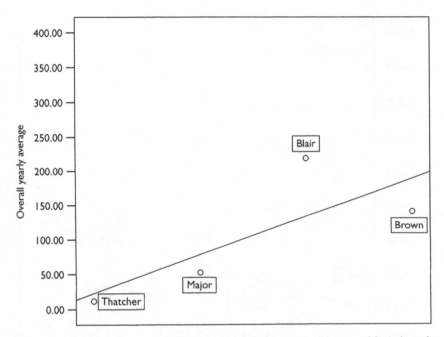

Figure 1.4 Yearly average visibility of UK Prime Ministers' personal lives based on four indicators over their period in office

This evidence shows that there is both a variation between countries and between leaders within countries. So, when trying to explain the findings, we need to find a way of accounting for why the personal lives of some national leaders receive more exposure than others but also why it varies between countries.

Explaining the exposure of the personal lives of national leaders

I want to argue that any explanation of these findings cannot be reduced to a single factor, such as a development in the media system, but, rather, is the result of an interplay of micro and macro factors relating to the leaders as well as the media and political environments of each country (see also Adam & Maier,

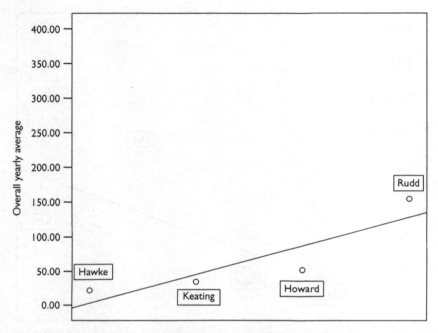

Figure 1.5 Yearly average visibility of Australian Prime Ministers' personal lives based on four indicators over their period in office

2010). There is, though, no consensus in existing studies about the range of possible causal conditions that might lead to a growth in the consensual exposure of national leaders' personal lives. I want to suggest that exposure is the result of a leader's propensity to adopt an open personal style, and of conditions in the media environment which mean that media outlets are eager and willing to publish such details, and in the political environment which incentivizes such self-disclosure. Some of these factors, it should be noted, change over time. With this in mind, I want to explore a number of likely specific causes.

There are a range of possible micro (agent-related) and macro (systemic) factors that help explain the differences shown in table 1.9. Some have already observed that women politicians are less likely to 'go personal' than their male counterparts (Van Zoonen, 2006), although with so few women in this sample it is not pos-

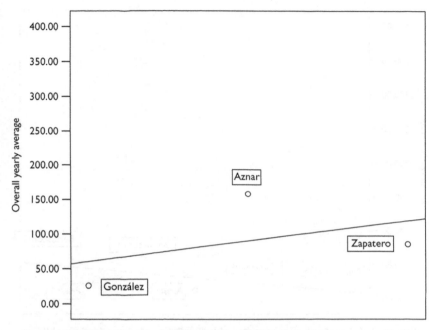

Figure 1.6 Yearly average visibility of Spanish Prime Ministers' personal lives based on four indicators over their period in office

sible to say whether mediated visibility can be attributed solely to the gender of the leader in question; that said, other personal factors need to be considered. Those towards the top of the list in table 1.9 seem younger. One explanatory factor might be generational differences between leaders. Younger leaders, members of the so-called 'baby boomer' generation who have grown up in the 1960s and afterwards, feel more at ease making their personal life public. Wouters, for example, argues that in the 1960s and 1970s many western democracies witnessed an informalizing process in which much conduct that had been forbidden was permitted, and ways of behaving in public changed fundamentally (Wouters, 1986, p. 1). These baby boomer leaders might be more relaxed with open display of emotions and personal disclosure than leaders of an older generation (see Furedi, 2004). Older leaders, brought up in a generation before the informalization of the 1960s

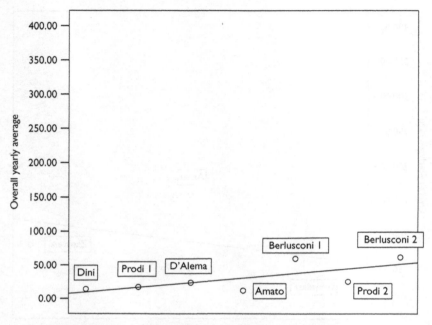

Figure 1.7 Yearly average visibility of Italian Prime Ministers' personal lives based on four indicators over their period in office

took hold, might be more reserved and, therefore, such informal personal disclosure might be seen as inappropriate.

Another factor might be the position of the leader on the left–right ideological continuum. Those leaders who are more centrist may not seek to differentiate themselves from their rivals on policy but will perhaps tend to rely on personal rather than programmatic appeals to distinguish themselves. The observed increased clustering of political actors on the ideological centre ground might mean such trends are more pronounced today than in the past (see Benoit & Laver, 2006, for a discussion of party positions). A further factor might be the leader's need to bond personally with voters in order to secure support, rather than relying on party attachments. Langer (2010) and Holtz-Bacha (2004) show how leaders in the UK and Germany disclose personal information in order to humanize themselves for voters – in other words, 'to

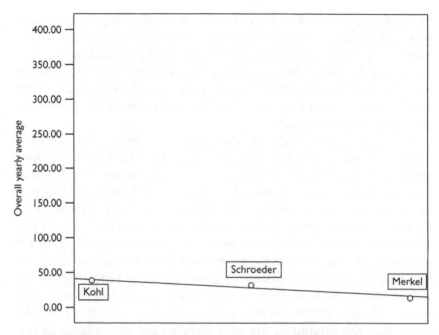

Figure 1.8 Yearly average visibility of German Chancellors' personal lives based on four indicators over their period in office

appear more personable, more like the lay person, and thus seemingly close and familiar to voters' (2004, p. 49). Leaders who have spent relatively little time in the public eye need to let the voters know who they are when seeking high office, and are likely to seek to try to bond with voters by revealing personal information and attracting the interest of the media (Hayden, 2002; Langer, 2012; Stephanopoulos, 1997; Wayne, 2000).

These factors need to be considered alongside systemic factors: there seem to be more Presidents towards the top of table 1.9. It is often argued that a more personalized style of politics is evident in democracies in which the national leader is directly elected, such as France and the US, as opposed to in parliamentary democracies, where voters choose a party or parties to govern. It could be that leaders who are elected in person need to be more open than those in parliamentary democracies. This need could be enhanced by declining party membership and decreasing loyalty amongst voters. McAllister notes, for example, that if party cues are weak, voters will tend to rely more on the appeal of personalities of candidates in deciding who to vote for (McAllister, 2007, p. 583; see also Adam & Maier, 2010). Where party membership and loyalty are low, these might be incentives to reach out to the electorate through personal appeals.

The final factor might be the extent to which a democracy has an established and/or growing tabloid media sector. Tabloid media outlets can have an influence on media systems as a whole (see Sparks & Tulloch, 2000). The larger the tabloid media sector, the more its potential to shape the milieu of a media environment. By this, I do not mean that all media outlets suddenly act in the same way – that is clearly not the case – rather, the tabloid media normalize the focus on personal lives of those in the public eye, it becomes mainstream, a taken-for-granted part of reporting for the whole system, and not seen solely as a preoccupation of a certain sector (Zaller, 1999). Drawing on secondary sources, I would argue that the tabloid media may have its greatest impact in the US and UK. Here we see a highly competitive, aggressive tabloid media sector, a competitive commercial television environment and an expansion of new media outlets which focus on celebrities' lives (Calabrese, 2000; Franklin, 1997; Sparks, 2000). The traditional tabloids face competition from television shows, and online gossip websites and blogs. This creates a potent combination which influences the other media. In the US, Williams and Delli Carpini (2000) argue that there has been a death of gatekeeping amongst serious media outlets. There has been a growth of the celebrity magazine sector in France and Spain, but the sector is not as large (Bueno et al., 2007; Kuhn, 2007). Similarly, the sector's influence is weaker in Italy, Germany and Australia (Goot, 2012; Klein, 2000).

However, it is not enough simply to list a range of possible factors; we need to say how they work together to produce the outcome in table 1.9. It might be that each individual condition is necessary and sufficient to produce the outcome, but it might be that not all are. All too often, research says nothing about how causes might work together to produce an outcome. Using fuzzy set qualitative comparative analysis (fsQCA) allows researchers to explore the impact of combinations of conditions which have the potential to shape the outcome. The basic principle of fsQCA is that it seeks to establish set-theoretic relationships between outcomes and configurations of causal conditions. FsQCA identifies causal configurations that produce an outcome rather than trying to detect the 'best predictors of the outcome based on statistical estimates of the net effect of each variable' (Ragin, 2008, p. 157). In order to produce these configurations, or recipes, the researcher needs to go through a series of stages which are briefly outlined here but explained in more detail in the appendix. The first step in a fuzzy set analysis is to turn the outcome (the result one wants to explain) into set membership scores via a process of calibration. Calibration is the process by which raw scores, in this case the score for each leader, are converted into a set membership score. This involves establishing the divide between membership and non-membership before allocating each person a membership score. For example, in a four-value set, full members are given a score of 1, full non-members a score of 0, those more in than out a score of 0.7, and those more out than in a score of 0.3. The researcher determines set membership based on theoretical and substantive knowledge (see Ragin, 2000, p. 166). Having allocated fuzzy membership scores for the outcome, the set membership of each causal condition are calibrated and scores allocated. Once this process is complete and all relevant causal conditions are calibrated, a truth table can be produced and the data can be analysed using the fsQCA software. The membership score for each leader listed in table 1.9 was calibrated. Leaders were considered members of the fuzzy set *'leaders whose personal lives are highly visible'* (the outcome) if they had a mean score of 101 or more. The score for full membership was 200, or twice the mean. For mostly but not fully members, scores were between 150 and 199; for more or less in, scores were between 101 and 149. The threshold for full non-membership was set at 25. For more or less out, scores were set at 50 to 100, and for mostly but not fully out, between 26 and 49. The membership scores for each of the

Table 1.10 Causal recipes for the visibility of national leaders' personal lives

Causal recipe	Raw coverage	Consistency
tabmedpres*pressystem*ptymemb*bonding*boomer	0.224138	1.000000
tabmedpres*ptymemb*bonding*centrist*boomer	0.387931	0.900000
pressystem*ptymemb*bonding*centrist*boomer	0.215517	1.000000

causal conditions outlined above were also similarly calculated. These scores were used to produce a truth table which could be analysed – further details are provided in the appendix.

Table 1.10 presents a series of combinations or recipes that explain the outcome – namely the extent of consensual exposure of leaders' personal lives. The solution discussed below is the so-called 'intermediate solution'; it is the preferred solution for Ragin as it 'strike[s] a balance between parsimony and complexity, based on the substantive and theoretical knowledge of the investigator' (Ragin, 2008, p. 175). In total, there are three possible causal recipes, based on the conditions discussed above. In other words, there are three possible combinations that explain the same outcome. In all three we can see that micro personal factors work together with macro environmental factors. If we take each recipe in turn, the first suggests that if a country is a presidential democracy where the national leader is directly elected (pressystem), with a large tabloid presence in the media environment (tabmedpres), with low party membership and loyalty (ptymemb), and the leader needs to bond personally with voters (bonding) and is young, part of the so-called 'baby boomer' generation (boomer), then there will be a high level of personal exposure. In the second recipe, being a presidential democracy is not necessary; here, having a large tabloid media presence in the media environment (tabmedpres), with low party membership and loyalty (ptymemb), and a leader who tries to personally bond with voters (bonding), is a baby boomer (boomer) but is also on the ideological centre ground (centrist), then there will be a high level of exposure. In the final recipe, a large tabloid media presence is not necessary; here, being

Table 1.11 Causal recipes for the lack of visibility of national leaders' personal lives – the negation

Causal recipe	Raw coverage	Consistency
~pressystem*~bonding*~centrist*~boomer	0.246753	1.000000
~tabmedpres*~bonding*~centrist*~boomer	0.272727	1.000000
~tabmedpres*~pressystem*bonding*~centrist	0.409091	0.926471

a presidential system (pressystem) with low party membership and loyalty (ptymemb) and a leader who tries to bond personally with voters (bonding), is a baby boomer (boomer) and a centrist (centrist), will lead to a high level of exposure. The first recipe helps explain, for example, the high incidence of personal exposure of some US leaders, like Bill Clinton, George W. Bush and Barack Obama; the second recipe helps explain incidences in the UK and Australia – Tony Blair, Gordon Brown and Kevin Rudd could be seen to fit into this. The final recipe helps explain why leaders such as Nicolas Sarkozy gained personal coverage. All the recipes have a high level of consistency, 0.90 or higher; in other words, there is a very high degree of agreement between instances of the outcome and the recipes displayed, and the raw coverage of each recipe, while on the low side, covers a large enough number of instances of the outcome to be compelling (Ragin, 2008).

FsQCA also allows an exploration of the negation of the outcome – in other words, explaining why levels of exposure of leaders' personal lives are low or absent. The table provides three possible recipes to explain low levels of exposure. The first suggests that where the country is not a presidential democracy (~pressystem), the leader does not need to bond personally with voters (~bonding), is more ideologically extreme and not on the centre ground (~centrist) and is part of the pre-boomer generation, not a baby boomer (~boomer), then exposure of the personal lives will be absent. This combination of conditions explains, for example, the lower levels of exposure of Margaret Thatcher and John Major in the UK and Bob Hawke, Paul Keating and John Howard in Australia. None of these leaders was directly elected, none was a baby boomer, and programmatically they were all more to the right or left of the political centre ground. In addition, as each was a leading member of a political party and had been in politics for some time, there was also less need to build personal bonds to ensure support.

The second recipe suggests that if the tabloid presence in the media environment is small or absent (~tabmedpres), the leader does not need to bond (~bonding), is more ideologically extreme (~centrist) and is part of the pre-boomer generation (~boomer), then exposure will also be absent. This recipe helps explain the lack of personal coverage of François Mitterrand in France; Helmut Kohl and Gerhard Schroeder in Germany; Silvio Berlusconi and Romano Prodi in Italy; and Felipe Gonzalez in Spain. None of these leaders was a baby boomer, and programmatically they were all more to the right or left of the political centre ground. Further, as each was a leading member of a political party and had been in politics for some time, there was less need to build personal bonds to ensure support. Finally, there was no major tabloid media sector to normalize the focus on the personal lives of those in office.

The final recipe suggests that where the national leader is not directly elected (~pressystem), the tabloid presence in the media environment is small or absent (~tabmedpres) and the leader is more ideologically extreme (~centrist), then coverage of the leader's personal life will still be absent even if the leader does seek to bond with voters personally (bonding). The final recipe accounts for the lower exposure of the personal lives of Angela Merkel in Germany and José Zapatero in Spain. While these leaders are baby boomers, none was directly elected, programmatically they have been more to the right or left of the political centre ground and there is no major tabloid media sector to normalize the focus on the personal lives of those in office. These recipes, therefore, help to explain the low incidence of personal exposure amongst not only the older generation of leaders in table 1.9, but also leaders in Germany, Italy and Spain.

In sum, there is no single explanation for the differences in exposure of leaders' personal lives between countries, and over time within the same country. The tables show that each explanation combines conditions related to the individual leader, and to the media and political system. This explains why certain leaders receive personal coverage while others do not. It highlights the importance of certain trends over time: informalization; the decline of party membership/loyalty and weakening parties; the decline of ideological difference; the rise of the tabloid influence; and structural constants – namely, whether the country is a presidential system or not. Where these processes occur, they lead to a greater focus on the personal lives of political leaders.

Conclusion

This chapter has explored the consensual exposure of leading politicians' personal lives, focusing on specific aspects of national leaders' personal domains. It has shown that there are significant variations in the extent to which the different domains receive publicity across countries and between leaders. The composite indicator of yearly average exposure shows that it is most prevalent in the UK, the US and France and least prevalent in Spain, Australia, Italy and Germany. The chapter also showed that exposure varied considerably between leaders over their period in office but, in all but one country, the publicity surrounding leaders' personal lives had increased over time. In countries such as France, for example, the rise in the level of publicity has been quite dramatic, while in others it was much less pronounced. There is no single structural reason for this difference but, rather, a complex interplay of factors operating at macro and micro levels. The fsQCA analysis suggested that three possible causal recipes explain national leader differences; these combined conditions related to the individual leader and to the media and the political system. Being baby boomers, centrists and having to bond with supporters are necessary but not sufficient without either political or media structural factors. Where these conditions were absent, the exposure of leaders' personal lives was lower. It seems that consensual exposure of non-scandalous personal content flourishes nationally where you have the combination of conditions noted above, but that there are variations between leaders that are also significant. The US and UK tick many of the causal boxes in having a media and political environment which enables exposure of personal lives, and leaders who seem at ease with personal disclosure, but this does not mean that every leader automatically receives a similar level of exposure or, indeed, seeks it.

2

Digging for Dirt: Publicizing Politicians' Sex Lives

Not all publicizing of politicians' personal lives is necessarily initiated or welcomed by them. This is particularly true for publicity of their sexual relationships, which they understandably might want to keep private if they involve infidelity. However, studies suggest that the media in some democracies are keen to publicize such intensely personal information without the consent of the people involved. In the US, for example, some authors note that media outlets are now by and large willing to report any 'unsourced and unsubstantiated rumour', especially when it is about politicians' extra-marital affairs or sexual orientations (see Ross, 1988; Sabato et al., 2000, p. 71). Similar observations have been made in the UK (see Parris & Maguire, 2005; Tumber 2004). However, this is far from a ubiquitous situation across countries. Other studies suggest that in France, Germany, Italy and Spain, journalists largely see the reporting of the extra-marital sexual antics of politicians as 'taboo' (see Cepernich, 2008; Esser & Hartung, 2004; Holtz-Bacha, 2004; Jimenez, 2004; Kuhn, 2004). In Australia, Tiffen notes that there has been relative restraint when reporting the infidelity of politicians (1999). It might well be, as Castells observes (2004; see also Barker, 1994), that when it comes to the reporting of extra-marital sex lives the US stands at one extreme in its lack of reverence, with continental European democracies at the other, and the UK somewhere in between, but more systematic comparative research is needed to determine the extent to which this is the case. The first part of this chapter examines revelations surrounding extra-marital affairs; the second part looks at non-consensual exposure of sexual orientation, the phenomenon known as 'outing'. In both cases, the chapter compares exposure in different democracies to ascertain whether extra-marital sex lives and sexual orientation are indeed publicized more frequently in the US and UK than in other countries, and why that might be.

Publicized infidelity across democracies

As noted, politicians' sexual relations, especially if those relations are with somebody other than their partner, can be considered an aspect of their personal lives they want to keep private from the media and public. It is the exposure of this latter type of sexual relationship that is often termed a sex scandal as it involves a transgression of the 'prevailing norms or codes governing the conduct of sexual relations' (Thompson, 2000, p. 120). Indeed, it is often the very transgression of 'prevailing norms' that certain media outlets in some countries find so newsworthy. It should be noted there are different forms of transgression; this section focuses on the exposure of sexual relationships that are considered lapses in moral probity but that take place between consenting adults, even if briefly. It excludes cases of politicians involved in inappropriate sexual conduct where there is no relationship or the relationship is not between adults. The table below shows all *publicized* cases of infidelity by elected officials from 2000 to 2009.

What is most striking about table 2.1 is the extent to which infidelity is publicized in the US and the UK when compared to other democracies. The US has 30 cases and the UK 14, which, together, accounted for 44 of the 57 publicized cases of infidelity over the ten-year period – that is, around 77 per cent. Next highest, but some way behind, was Australia with 5 cases, and then the four continental European democracies, with a total of 8 cases between them. Despite high-profile revelations in 2010 about Prime Minister Berlusconi's indiscretions in Italy, or those

Table 2.1 The number of cases of publicized infidelity 2000–2009

	Number of cases	Per cent
US	30	52.6
UK	14	24.5
Australia	5	8.8
Germany	3	5.3
Italy	3	5.3
Spain	2	3.5
France	0	0
Total	57	100.0

Source: author compiled. Line indicates cross-over point for fuzzy set membership.

of then-President Sarkozy, the findings really emphasize that the exposure of politicians' infidelity is largely a phenomenon of the US, and to some extent the UK, and has not become widespread across democracies in the last ten years. This amplifies the findings of some of the above studies, clearly showing that exposure of private peccadilloes of politicians is a largely US–UK phenomenon and almost absent in other democracies. But why is this the case?

One possible explanation, often mooted, is the difference in attitudes towards the transgression of sexual norms in Protestant and Catholic countries. In Protestant political cultures, the argument goes, disapproval of infidelity may be more entrenched than in Catholic cultures, which have a more relaxed attitude towards extra-marital affairs. For example, in the US, some surveys have found high levels of disapproval towards extra-marital sex amongst respondents (see Sachleben, 2011). There are, though, problems with such a perspective (see also Adut, 2008). Research by Norris and Inglehart (2004) reveals that Protestant societies are not significantly more ethical than Catholic societies and, on key moral issues, Catholic societies are more conservative than their Protestant counterparts. Further, such an emphasis on the impact of religious cultures underplays secularization. Norms are not fixed, and attitudes towards sexuality have changed across western democracies in both Protestant and Catholic cultures since the 1960s. In many western European democracies, religion holds little sway over the population's moral outlook (Norris & Inglehart, 2004).

Another possible explanation for the absence or presence of publicized infidelity might be the deferential nature of a society towards political authority (Inglehart, 2000). It could be argued that, in continental European democracies, politicians, especially leading politicians, are treated with greater deference than in Anglo-Saxon democracies. However, there are problems with such generalizations. First, Australia does not fit neatly into such an explanation, even though it has similar low levels of exposure to those in continental Europe; and second, such generalizations inevitably simplify public attitudes. Public-opinion polling across numerous countries – some examined in this book – suggests that politicians are often distrusted and may not be held in high regard, and there is certainly no evidence of overt deference in continental European democracies (see Nye, 1997). Finally, it could be that in some countries adultery is not seen as transgressing any norms, or politicians in some countries are more likely to commit adultery. However, research on scandals shows that extra-marital affairs are seen as a transgression of moral norms across a range of democracies, not just in the US and UK, and politicians in other democracies are no less likely to have affairs or lead double lives than their counterparts in the US and UK (see Thompson, 2000). For example, in France, François Mitterrand's relationship with Anne Pingeot was widely known about in journalistic circles but went unreported, and it was not until 1994, a few months before President Mitterrand left office, that *Paris Match* broke the news, with the President's permission, that he had had a child out of wedlock some twenty years earlier (Adut, 2008; Kuhn, 2004).

If these potential mono-causal explanations are problematic, the existing research in political communication puts forward some alternative reasons for why intrusion occurs or does not in various national contexts. If we take explanations for the occurrence of sex scandals in US politics, Thompson (2000) suggests they are the result of four factors. The first is a changing journalistic culture which means journalists and their editors are less reticent in publishing details about politicians' sex lives (2000,

p. 147). The second factor is a changing political culture, which has seen a greater emphasis placed on questions of character, with scandal becoming a weapon used by political rivals in a struggle for political advantage. The third is a change in societal norms and expectations concerning sexual conduct, seen in a 'growing sensitivity to certain forms of male behaviour which might have been regarded as normal or acceptable in previous decades' but are now deemed unacceptable (2000, p. 148). The fourth factor is a trend towards the legalization of political life. In the wake of scandals, there has been introduction of new ethical standards for politicians, as well as laws on sexual harassment and complaints procedures for those working for politicians (2000, p. 148). For Thompson, these factors combined have led to a rise in the visibility of political sex scandals. Adut (2008) argues that the presence of sex scandals in US politics today is the result of a combination of specific factors: declining modesty in American society and the politicization of sexuality, both of which have been enabled by the 'sexual liberalization of the sixties' (Adut, 2008, p. 181). These factors meant that politicians' sexuality and sexual transgressions could be discussed with a lack of embarrassment and frankness not possible before, but also that they could be defined as wrongdoings.

In the UK, studies have similarly pointed to a number of possible causes. Tumber, for example, suggests attention to what he terms 'personal morality' in the press is the result of its deliberate 'audience building strategy' (2004, p. 1124). Whether in politics or the world of business, such scandal stories are attractive to news outlets that are trying to grow their audience share. Another factor Tumber raises is the tabloidization of the press, which has seen the broadsheet press go downmarket following the tabloid press news agenda, leading to a prevalence of tabloid entertainment values and a disregard for the principles of reporting (2004, p.1124).

In France and Germany, a number of possible reasons for the absence of sex scandals have been proffered. Kuhn (2004, 2007) suggests the lack of coverage of politicians' private lives in France is the result of three factors. First, there is a journalistic culture which regards aspects of politicians' private lives as off-limits, combined with an absence of a tabloid culture; second, there is a societal acceptance that sexual behaviour of public figures is a private matter; and third, there are legislative constraints that protect the privacy of public officials. The absence of sex scandals in Germany is due, Esser and Hartung argue, to a combination of factors: a 'tacit agreement' between journalists and politicians that journalists do not disclose any details about politicians' private lives, combined with legal protection for the privacy of politicians and a high respect for them amongst journalists (Esser & Hartung, 2004; see also Esser, 1999). All these studies, when examining occurrence of sex scandals, suggest that the outcome is not attributable to a single factor but a combination of factors or, more precisely, a combination of political, media and socio-cultural factors. These, though, remain lists of plausible causes; there is no sense of how they work in combination with each other, or which are necessary or sufficient. That said, they form a good basis for identifying a range of possible causal conditions to explain the findings in table 2.1.The next section looks at a range of what I see as the key conditions explaining why this type of exposure is largely seen in the US and the UK and absent in the other democracies. As in the last chapter, I then use fuzzy set qualitative comparative analysis to explore the causal recipes which explain this outcome.

Explaining differences

Drawing on the literature above, a range of possible causal conditions can be discerned that help to explain the publicizing of extra-marital sexual relations in different countries. There are politically related conditions, such as the greater emphasis on character in US politics and the growing legal control of political life in the US. There are media-related conditions such as commercial pressures on the media and the tabloidization of the press in the UK, or the absence of tabloidization in France. There is also the culture of journalism, which either undermines respect for politicians and their privacy amongst journalists, as in the US, or separates private from public in matters of sex, as in the cases of Germany, France and Spain. There are legal conditions, such as the presence of legal protection for politicians' privacy, as in continental European democracies. Finally, there are socio-cultural conditions, such as societal norms surrounding sexual behaviour of politicians, which might mean that infidelity is seen either as a private matter, as in France, or something of public interest as in the US. Drawing on these causal conditions, I want to put forward a refined range of conditions conditions whose presence or absence contributes to the publicizing of politicians' infidelity. The differing levels of exposure, I want to argue, are possibly the result of five conditions, which work in concert with each other: weak legal privacy protection for public figures; a weak journalist/media consensus on privacy (these two conditions together forming a weak privacy culture); an established tabloid media sector; highly partisan and adversarial media; and the presence of politicians with a socially conservative agenda, such as the Christian right. In what follows, the influence of these conditions is discussed in more detail.

The first factor helping to explain the differences between countries, as shown in table 2.1, is whether a country has a weak, or conversely a strong, privacy culture. A privacy culture consists of two factors. The first is the presence or absence of legal privacy protection for public figures which constrains the media's ability to intrude into their private lives, and the second is the strength of consensus amongst journalists, and media outlets more generally, about the appropriateness of intrusion and exposure. I want to start by examining the presence or absence of national laws which constrain media activity.

Legal privacy protection

While the exact privacy rights afforded to public figures vary between countries, a clear divide can be seen between the statutory protection given public figures in so-called 'civil law' nations, such as France, Germany, Italy and Spain, and the protection given in common law nations, such as Australia, the UK and the US (see

Shackelford, 2011; Whitman, 2004). In Australia, the UK and the US, the common law provides varying degrees of protection for those in public life. Although not a privacy law, libel law provides some protection, but recourse to libel is not straightforward, the cost can be prohibitive and the outcome far from guaranteed, with the awards increasingly small in the UK (Lauterbach, 2005). Politicians rarely attempt to sue media outlets. In the US, politicians are treated differently from ordinary citizens when it comes to libel. The onus is put on the politician to prove that what has been written not only is untrue, but was 'published in the knowledge that it is untrue or recklessly as to the truth' (McCormick, 2005). There have been cases where politicians have sought to sue the media but these are rare and not always successful, as in the case of former US Congressman Gary Condit. In the UK and Australia, politicians are not treated any differently from anyone else but the potential costs of suing, both financial and in damage to reputation, outweigh any benefits. In the UK, John Major sued *Scallywag* magazine over allegations that he had had an affair with a manager of a catering firm, but very few choose to engage in such acts due to the attention they are given in the media (see also Corner, 2003, on Jeffrey Archer). More recently, Cherie Blair, the former Prime Minister's wife, threatened to sue the *News of the World* over allegations that she had had a feud with Sarah Brown, wife of then-Blair-rival Gordon Brown, but, mainly, politicians have tended to put up with such stories. In Australia, Liberal Party politicians Peter Costello and Tony Abbott successfully sued Random House over a book which made allegations about their private lives, but this is very much the exception (Blenkin, 2002). However, the publicity surrounding the cases only serves to place the allegations further in the public eye. This is not to suggest that there are no other options. Politicians, especially those with a high public profile, have resorted to other means. In the UK, some politicians have attempted to protect themselves from future disclosures by third parties via confidentiality clauses. These have been inserted into employment contracts, preventing employees from publicly disclosing their experiences. In 2000 when the *Mail on Sunday* announced it would serialize an unpublished account by Rosalind Marks of her life as the Blairs' nanny, Cherie Blair threatened to sue Ms Marks, who had signed a confidentiality agreement before starting her job. Eventually matters were settled when Ms Marks agreed to provide the Blairs with all copies of the manuscript she had in her possession. In the UK, politicians can also ask a judge to issue an injunction preventing publication of information on grounds of breach of privacy under the Human Rights Act, which has been incorporated into English law, although this can be challenged by the media in the court. A number of politicians have sought an injunction to prevent press publication without success. In 2004, for example, Lord Coe's request for an injunction to prevent the tabloid press from publishing his former lover's account of their relationship failed. The Judge commented that, as 'a public figure recently in the news he could not expect the right to privacy, given that some details of the case were already in the public domain and involved an extra-marital affair' (Bourne, 2004). Public figures can also complain to the media outlets directly or to industry ombudsmen such as the Australian Press Council or Press Complaints Commission (PCC) in the UK, but such bodies tend to be weak and their rulings can be flouted by certain media outlets; the UK would provide a prime example of this and the PCC has been closed down (see Fielden, 2012; Rozenberg, 2004). Public figures in common law nations are provided with some privacy protection but in no way could it be considered as the same level of protection as in civil law nations, even with the inclusion of the Human Rights Act into law in a UK context.

In France, Germany, Italy and Spain, public figures generally receive a great deal of legal privacy protection. France provides some of the most robust privacy protection for public figures in the world (Shackelford, 2011). Privacy protection was officially written into the French Civil Code in 1970 (Roberts, 2002; Shackelford, 2011). Article 9 of the Civil Code states that 'everybody is entitled to the respect of his private life . . . ' (Bilger-Street, 2010, p. 3). It gives citizens the 'rights to take any steps to prevent or put a stop to an attack on "core privacy interests"' (Roberts, 2002, p. 30). These interests are: love life; information concerning the human body (emotional and health status); financial status; religion; home and family life; and personal messages (Roberts 2002, p. 30; Trouille, 2000). The Civil Code extends to all citizens, including politicians, and provides them with a high level of protection (see also Kuhn, 2004). There are also laws giving members of the public rights to their own image. The law leaves French media vulnerable to litigation on the grounds of privacy intrusion and use of an image without express permission (see Chalaby, 2004). For example, Nicolas Sarkozy and Carla Bruni sued Ryanair in 2008 for using a picture of them, together with the caption 'With Ryanair, all my family can attend the wedding.' Ryanair was ordered to pay damages (Sweney, 2008).

As in France, German law provides public figures with a high degree of privacy protection. Although not as protected as ordinary citizens, those permanently in the public eye enjoy 'personality rights' under civil law and the country's post-World War Two constitution (Whitman, 2004). These general rights of personality provide public figures with significant control over their image (as in France), and privacy protection for their home life and from unwarranted intrusion in public spaces if secluded (Klein, 2000; Shackelford, 2011). The onus is on the media to prove that such intrusion is in the public interest (Esser & Hartung, 2004; Holtz-Bacha, 2004).

In Italy, there is no specific privacy law, although privacy is protected by a clause in the constitution which provides the public, including politicians, with certain privacy rights (Frost, 2000), and guarded by the Codice in Materia di Protezione dei Dati Personali. These rights are employed by politicians to limit unauthorized exposure of their private lives. In Spain, individual privacy is protected by the constitution and by the Penal Code. The Constitutional Tribunal establishes the right to privacy as a basic right. Sentences 137/1985 and 57/1994 afford individuals certain privacy rights (Bueno et al., 2007). Parts of the Spanish Penal and Civil Code also offer citizens protection from privacy intrusion. The principal protection comes from the Civil Code of 1982 which 'protects the right to honour, personal and family privacy and to one's own image' (Sanders & Canel, 2004, p. 204). Two key issues arise in deciding whether the law has been breached: the first is whether consent existed and the second whether any illegitimate intrusion occurred (2004, p. 204). While the judiciary has much discretion in interpreting the law, and rights to privacy are counterbalanced by rights protecting freedom of expression, the legal protection of privacy is fairly strict (2004). The privacy of minors is especially protected. The Law on the Legal Protection of Minors of 1996 requires parental permission for the publication of images of children.

The strength of an ethical consensus

The second factor that needs to be considered is the strength of an ethical consensus on the appropriateness of exposure. In France, Germany, Italy and Spain, non-consensual media exposure of the personal lives of politicians is not just potentially illegal but is seen as ethically inappropriate amongst a large section of media professionals, unless justified in very specific terms. Journalists are generally aware of what these justifications are without constant recourse to the courts. Such attitudes are revealed in existing national studies (Chalaby, 2004; Esser & Hartung, 2004; Kuhn, 2007; Sanders & Canel, 2004). In these countries, a strong consensus has emerged amongst journalists, and the media more generally, that such reportage is ethically dubious unless there is a public-interest motive. Morrison and Svennevig (2007) observe that public interest is one of the key defences for privacy intrusion. The public interest acts as a guide to when and in what circumstances it is appropriate for the media to intrude upon the private lives of individuals, and when it is not. The exposure of marital infidelity can be seen as justified if it can be considered in the public interest.

In France, Germany, Italy and Spain there is greater consensus about what constitutes – or at least what does not constitute – the public interest. This does not mean that there is unanimity – of course, there are disagreements, but there is, I would argue, much less contention amongst media professionals about what is or is not in the public interest compared to the US and UK. In continental European democracies, there is a strong shared belief across media outlets that reporting politicians' extra-marital sex lives for their own sake is not in the public interest. In France, there was much speculation about whether Jacques Chirac had an illegitimate child with a Japanese translator but this was never made public (see Astier, 2003). News of affairs only surfaces in contexts where it is legitimate to raise it. For example, Roland Dumas's affair with Christine Deviers-Joncour was only made public in relation to an ongoing legal investigation into financial corruption in 1998 (see Trouille, 2000). In Germany, there was much gossip amongst journalists that Chancellor Kohl was having an affair with his long-term personal assistant, Juliane Weber. The gossip was not made public in the mainstream media until the death of Kohl's wife, Hannelore, in 2001, and even then it was only the news magazine *Stern* that suggested that the couple had had marriage difficulties (Gimson, 2001).

In continental European democracies, this consensus is reinforced, of course, by sanctions, and acting inappropriately may have severe consequences. The presence of privacy laws means that there are legal penalties and it is quite likely that journalists would have to justify any intrusion in court, with potentially high penalties if it is deemed unwarranted. Unlike in the US or the UK, the hypocrisy of a politician is not justification for intrusion. Breaching this consensus may have other consequences too. In Germany, for instance, journalists who step outside this consensus and violate the codified norms surrounding exposure of private lives may find themselves isolated within the press corps. As one German journalist noted, 'if someone breaks the rules here and reports private matters, one is immediately expelled from the famous background circles [unofficial meetings of politicians and journalists]' (cited in Klein, 2000, p. 189). In France and Italy, political journalists have often been privy to any extra-marital indiscretions of politicians but have not tended to report them (Kuhn, 2004; Roncarolo, 2004). In France, reporting such revelations would certainly have a damaging impact on their career. For example, the Editor of *Paris Match* was fired in 2005 allegedly for putting the wife of the then Interior Minister, Nicolas

Sarkozy, and her lover on the front cover of the magazine (see Adut, 2008; Dakhlia, 2010). In March 2010, in the aftermath of rumours of that both Nicolas Sarkozy and Carla Bruni were having extra-marital affairs, *Le Journal du Dimanche*, where the rumours had first been posted, wrote a letter of apology for the hurt it had caused the President and said it would find those responsible. Barely a month later, the journalist who had posted the rumour on his website, in the hope of increasing ratings, was sacked, as was his boss (Kirby, 2010). In Spain, the magazine *Dos Minutos* was forced to apologize and to agree not to reproduce paparazzi pictures of the then Prime Minister José Zapatero and his family on holiday in Menorca, after Zapatero and his wife, Sonsoles Espinosa, threatened the magazine with legal action for infringement of their children's privacy. The magazine had used the images of the new Prime Minister and his family in a 2004 four-page spread under the headline 'Zapatero: First Vacation as President'.

In Australia, some have suggested that there are different attitudes to privacy intrusion compared to the US and UK (see Tiffen, 1999); indeed, Flemming (2006) remarks that Australian journalists have long been more concerned with politicians' abuse of power than with their personal infidelity. It might well be that a strong consensus on what is in the public interest exists amongst journalists but, if so, it is not underpinned by statutory privacy protection but by other factors. In Australia, there has traditionally been a high level of unionization amongst journalists; one estimate put the proportion in the mid-1990s at 86 per cent. Although this figure may have declined, it is still higher than in the UK and the US (Henningham, 1998). Further, the Australian Journalists' Association has played an important role in the development of a national ethics code (Henningham, 1998). These factors have perhaps led to a stronger consensus about inappropriateness of certain revelations. For example, Breit et al. (2002) write about the exposure of an affair between Australian Labor Party politician Cheryl Kernot and Liberal MP Gareth Evans in 2002. They note that it had been widely known about amongst journalists for five years before it was revealed in the mainstream media, and then it was only revealed by a freelance journalist after Kernot had omitted the detail from her autobiography (Breit et al., 2002). Such evidence shows greater reticence amongst certain sections of the Australian media, especially the Canberra press gallery, about breaking such news. More recently, there is evidence of greater willingness of certain elements of the press to report the private lives of politicians. In 2009, New South Wales Health Minister John Della Bosca resigned after the *Daily Telegraph* revealed he had had a six-month extra-marital affair. Later in the same year, television station Channel 7 carried an interview with waitress Michelle Chantelois, who claimed to have had a long-term affair with South Australia state premier Mike Rann (Wright, 2009). These examples might indicate that the consensus is weakening, but it still seems stronger than in the US and the UK.

In the UK and the US, the consensus about what is or is not in the public interest is a lot weaker. While certain outlets share their continental European and Australian colleagues' views, especially the broadcast media and serious press, a substantial section of media professionals define the public interest loosely – in some cases, as anything the public or their readers are interested in (see Morrison & Svennevig, 2002, 2007). As one interviewee observed in Morrison and Svennevig's study of press attitudes to privacy, such a loose definition allows 'anything to be published which is going to sell newspapers' (2002, p. 7). There are ethical guidelines, but these are easily ignored. Journalists generally do not have to justify intrusion in court and there have been few penalties. Adjudications by self-regulatory bodies, where they happen, occur months after the event and certainly do not prohibit intrusion. Indeed, the ineffectiveness of self-regulation has led some to call for statutory regulation of the UK press (Bingham, 2007).

So, in the US and UK, there are those outlets that are reluctant to publish allegations and revelations without a strong public-interest reason and those that are much less circumspect, and this is a really clear divide that does not exist to the same extent in continental European democracies. In the UK, the serious press and the broadcast news are least likely to expose marital infidelity for its own sake. The BBC has been reluctant to cover sex scandals broken in the tabloids (Tumber, 2004). In the US, some studies point to continued, although weakening, reticence of the 'serious' press when it comes to reporting the private peccadilloes of politicians (Entman, 2012; Sabato et al., 2000). Quite often, allegations might be common knowledge but there has been a reluctance to report what is seen as inappropriate news. One reason why those working for serious news outlets have generally been reluctant to seek out sex stories is their self-conception as professionals (Tumber, 2004). In the US, while many journalists knew about Clinton's extra-marital sex life, few thought it worthy of publication. They also sought to avoid scandals not only because they saw them as 'low brow', 'unworthy of their attention', but also because of, as Sabato and Licther note, 'their revulsion at the tabloid and ideological forces pushing the stories to the fore' (cited in Tumber 2004, pp. 1125–6). The serious press did not initially run stories about Clinton's alleged relationship with Paula Jones, only reporting it when it emerged as a big story (Williams & Delli Carpini, 2004). *Newsweek* sat on the Lewinsky story rather than publish it (see chapter 4). However, evidence seems to suggest that such a hard stance is weakening, and the serious press is increasingly willing to report such stories when they emerge (Williams & Delli Carpini, 2000; 2004). Sabato et al., writing after the Clinton–Lewinsky scandal, note that the 'serious' media now see extra-marital sex lives of politicians as legitimate news stories, if certain conditions are met. They quote an executive editor of the *Washington Post*, who remarked that the paper imposed two standards on such stories: 'First, can it be proven to be true? And second, is it relevant to the candidacy?' (cited in Sabato et al., 2000, p. 2). This is not to suggest that such decisions are easily taken; there is evidence of much agonizing prior to decisions being reached, but decisions to publish are increasingly being taken (Riffe, 2003).

In sum, this section highlights some of the key differences and similarities that exist in national journalistic cultures' attitudes towards the privacy of public figures. Key is the attitude to when it is or is not acceptable to intrude into the private lives of public figures. Here we can see a clear difference between the US and the UK, where consensus is weak, and continental European democracies – and to some extent Australia – where the consensus is stronger, in part because of the presence of privacy laws in Europe. This does not mean that the consensus may not weaken, but there is not yet a global convergence.

The size of the tabloid media sector

The first two conditions might not be enough without the presence of a type of media outlet which is willing to intrude into the personal lives of politicians. The tabloid media are more likely to intrude into politicians' private lives on a regular basis than other types of media (Stanyer & Wring, 2004). However, more than this, the larger the tabloid media sector, the more intrusion there will be; this is driven by competition between tabloid media outlets. In the US and the UK competing tabloid media outlets have had no qualms in reporting politicians' infidelity. In the US, tabloid exposés are fairly common. For example, it was the *New York Daily News* that broke the news of Bob Dole's affair in 1996 (Paterno, 1997; Sabato et al., 2000). Sabato et al. note that rumours about Newt Gingrich's extra-marital affair were circulating long before the actual revelations. In 1995, a *Vanity Fair* article identified Callista Bisek as Gingrich's favourite breakfast companion. Solid evidence was not disclosed until 1999, when the *Star* published photographs of the pair together (Sabato et al., 2000, p. 11). In 1992, the *Star* published Gennifer Flower's kiss-and-tell exposé of her affair with Bill Clinton; in 2008, the *National Enquirer* published Rielle Hunter's revelations about her affair with the Democrat presidential hopeful John Edwards and their love child, and the *New York Post* printed details about Laura Fay's affair with Congressman Vitto Fossella and their illegitimate child (see Sipes, 2011). In the UK, recent tabloid exposés of politicians' extra-marital sexual relations include: an MP leaving his wife, who had been diagnosed with cancer, for his lover (James Gray); an MP badgering his lover into having an abortion (Boris Johnson); an MP having an affair with an SAS war hero's wife (Paul Keetch); an MP leaving his wife and young family for a male interior decorator (Greg Barker). The UK tabloids seem prepared to go to any lengths to get personal information on public figures, as recent scandal has shown. They regularly pay to obtain private information, whether from a member of the public or from a private investigator. Cheque-book journalism has a long history in the UK (Bingham, 2009). For example, in 2006, the *Mirror* paid for revelations on the then Deputy Prime Minister John Prescott's tryst with Tracey Temple, publishing every detail about the couple's antics, including, perhaps most memorably, Tracey's claim that Prescott's manhood was the size of a cocktail sausage.

Weekly tabloids such as the *National Enquirer* and the *Star* in the US, and the daily and Sunday tabloid press in the UK, and the myriad of online outlets, will print any allegations about a politician's transgressions of marital norms and will only in certain instances have to deal with the courts. In the UK, they may well face a libel trial, but they have deep pockets and the damages awarded are much smaller than at their height in the 1980s. The size of the tabloid sector in each country, with its focus on celebrities' personal lives, guarantees that it is important for the flow of such material. The key difference between the US, the UK and continental Europe is the size of the tabloid media sector. Further, as chapter 1 has shown, aggressive large-scale tabloid competition impacts on the whole media environment. Australia, at first sight, poses a conundrum in this respect: it has a tabloid press but a low number of publicized cases. This could be explained by historical homogeneity of the Australian press and the fact that there is not a large-scale competitive tabloid press, in comparison to, say, the UK (see Goot, 2012). Perhaps the most well-known tabloids are the *Daily Telegraph*, based in Sydney; *the Herald Sun*, in Melbourne; the *Courier Mail*, Brisbane; and the *Advertiser*, Adelaide. Although they have an online presence, they have distinct city markets. This is not to say that the tabloid press has not exposed the extra-marital antics of leading politicians – one can think perhaps of the *Daily Telegraph*'s exposé of John Della Bosca's affair in 2009, mentioned earlier – but, over a twenty-year period, these remain largely isolated examples.

Adversarial partisanship

A fourth condition is related to the political motivations of a particular media outlet. The media in some countries not only support one political party but also frequently attack the parties they oppose: they are adversarial partisan supporters. Intensely adversarial partisan media might be more keen to expose the sexual peccadilloes of their political opponents for partisan gain than media that have weaker party ties or in which levels of 'neutral' professionalism are strongest. The number of reported cases of infidelity might thus be a result of the degree to which different media institutions within the media system, especially the press, are partisanly aligned. The levels of press–party parallelism in the different countries might help explain the differing degree of exposure. The model of neutral professionalism is perhaps weakest in Italy, where the Italian press often takes an 'activist role mobilising their readers to support political causes and participate in political events' (Hallin & Mancini, 2004, p. 103). In Spain and France, levels of professional neutrality are somewhat higher. In Spain, Hallin and Mancini note that the influence of the US model of neutral professionalism has been great, while in France, this model has been 'embraced' but has not displaced a tradition of commentary (2004). In Germany, the press very rarely identifies with a single political party and tends not to campaign openly for political parties during election campaigns, Hallin and Mancini observe; papers avoid clear political tendencies, reflecting a wide spectrum of political views (2004). In the US, the principle of journalistic neutrality is strong. In the UK, press–party parallelism is relatively strong, especially at election times (2004); similarly in Australia, where the press tends to be vocal in support for the main political parties (Jones & Pusey, 2010).

The rise of the Christian right

The final condition is the rise and presence of the conservative Christian right or New Religious Right and its moral agenda (see Williams, 2010). The Christian right are profoundly conservative on social issues (Wilcox & Robinson, 2010). This conservatism can be seen in the championing of the traditional pro-family initiatives, and in the opposition to many of the social reforms of the 1960s, such as those on abortion and the relaxation of divorce laws, by many Republican politicians. From the 1980s the Christian right, in the US, placed personal morality on the political agenda, and that of the Republican Party, in a way it had not been before (Eisenstein, 1982; Petchesky, 1981). One of the consequences of this has been that the moral behaviour of politicians, especially their adherence to the norms governing sexual conduct and the family, has become an important political issue. In such an environment the media are often keen to expose the moral hypocrisy of those politicians who espouse family values[1] in public while carrying on extra-marital affairs in private. In 2009, the extra-marital affairs of leading conservative politicians, South Carolina Governor Mark Sanford and Nevada Senator John Ensign were revealed in the national media. This followed on from revelations of infidelity by Louisiana Senator David Vitter, Mississippi Representative Chip Pickering and Washington State Assembly member Richard Curtis in 2007. In a survey of US editors' newsroom policies, while only 39 per cent said they would disclose a candidate's extra-marital affair, that figure rose to 84 per cent of editors if the politician was a family-values candidate (cited in Riffe, 2003, p. 100; see also Splichal & Garrison, 2000).

Although the New Right has been present in UK and Australian politics (Hollander, 2008; Marks, 1986), the presence of the Christian right and social-issue conservatism has not been nearly so strong. Similarly, in continental European democracies there are political parties that are socially conservative in outlook but the Christian right has not been a political force in the way it has been in the US, and personal morality not as contentious a political issue.

Causal recipes

Having examined the potential causes, I want to explore how these causes work together to produce high levels of publicized infidelity

Table 2.2 Causal recipes explaining high levels of publicized infidelity

Causal recipe	Raw coverage	Consistency
newright*wkprvprocult*tabmedpres	0.538462	1.000000
polaligpres*wkprvprocult*tabmedpres	0.615385	0.842105

using fuzzy set qualitative comparative analysis. Table 2.2 shows the causal recipes that explain high levels of publicized infidelity. As in chapter 1 the table presents what is termed the intermediate solution – that is, the solution that Ragin recommends in that it only allows alternative counterfactual combinations that conform to our knowledge of the situation in the simplification process (Ragin, 2008; further details in the appendix). It should be noted that countries were considered members of the fuzzy set '*democracies where politicians' infidelity is highly publicized*' (see table 2.1) if they had more than one publicized case every year between 2000 and 2009 – that is, a minimum of 10. The threshold for full membership was set at 20, at least 2 cases per year, or more; for mostly but not fully in, between 16 and 19 instances; for more or less in, a minimum of 11 cases but no more than 15. The threshold for full non-membership was set at 0, that is, no cases at all over the period; for more or less out at 5 to 9 cases; and for mostly but not fully out, at 1 to 4 cases (further calibration details and the truth table can be found in the appendix). The first thing to say is that there is more than one recipe that explains high levels of publicized infidelity.

The first suggests that high levels of publicized infidelity result where there is the social conservatism of the Christian right (newright), there is weak privacy protection for political elites (wkprvprocult) and a large tabloid presence in the media environment (tabmedpres). This is clearly the case in the US, where Christian social conservatism and moralizing have become key features of politics. There is an alternative pathway to the same outcome. The second recipe suggests democracies might also witness high levels of publicized infidelity where there is a strong presence of an adversarial politically aligned press (polaligpres), a

Table 2.3 Causal recipes explaining the absence of high levels of publicized infidelity – the negation

Causal recipe	Raw coverage	Consistency
~newright*~wkprvprocult*~tabmedpres	0.772727	1.000000
~newright*polaligpres*~tabmedpres	0.409091	0.857143

weak privacy culture (wkprvprocult) and a large tabloid presence (tabmedpres). In the UK, the press are partisan actors that regularly attack governments and their political opponents – especially the tabloid press. Here, exposure can be seen as part of a newspaper's political agenda. All the recipes have a high level of consistency, over 0.84 – the recommended cut-off is 0.80 – in other words, there is a very high degree of agreement between instances of the outcome and the recipes displayed, and the raw coverage of each recipe shows there are a large number of instances of the outcome (Ragin, 2008).

FsQCA also allows us to explain the negation of the outcome – in other words, why publicized infidelity is low or absent in a particular country. Table 2.3 provides two causal recipes: the first shows that if there is no Christian right (~newright), a strong privacy culture that provides protection for political elites (~wkprvprocult) and a small tabloid media sector (~tabmedpres), then exposure of infidelity will be low or absent. This combination of conditions explains, for example, the lower levels of exposure in Germany and Spain. The second recipe suggests that if there is no Christian right (~newright), and the tabloid media sector is small (~tabmedpres), then there will be an absence of high levels of publicized infidelity, even if there is a politically aligned press (polaligpres). The politically aligned press found in Australia and some continental European democracies, like France and Italy, is not enough on its own to trigger exposure on the scale of the UK.

In sum, different combinations of factors have produced a similar outcome: the social conservatism of the Christian right in the US and the adversarial partisan nature of the British press combined with a weak privacy culture and a large and influential scandal-oriented tabloid media lead to the high levels of publicized infidelity.

Breaking into the closet

The homosexual relationships of assumed heterosexual politicians are subjects that the politicians concerned may want to keep private, but also something that certain media outlets in some countries are keen to reveal. This section focuses on the non-consensual exposure of married and assumed heterosexual politicians as gay. 'Outing', a term widely used, refers to the exposure of a person, assumed to be heterosexual, as homosexual, without their consent. Such information has tended to come to public attention in several ways: as the by-product of another investigation, for example by the police, or as the result of a deliberate act of exposure by the media. Table 2.4 shows all cases of outing of politicians while in office over a ten-year period, whether linked to other investigations or not.

The table shows that nearly 60 per cent of cases over the period occurred in the US, and approximately 30 per cent in the UK. There is a particularly striking absence of cases in the other

Table 2.4   The number of cases of 'outing' 2000–2009

	Frequency	Per cent
US	11	57.9
UK	6	31.6
Germany	1	5.3
Australia	1	5.3
France	0	0
Italy	0	0
Spain	0	0
Total	19	100.0

Source: author compiled. Line indicates cross-over point for fuzzy set membership.

democracies over this period. Why are cases of outing focused mainly in the US? I want to suggest that many of the same conditions that led to high levels of publicized infidelity also explain the levels of outing in various democracies. The first possible factor is the level of legal privacy protection and the journalistic consensus, as already discussed. Under continental European privacy laws, 'outing' a politician would be a breach of the law unless it could be proven to be in the public interest. Revelations that have occurred seem linked exclusively to other acts or events. We can see examples of this in Germany and France. In 1995, Christian Democratic Union (CDU) Party Interior Minister for Saxony and former pastor Heinz Eggert was outed in the news magazine *Der Spiegel*, but only as part of an investigation into complaints that he was sexually harassing his male staff. Revelations in 2003 that the Mayor of Hamburg, Ole von Beust, was gay emerged in the media only after he went to the police to complain that he was being blackmailed by a former employee. Similarly, in France, revelations that government minister Frédéric Mitterrand was gay, while no secret, came to public prominence only in relation to allegations that some of his lovers were under-age. In the US, such privacy protection of those in public life is absent.

The size of the tabloid sector and its influence in a competitive media environment is also potentially significant. In the US, in 1989, Massachusetts Democrat House Member Barney Frank admitted to paying for sex with a male prostitute after the prostitute tried to sell his story to a tabloid newspaper (Carlson, 1989). The serious press has also engaged in its own exposés. In 2004, the then-married New Jersey Governor, James McGreevey, was forced to admit that he was gay after his local newspaper reported he had had an extra-marital affair with a male aide, as part of an investigation into corruption in the Mayor's office. Spokane Mayor Jim E. West confessed to being gay after his local newspaper, investigating child sex abuse, revealed he was a user of a gay website (see Robinson, 2009). In 2007, the Idaho Republican Senator Larry Craig was outed as gay in the press, after he was arrested for allegedly inappropriate conduct in a men's room in Minneapolis-St Paul airport (Kane & Murray, 2007). In some instances the media are not adverse to printing unproven allegations. In 1998, an alternative Buffalo newspaper, the *Beat*, reported rumours that Democrat Representative Bill Paxon, who had retired unexpectedly, did so because an opponent had threatened to reveal Paxon's homosexual affair with a Washington journalist who had committed suicide a few days earlier (Sabato et al., 2000, pp. 47–8). Paxon's denials on local radio only seemed to feed coverage of the story, which was covered by leading newspapers such as the *Washington Post* (2000). Rumours about sexual orientation also dogged Republican Representative John Kasich, suggesting that he was having an affair with his male chief of staff with whom he shared a Washington house (2000). Despite denial, the rumours were reported in *Time* magazine. Indeed, allegations elsewhere are often used as hooks to discuss the rumours further (2000). In 2011, rumours that Texas Governor and Republican presidential hopeful Rick Perry had had a homosexual affair and was gay appeared on gossip blogs and websites.

As with cases of publicized infidelity, presence of the conservative Christian right may also be important. As noted the Christian right, in the US, placed personal morality on the political agenda, creating an environment in which the media are often keen to expose the moral hypocrisy of those politicians that espouse family values. As also discussed, the level of social-issue conservatism in UK and Australian politics has not been nearly as strong.

Finally, there is the presence of gay rights activists. Activists have played a key role in outing politicians, especially in the US. Certain gay rights activists demand that all gay men and women 'come out', and define those in the closet as 'stalling the progress' of gay equality by hiding their identity (Boling, 1996, p. 144). Boling notes that there are numerous justifications used for outing; the following are some of the key ones taken from her book (see also Chekola, 1994; Gross, 2003). Those in the closet are benefiting from the struggle but are taking a free ride. How can being gay be private when being straight is not (Boling, 1996, p. 145)? Sex is private but sexuality is not. Homosexuality is a matter of 'identity, community and culture rather than private sex acts' (1996, p. 145). Other activists focus on closeted homosexuals in public life who 'voice or pursue homophobic ideas or policies'; they argue such actors forfeit their right to keep their sexual identity private, as their actions can be judged hypocritical (1996). Others suggest that outing can be justified as a necessary part of getting heterosexual society to take gay rights seriously and bring about wider reform (1996). What is provided is a complex series of justifications put forward by a range of activists, but all seek to override the wishes of the closeted individual and make public their sexuality for the greater benefit of the gay community generally (1996). In the US, Mike Rogers's blog (blogactive.com) seeks to out politicians who are said to be in 'the closet'. It follows on from the short-lived magazine *Outweek* which started in the late 1980s, the idea of gay activist Michelangelo Signorile. Republican Senator Mark Hatfield became the first politician to be outed by activists in 1989. Blogactive.com provides a list of Senators, Representatives, congressional and presidential staffers and local politicians who are in the closet, but particular ire is reserved for those seen as hypocrites: those in the closet who champion family values or oppose gay rights. Larry Craig's actions received widespread coverage in the media. Craig, an opponent of gay marriage rights, had also been the target of outing website blogactive.com that suggested that Craig had had sexual encounters with men dating back to 2006. The motivation for outing Senator Larry Craig and Representative Edward Schrock was their hypocrisy on issues of gay rights (M. Fisher, 2007). In 2009, Kirby Dick's documentary *Outrage* set out to expose as hypocrites a number of closeted politicians who opposed gay rights legislation while secretly being gay. In the words of one openly gay politician in the film: 'there is a right to privacy but not a right to hypocrisy'. The film revealed how closeted individuals on Capitol Hill opposed gay rights legislation.

Table 2.5 shows the causal recipes that explain the levels of outing in the US compared to the other democracies. It should be noted that countries were considered members of the fuzzy set *'democracies where politicians' sexual orientation is highly publicized'* (see table 2.4) if they had more than one case of outing every

Table 2.5 Causal recipes explaining high levels of outing

Causal recipe	Raw coverage	Consistency
newright*wkprvprocult*tabmedpres*activist	0.714286	0.714286

Table 2.6 Causal recipes explaining the absence of outing – the negation

Causal recipe	Raw coverage	Consistency
~newright*~activist	0.750000	1.000000

year between 2000 and 2009. The threshold for full membership was set at 20, at least 2 cases per year, or more; for mostly but not fully in, between 16 and 19 instances; for more or less in, a minimum of 11 cases but no more than 15. The threshold for full non-membership was set at 0 – that is, no cases at all over the period; for more or less out, at 5 to 9 cases; and for mostly but not fully out, at 1 to 4 cases (further calibration details and the truth table can be found in the appendix).

There is a single recipe that explains levels of outing in the US. Table 2.5 shows outing occurs where there is the presence of the social conservatism of the Christian right (newright), there is weak privacy protection for political elites (wkprvprocult), a strong tabloid presence in the media environment (tabmedpres) and a large presence of gay rights activists (activist). It seems that the media and activists are often keen to expose the moral hypocrisy of those politicians who attack homosexual rights in public while having gay relationships in private. Although the recipe consistency was lower than 0.8, a lower cut-off point of 0.7 was used in this instance as the truth table row is important as it covers the only case (Ragin, 2008). The raw coverage of the recipe includes a sufficiently large number of instances of the outcome to be compelling.

Table 2.6 shows why outing is low or absent in a particular country. The table provides a single causal recipe: if there is no Christian right (~newright) and low presence of gay rights activists

(~activist), then there will be no outing, irrespective of the other conditions. This might go some way to explain why exposure in the UK has been low over the last decade. In the UK, both these factors have been absent even though others might have been present. Tabloid media outlets which have traditionally had no qualms in exposing politicians' sexual orientation seem perhaps to be more reticent to expose than in the past. The 1990s saw a rash of tabloid exposés of married MPs. In 1994, Conservative MPs David Ashby and Michael Brown were exposed. Brown resigned as government minister in the Major government after the *News of the World* reported his affair with a 20-year-old man. In 1997, Conservative MP Jerry Hayes was outed by the tabloid press when he was photographed with his 18-year-old boy friend – the age of consent for gay men at the time was 21. In 1998, when threatened by the *News of the World*, government minister Nick Brown admitted he was gay, and so did the Cabinet minister responsible for Wales, Ron Davies, who was mugged while cruising on London's Clapham Common (Barnett & Gaber, 2001). These revelations, and others elsewhere, prompted the *Sun* newspaper to run a front-page editorial under the banner headline 'Tell us the truth Tony, are we being run by a gay mafia?', together with pictures of several gay ministers and a telephone number for MPs and ministers to call if they wanted to come out (2001, pp. 17–18; see also McNair, 2000). However, in the wake of this headline, the *Sun* declared it would no longer out public figures. This does not mean the tabloid press no longer outs MPs, but this practice may no longer be on the same scale. Similarly, activist groups may well have been less committed in outing politicians than previously. While the gay rights group OutRage! was active in the 1990s, its founder Peter Tatchell recently claimed that the anger over the hypocritical stance of closeted gay MPs has dissipated, with full equalization of the age of consent obtained in 2000 and civil partnership legislation (see Strudwick, 2010).

It seems that in the US the anger about the real or perceived hypocrisy of Christian conservative politicians who preach one thing and do another has become an important rationale for justifying such exposure by gay activists and the mainstream media.

Conclusion

This chapter has shown that extra-marital sex lives are, indeed, publicized more frequently in some countries than others. The chance of infidelity being revealed without consent is far greater for politicians in the US and UK than in any other democracy examined in this study. High levels of publicized infidelity are not the result of a single factor, such as a prudish Protestant political culture or over-sexed politicians, but the outcome of a combination of media-political and cultural conditions. High levels of publicized infidelity were the product of two possible causal recipes: the first involves a combination of social conservatism of the Christian right, weak privacy protection for political elites and a strong tabloid presence in the media environment. The second recipe involves a politically aligned media, a weak privacy culture and a strong tabloid presence. Both recipes show that media conditions are only sufficient to produce the outcome when combined with political and legal conditions. Without this combination of conditions, the outcome does not result. The chapter showed that where the tabloid media sector is weak or absent, there is a strong privacy culture and an absence of the Christian right and its social conservatism, a country is unlikely to experience high levels of publicized infidelity, irrespective of the level of partisanship in the press.

The chapter also shows that outing of elected politicians was most frequent in the US. This was the result of a combination of conditions – namely, the social conservatism of the Christian right, weak privacy protection for political elites, a strong tabloid presence in the media environment, and a large presence of gay rights activists. Together, these conditions explain the outing of those gay politicians who wished to keep their sexuality private. An absence of the Christian right and gay rights activists, irrespective of the other conditions, seems to have been enough to ensure that outing of politicians would be kept to a minimum.

3

Changing Exposure: Critical Moments and the Uncovering of Politicians' Infidelity

Although recent studies of political scandal remind us that the exposure of marital infidelity is not new (see, for example, Clark, 2003; Ross, 1988; Thompson, 2000), the extent to which exposure has increased over time, if at all, is still not clear. Without comprehensive time-series data from which to draw any firm conclusions, it is impossible to know if there are any trends. This chapter examines the exposure of infidelity over time, focusing on a forty-year period from 1970 to 2009, looking particularly at the US and the UK, which, as the previous chapter revealed, are where most publicized cases occurred between 2000 and 2009. The chapter seeks to understand the extent to which the exposure of politicians' infidelity has changed over time, and why.

Publicized cases of infidelity – 1970s onwards

Although known about in journalistic circles, the extra-marital sex lives of leading politicians were largely ignored or not seen as worthy of exposure in the national media for much of the twentieth century (see Bingham, 2009; Summers, 2007[2000]). It was not until the 1970s, some have argued, that the media in the US began to cover politicians' peccadilloes (Ross, 1988). For example, the extra-marital affairs of Presidents Harding, Roosevelt, Kennedy and Johnson were not publicized in the media in the same way as Bill Clinton's. Ross argues that reticence in reporting extra-marital sex lives of politicians came to an end in the US in 1969 when Ted Kennedy drove his car off a bridge and left his passenger, Mary Jo Kopechne, to drown. The Chappaquiddick incident, Ross argues, triggered a re-examination of the extra-marital sex lives of the other Kennedy brothers (1988, p. 193; see also Bauer, 2008). In the UK, Bingham (2009) notes that although the Profumo scandal occurred in 1963, it was effectively a one-off until the Lambton and Jellicoe scandals of the early 1970s. Similarly, in Australia prior to the 1970s, extra-marital antics rarely, if ever, made the news; Prime Minister Ben Chifley's affair with his secretary was never mentioned, and Prime Minister John Gorton's sexually inappropriate behaviour towards a female journalist received only minor coverage (Tiffen, 1999). It was not until Jim Cairns's affair with one of his personal staff in 1975 that extra-marital antics gained more attention (Blenkin, 2002; Tiffen, 1999). Indeed, an examination of secondary sources found few cases of publicized extra-marital affairs in the six decades preceding the 1970s (see Parris & McGuire, 2005; Ross, 1988; Tiffen, 1999); that said, it is still unclear how numerous cases were in the 1970s, the 1980s and 1990s.

Figure 3.1 shows the number of publicized cases of marital infidelity involving elected politicians in seven democracies over four decades; the decade averages are shown in table 3.1. Figure 3.1 clearly shows very little difference between the countries in the 1970s and 1980s – the number of publicized cases in the US and UK were higher but not substantially so. The marked difference between countries starts in the 1990s and continues in the 2000s where a clear divergence can be seen.

Table 3.1 shows show more clearly the actual number of cases per decade and the average number of cases per year during each decade. In the 1970s and 1980s, in the UK and the US, there was on average 1 case every three to five years. The average number of cases dramatically increases, though, in the 1990s in both countries. In the UK there were 2 cases every year in the 1990s and nearly 1.5 cases in the US. In the 2000s the average number of publicized cases in the US continued to increase, reaching 3 cases per year, although in the UK the number of cases fell slightly.

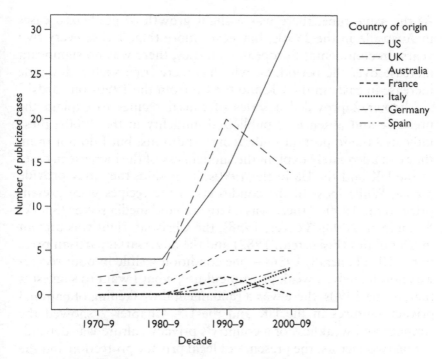

Figure 3.1 Publicized cases of politicians' infidelity over time: 1970–2009

Table 3.1 The actual and annual average number of cases of publicized infidelity per decade: 1970–2009

	Decade								Total
	1970-9		1980-9		1990-9		2000-9		
	N	Av	N	Av	N	Av	N	Av	
US	4	0.4	4	0.4	14	1.4	30	3	52
UK	2	0.2	3	0.3	20	2	14	1.4	39
Australia	1	0.1	1	0.1	5	0.5	5	0.5	12
Germany	0	0	0	0	1	0.1	3	0.3	4
Italy	0	0	0	0	0	0	3	0.3	3
France	0	0	0	0	2	0.2	0	0	2
Spain	0	0	0	0	0	0	2	0.2	2
Total	7	0.7	8	0.8	42	4.2	57	5.7	114

Source: author compiled.

At the same time, there was a slight growth of publicized cases in Australia in the 1990s, but never more than 1 case every two years. In continental European countries, there was no significant increase over the period. So why has there been such a dramatic increase in cases in the UK and the US from the 1990s onwards?

Chapter 2 provided a series of causal recipes to explain the presence and absence of publicized infidelity in the 2000s; these indicated the important underlying conditions, but I do not think they can adequately explain the suddenness of the increase in cases in the UK and the US in the 1990s. That said, they may provide a clue. While most of the conditions in the recipes were present prior to the 1990s – there was a large tabloid media sector (Sparks & Tulloch, 2000; Weaver, 1998), the Christian right was present in US politics (Eisenstein, 1982) and the adversarial partisan press in the UK (Tunstall, 1996) – one condition visible in both recipes was not: namely, a weak privacy culture; what I want to suggest is that, in the 1990s, there was a fundamental weakening of national privacy cultures in the UK and the US. Chapter 2 showed the strength and weakness of a country's privacy culture was dependent on two factors: the presence of legal privacy protection and the strength of the ethical consensus amongst national media about privacy intrusion. Something seems to have fundamentally undermined the latter factor – namely, the reticence to expose politicians' peccadilloes unless there is a strong public-interest motive. More specifically, I want to make the case that two 'critical moments' can be identified where the ethical consensus on privacy intrusion was undermined and weakened, leading to a surge of revelations of infidelity. A critical moment is a point at which a transition starts or gathers momentum, a tipping point which opens up new possibilities, or a fateful moment which fundamentally alters a given state of affairs (Giddens, 1991). In their 1975 article, Kraus et al. introduce the idea of critical events. They note: 'critical events analysis seeks to identify those events which will produce the useful explanations and predictions of social change' (Kraus et al., 1975, p. 196). Although they say little about the historical context of these events, I would argue they can be understood in such a way. A critical moment is an event or series of events in close proximity, but its significance, the extent to which it changes practice, can only be fully understood in historical context. Not all events can be termed critical moments. In any timeline, not all events are as significant as each other; some have a greater impact and can be retrospectively seen as critical moments because things change afterwards. They are points in time after which things are different.[1]

Two major incidents in the 1990s go some way to explaining the surge in the number of publicized cases. First of these is the so called 'back-to-basics' speech delivered by the then UK Prime Minister John Major in October 1993. The other event is the 1998 push for the impeachment of President Clinton by Republican Congressmen in the wake of the Clinton–Lewinsky scandal. In the ten years prior to the 1993 speech by John Major there were 5 publicized cases of politicians' infidelity, but 20 in the following ten years. Similarly, in the US, there were 7 cases of publicized infidelity in the ten years up to 1998 and 32 in the ten years afterwards. What follows is an examination of these game-changing events, which in effect normalized non-consensual exposure.

Back to basics

In his speech to the 1993 Conservative Party conference, Prime Minister John Major delivered the now immortal lines: 'It is time to return to those old core values: time to get back to basics, to self-discipline and respect for the law, to consideration for others, to accepting responsibility for yourself and your family, and not shuffling it off on the state' (Jones, 1995). Although subsequently denied, the speech was widely spun as the Prime Minister's wish to roll back the permissive society, and interpreted in the media as a call for a re-entrenchment of family values in society (1995). The speech was at the end of a conference which had seen criticisms of the unemployed and single-parent families by Conservative ministers. For many in the press, and the tabloid press in particular, lectures about family values by government ministers were seen as especially suspect, given the revelations about government ministers' private lives the previous year (Mortimore, 1995). In 1992,

the then Heritage Minister David Mellor's affair with actress
Antonia de Sancha was revealed in the *People*. Over a nine-week
period in the summer, details of the trysts, supplied by de Sancha,
were drip-fed by the paper, including Mr Mellor's fondness for sex
in his Chelsea football kit. Mellor finally resigned in September
1992 (Tunstall, 1996).

   Major's 1993 speech, together with his government's policy
proposals, acted as a catalyst for a series of further exposés of the
extra-marital sex lives of Conservative government ministers and
MPs. In the months following the speech, there were revelations
about government Transport Minister Steven Norris having five
mistresses. January 1994 saw revelations about the extra-marital
sex life of the Junior Minister for the Environment, Tim Yeo,
who resigned after the *News of the World* revealed he had had
an illegitimate child with a Conservative councillor – Yeo had
taken a particularly strong line on single mothers on state benefits (Thompson, 2000). Political journalist Nick Jones's account
of the events surrounding the Yeo resignation captures some of
the indignation of the tabloid press at John Major's attempts to
stand by his minister, and suggests it was a personal matter. The
Sun, in one of its editorials, argued that the press had every right
to publish stories about politicians' infidelity – after all, voters
based their judgements on the public image of MPs, 'that's why
so many politicians include happy family photos on their election literature. And that's why MPs don't like the press spilling
the beans when they're caught not practising what they preach'
(Jones, 1995, p. 5). Not long after, the extra-marital infidelity of an assortment of junior ministers and MPs was exposed.
Hartley Booth, Parliamentary Private Secretary to a Foreign Office
Minister, resigned after an affair with a House of Commons
researcher became public. Minister of Aviation and Shipping Earl
Caithness resigned after his extra-marital antics were reported
in the press and his wife committed suicide. It was also revealed
the same year that MP Gary Waller had fathered a child out of
wedlock. The hunt was on amongst the tabloid press to find more
cases of Tory moral turpitude. In 1995, Richard Spring, MP and
ministerial aide to the Northern Ireland Secretary, was revealed to

have had a three-in-a-bed romp. In 1996, the extra-marital affairs of MPs Robert Hughes, Rod Richards and Rupert Allason were publicized. In 1997, the last year of the Conservative Government, the MPs Piers Merchant, Allan Stewart and Michael Hirst were all implicated in sex scandals. In total, between 1993 and 1997 when the Conservatives left office, the infidelity of five government ministers and seven MPs was exposed; these figures do not include other sexual transgressions. One particularly graphic event, not included in figure 3.1, was the accidental death of Conservative MP Steven Milligan by autoerotic asphyxiation in 1994; he was found dead in his home in women's underwear with a satsuma in his mouth.

Backlash against moral conservatism

A similar reaction against perceived moral hypocrisy can be seen in the media reaction to the Republican-controlled House of Representatives' decision to impeach President Clinton in 1998. Particular anger was directed at certain conservative Representatives on the Republican right who had been vocal critics of Clinton's womanizing, who had attacked Clinton's philandering in their own campaign commercials, and who had denied House members the opportunity to vote for a resolution to censure rather than impeach Clinton (see Berke, 1998; Davis, 2006). This is not to say that the media reaction was co-ordinated, but evidence from a range of sources points to perceived hypocrisy being a key factor driving revelations. It was certainly a justification put forward by the pornographer Larry Flynt (Davis, 2006). Flynt employed two full-time investigators to scrutinize the 2,000 responses to an advert he placed in the press which offered $1 million to anyone who would disclose details of their affair with a Member of Congress or high-ranking government official (Shepard, 1999). The advert read: 'Have you had a sexual encounter with a current member of the United States Congress or a high-ranking government official? . . .Can you provide documented evidence of illicit sexual or intimate relations with a Congress person, Senator or other prominent office holder?' (cited in Goldenberg, 2007).

With the responses, Flynt and his researchers produced the *Flynt Report*, exposing the sexual activities of Republican Congressmen: the 82-page magazine revealed Republican politicians who had or were having extra-marital affairs (Calvert, 2000). The *Flynt Report* revealed that Republican Congressman Bob Barr, an opponent of abortion, had forced his ex-wife to have an abortion. Flynt was joined by 'serious' news outlets that also saw the condemnation of Clinton as deeply hypocritical. The *Idaho Statesman* revealed that Representative Helen Chenoweth had had an affair with a married man. The *Statesman* decided to expose Chenoweth's six-year affair because she had run a series of TV ads attacking Clinton for his relationship with Lewinsky ahead of the 1998 midterm elections (see Sabato et al. 2000, p. 115). The *Indianapolis Star and News* took up the story, broken by a small magazine *Nuvo*, that Indianapolis Congressman and long-time Clinton critic Dan Burton had had a child out of wedlock (Davis, 2006; Kurtz, 1998; Sabato et al., 2000). Washington magazine *Roll Call* broke perhaps the most significant story, about Bob Livingston, who was forced to admit to a string of extra-marital affairs, resulting in him giving up his ambition to be House Speaker (Calvert, 2000). Salon.com revealed that Henry Hyde, the Republican Congressman presiding over the House Judiciary Committee hearing articles of impeachment against Bill Clinton, had an extra-marital affair in the 1960s (Calvert, 2000; Sabato et al., 2000; see also Robertson, 1998).

These two events can be seen as critical moments in the decline of reticence in a way that previous highlighted cases were not. The Chappaquiddick incident in July 1969 was important but was an isolated event; the same can be said for the exposure of Gary Hart's extra-marital sex life in 1987 (see Ross, 1988; Splichal & Garrison, 2000). Similarly, in the UK, the Profumo scandal in 1963 was not a critical moment in the way the back-to-basics sex exposés were. Indeed, post-Profumo, with exception of the Boothby scandal in 1964, which saw the *Daily Mirror* pay damages for printing unproven allegations that a peer, Lord Boothby, was having a homosexual affair with a London gangster, there were no more revelations until 1973. The decade was more notable for an absence of the exposés that mark contemporary British political communication (see Bingham, 2009). These events are important points in the weakening reticence, and more incidents could be added, but they did not alter the media consensus.

Why did Major's back-to-basics speech and the Clinton impeachment lead to a weakening of journalistic reticence in a way previous incidents did not? They did so because the actions of some of the political class fundamentally outraged the media and generated a backlash. It was this large-scale backlash that was missing before. In the US, it was a reaction against the hypocrisy of conservative Republican Representatives who seemed to be condemning Clinton's extra-marital activity while some engaged in similar conduct themselves. US newspapers were not restricted by privacy protection legislation as their continental European counterparts are. In the UK, it was a reaction against the perceived hypocrisy of a Conservative government that trumpeted a return to traditional family values while its own ministers engaged in extra-marital dalliances. UK newspapers were similarly unhindered by privacy protection legislation. In both countries, sections of the media perceived Republican Representatives and the Conservative government's moralizing as hypocritical. Hypocrisy is one of the key justifications for intrusion in the US and UK where there is no strong consensus on what constitutes the public interest. Public displays of double standards are seen as providing a legitimate reason for exposure (see Sabato et al., 2000).

The other conditions shown in chapter 2 were, of course, also necessary, but not sufficient without the fundamental weakening of the ethical consensus on non-consensual exposure. If political elites in both countries had had strong legal privacy protection, as in continental Europe, then it is unlikely that the consensus would have broken as it would have had a legal underpinning. Secondary sources show that attitudes towards non-consensual exposure changed after these points. For example, a survey of US press journalists in 1993 and 1999 conducted by Splichal and Garrison – before and after Clinton–Lewinsky – found that attitudes towards coverage of the extra-marital affairs of politicians had shifted, with more journalists in 1999 saying they felt less strongly about the presence of such coverage (2000, p. 171). This change in attitude can be seen in the behaviour of US elite newspapers. In 1996 the *Washington Post* and other serious papers initially refrained from printing stories about presidential candidate Bob Dole's long-finished extra-marital affair because it was not deemed relevant to his presidential challenge (see Sabato et al., 2000; Entman, 2012). Paterno (1997) notes that executives at the *Washington Post* ignored the story because it was deemed old and irrelevant. In 2008, the *New York Times* was the first to publish allegations that Republican presidential nominee John McCain had had an affair with a lobbyist, Vicki Iseman – something it would perhaps have ignored ten years ago. Similarly, in 2012, ABC news programme *Nightline*, and the *Washington Post*, were the first to publicize allegations by Newt Gingrich's second wife, Marianne, that Newt had wanted an 'open' marriage, and had told her to put up with his affair with Callista Bisek – now his third wife. Although there are no similar surveys over the same time period in the UK, a comparison of research on scandal reporting before and after the back-to-basics scandals suggests journalists have become less inhibited in reporting the extra-marital trysts of politicians (King 1986; Sanders & Canel, 2006; Tumber, 2004).

This chapter has so far shown how critical moments go some way to explaining the sudden change that occurred in both countries. The back-to-basics campaign and the Clinton impeachment fundamentally transformed journalistic attitudes to politicians' extra-marital infidelity. Outlets that normally shied away from non-consensual exposure decided to expose the hypocrisy they witnessed; those that were formerly wary of crossing personal boundaries did so. It became acceptable to report on politicians' peccadilloes in a way that it previously was not. As chapter 2 has shown, these critical moments have normalized coverage of infidelity often on much more spurious grounds: it is now possible to publicize personal matters in a way that it previously was not, and to justify it in various other ways – or in any way a journalist sees fit.

Are current levels of exposure exceptional?

So far the chapter has shown a surge of cases of publicized infidelity in the UK and the US since 1970, but what happened before this date? Is exposure largely a contemporary phenomenon or is it something that has reoccurred from time to time? While it is not possible within the scope of this book to conduct primary historical research to address this question, there is a growing body of literature that can shed light on the exposure of marital infidelity during the eighteenth and nineteenth centuries.

In the US, from the times of the early republic, the literature suggests politicians have dug dirt on each other, revealing it for their own electoral advantage. For example, Benjamin Franklin complained in 1781 of those 'who will abuse you while you are serving them, and wound your character in nameless pamphlets' (cited in Jamieson, 1992, p. 233). Adut notes that personal rumour about extra-marital affairs was rife in American politics of the antebellum period, with 'every presidential candidate . . . rumoured to be either a bastard or the father of a second family' (Adut, 2008, p. 187; see Cogan, 1996). John Summers, in his article 'What Happened to Sex Scandals?' (2000), suggests that the scrutiny of the sexual character of office holders has varied dramatically over time. During the period from around the 1790s through to the 1890s, an office holder's sexual character was subjected to close scrutiny; however, for much of the twentieth century the exposure of sexual turpitude of those in high office had almost disappeared. He notes that the exposure of marital infidelity largely ceased between the presidency of Grover Cleveland in 1884 and, roughly, that of Bill Clinton some 100 years later. He observes that the 'foul gossip' identified by Theodore Roosevelt could still circulate in 1913 but it did so 'just under the surface' of public life (Summers, 2000, p. 825). Indeed, it is often remarked that extra-marital affairs of a string of US Presidents received no publicity, even though widely known about by journalists. For example, President Harding's affairs with Carrie Phillips and Nan Britton, Franklin D. Roosevelt's relationships with Lucy Mercer Rutherford and Missey LeHand, Eisenhower's romance with Kay

Summersby, Kennedy's affairs with Marilyn Monroe and others, and Lyndon Johnson's affair with Helen Gahagan Douglas went unreported. Roberts provides an example of the reticence that pervaded American journalism in the 1940s. He cites the example of *Washington Post* columnist Jerry Kluttz, who, before publishing news about the renewal of President Roosevelt's relationship with Lucy Mercer Rutherford, went to see the *Post*'s publisher Eugene Meyer. Meyer told Kluttz that the '*Post* will never use any stories . . . that would bring disrespect upon the president of the United States' (Roberts, 1997). It was only with the Clinton–Lewinsky scandal that, Summers (2000) argues, sexual character was once more subjected to close scrutiny (see also Adut, 2008; Ross, 1988; West & Orman, 2003). Summers's interpretation raises an intriguing question: can such a pattern be found in other countries? Unfortunately there are no similar studies that I have been able to find for the UK, but a picture can be constructed based on a series of secondary sources. What I want to suggest, drawing upon these secondary historical sources, is that media exposure in the UK has been erratic, appearing and disappearing from public gaze with peaks and troughs.

In the UK, like the US, there are examples of politicians' peccadilloes being made public through the eighteenth and nineteenth centuries (see Clark, 2003; Diamond, 2004; Thompson, 2000). Clark observes that allegations of sexual turpitude were a common part of late eighteenth-century politics. Political opponents, whether conservative or radical, Tory or Whig, accused each other of transgressing sexual norms. Accusations were circulated in pamphlets and in newspapers owned by or sympathetic to particular parties and politicians. Politicians could pay to have embarrassing revelations about their opponents placed in newspapers (Clark, 2003). For radicals, the transgression of sexual norms by those in power was evidence of the systematic corruption of the political class; for conservatives, the licentious acts of radical politicians were evidence of the moral anarchy which threatened the social order (2003). One high-profile politician accused of gross moral turpitude was radical Whig MP John Wilkes. Wilkes fought back, using his paper, the *North Briton*, to attack the King and the governments of Lord Bute and George Grenville (Thompson, 2000). Exposure of malfeasance, alleged or real, was a weapon in the power struggles between different political factions. Thompson also puts such exposure down to a number of other factors, such as the rise of the mass-circulation commercial press and professional journalists becoming less reliant on the financial support of politicians and political parties. It is in this context that scandal came to be seen as something factual, something that was uncovered (Thompson, 2000). High-profile divorces provided much fodder for a growing mass-circulation press.

Extra-marital indiscretions were reported, but it was often in subtle terms that would be lost on the audience of today. For example, in the Parnell case, the *Pall Mall Gazette* of May 1886 revealed that Parnell was living with the wife of a fellow MP, William O'Shea: when reporting his involvement in an accident, it noted that, when Parliament was sitting, 'the Hon. Member for Cork usually takes-up residence in Eltham' (the *Pall Mall Gazette*, 24 May 1886, cited in Parris & Maguire, 2005, p. 50), Eltham being where O'Shea's wife Kitty lived. In the 1880s there was a series of high-profile divorce trials which involved leading politicians of the day and which received widespread press coverage. In the UK, in 1886, one divorce case named Charles Dilke, a Liberal MP, as co-respondent, despite his denials (Parris & Maguire, 2005; Thompson, 2000). In a divorce case four years later, Captain O'Shea cited Charles Stewart Parnell as co-respondent (see Parris & Maguire, 2004; Thompson, 2000). With few reporting restrictions, every salacious detail was made much of in the press. The opponents of Irish home rule in the media were especially quick to pounce on Parnell's activities. However, as in the US, it seems for much of the twentieth century, at least until the Profumo scandal in 1963, the extra-marital dalliances of politicians received no coverage. There is agreement that David Lloyd George's relationship with Frances Stevenson, or Dorothy MacMillan's affair and alleged illegitimate child by another politician, would not have gone unreported today (Seaton, 2003; Seymour-Ure, 2003; Tunstall, 1996).

It is important to state, before we can speculate as to whether current levels of exposure are unique, that publicized cases in the eighteenth century need to be treated with caution. They were often no more than allegations and rumours, not the exposure of norm transgression we see today. As Thompson (2000) perceptively observes, the very notion of a scandal changes by the nineteenth century, so it is no longer simply the publication of libellous, seditious or obscene accusations, but the disclosure through the media of an event which involves some transgression of societal norms (2000, p. 52). Such a changing definition poses problems for pre-nineteenth-century temporal comparisons, therefore if we limit the comparison to the exposure of transgression of sexual norms from the mid nineteenth century onwards, the secondary literature shows that there were some high-profile examples, but they largely seem to be exceptions: the growing secondary literature in this area is not packed with examples. While any conclusion is highly speculative, the absence of examples does suggest that current levels of exposure may indeed be exceptional.

If the high levels of exposure are largely a contemporary phenomenon in the UK and the US, is the lack of exposure of politicians' infidelity a contemporary phenomenon in France and Germany, for example? Or is the current lack of exposure in these democracies exceptional? Studies reveal that the current level of rectitude when reporting the infidelity of public figures in contemporary Germany was absent in Wilhelmine Germany at the end of the nineteenth century and the beginning of the twentieth century. Hall, in his historical study *Scandal, Sensation and Social Democracy* (1977), observes that the press in Wilhelmine Germany used revelations about the private lives of leading political figures as a weapon in political struggles. He notes that journalists working for the SPD (Social Democratic Party of Germany), the main socialist political party, believed it was their 'duty to expose the hollowness of bourgeois claims to be the guardians of public morality' and their double standards (1977, p. 144). Likewise, leading members of the SPD were often the subjects of personal revelations by the conservative or establishment press. Perhaps the most high-profile exposé of the era concerned the sexuality of some of the Kaiser's close advisors. In 1906, journalist and editor of a satirical weekly periodical, *Die Zukunft* (The Future), Maximilian Harden, reported the revelations that several of the Kaiser's advisors, including Prince Philipp zu Eulenburg-Hertefeld and General Graf von Moltke, were homosexual or, in his words, 'sexually abnormal' (see Vargo, 2003). Harden was not a socialist but a supporter of Bismarck and long-term critic of the Kaiser and his style of government and saw exposure as a means of bringing it to an end. In 1902 he had threatened to expose Eulenburg unless he resigned from his political post. Provided with information by Eulenburg's opponents, he went on to make a series of further accusations in 1906 which ended in the libel courts. Both Eulenburg and Moltke sued, and the trials that followed, which included the testimony of General Moltke's estranged wife, received widespread coverage in the media not only in Germany but around the world (see Domeier, 2007). As in the US and UK, coverage of the personal lives of politicians seems thereafter to disappear from public view. In part this can be explained by the emergence of a law of personality in the late nineteenth century providing individuals with protection from insults and disrespect, and the extension of rights over one's image (Whitman, 2004). In other words, scandal politics of the late nineteenth century as detailed by Hall seems to have been kept in check by an emerging law of personality. By 1914 personality rights within German law had become quite extensive, granting those in public life significant protection, rights that did not disappear with the Nazis (see Ross, 2008; Whitman, 2004). After the defeat of the Nazis in 1945, citizens' personality rights were enshrined in the constitution of the new Federal Republic, as discussed in chapter 2 (see Holtz-Bacha, 2004; Whitman, 2004).

In pre-revolutionary eighteenth-century France, despite press licensing, unlicensed printed pamphlets circulated widely in Paris (Baecque, 1989). Particularly popular were the 'mémoires judiciaries' – the often melodramatic retelling of sensational trials involving the landed aristocracy (Maza, 1993). These scandal sheets were printed in their thousands and provided the public with the latest twists and turns in the trials of public figures, and were widely discussed (1993). They exposed the personal lives of the political class to the public gaze, with political opponents seizing such disclosures as evidence of a corrupt aristocracy. Exposure of the aristocracy's transgressions of norms was very much part of the effort to show the old ruling class were unfit to govern (Baecque, 1989). Revolutionary leaders were not spared similar accusations, as pamphlets were mobilized by different factions to spread rumours and denounce opponents (Popkin, 1990). Lindsay and Ricketson (2006) argue that it was precisely the activities of the press during the revolutionary period, and the lifting of Napoleonic-era censorship laws, that led to calls for privacy protection in French society by political elites in the early nineteenth century. The feeling was that it was necessary to provide citizens whose private lives had been intruded upon the right to legal redress. The idea of private life needing to be 'walled off' from the press, articulated by philosopher Pierre Paul Royer-Collard in 1819, was taken up by the courts in a series of cases in the nineteenth century, the most well-known involving salacious photographs of novelist Alexandre Dumas and his lover (Whitman, 2004). The outcome was a basic privacy law: privacy became regarded as a basic personality right (Lindsay & Ricketson, 2006, p. 134; see also Whitman, 2004). Indeed, when the French President Félix Faure died while engaged in sex with his mistress in 1899, the details were never made public. If we consider the exposure of transgression of sexual norms, then the secondary literature, like that focusing on the US and the UK, is not packed with cases. Of course, we need to exercise similar levels of caution – there are a few high-profile cases, but these seem to be exceptions. The relative absence of cases in France and Germany is not new but can be traced back to the emergence of strong personality rights that give legal protection to those in public life (Whitman, 2004) – rights that were added to over the course of the twentieth century, giving those in public life a substantial degree of legal protection which their colleagues in the US and the UK did not have (Whitman, 2004).

In the US and the UK, such statutory privacy rights were seen as an anathema to cherished freedom-of-expression norms

(Whitman, 2004). The rise of reticence in the twentieth century was not the result of legal privacy protection but other factors. Summers, in his study of press reporting of politicians' peccadilloes in the US, suggests that its absence for a large part of the twentieth century was the result of two key factors: the rise of professional journalism free from 'partisan moorings' of the past and with strong ethical guidelines (2000, p. 826), and the emergence of a centralized national political authority or order which was seen as being above the partisan fray and worthy of respect (2000). These factors, it could be argued, proved less robust than the legal framework established in France and Germany, and with their demise reticence disappeared too. Of course, the patterns in other democracies might well differ; the point here is to illustrate present developments in relation to a longer historical period and to speculate on the uniqueness of the present situation.

Dying and reviving? Reticence in Italy, Germany and the UK

Earlier, this chapter advanced the idea of critical moments as tipping points which bring about change. There have recently been a series of high-profile incidents in Italy, Germany and the UK which might have the potential to change practices around the exposure of politicians' sexual relationships. These are: the Berlusconi sex scandal in Italy; the Buntegate scandal in Germany; and the phone-hacking scandal at the *News of the World* in the UK. It might be too soon to say whether they indeed prove to be critical moments but I want consider whether each has the potential to become a critical moment or not. These high-profile incidents all stand out in a national context in terms of the scale of the revelations and their ability to shock; they are incidents that have gained much attention and whose consequences are still emerging, but nonetheless have the potential to change practices. This section examines the three cases above, assessing the evidence as to whether they might indeed have the potential to be critical moments.

Italian politics: becoming intimized?

The revelations surrounding Italian Prime Minister Silvio Berlusconi's private life have dominated the Italian media between 2009 and 2011, and raise the question of whether attitudes towards the privacy of politicians are changing in Italy. Berlusconi is not the first Italian leader to be rumoured to have had an active extra-marital sex life: it was widely alleged, although never reported, that Prime Minister Bettino Craxi had an affair with porn actress Moana Pozzi in the 1980s. There is, though, no evidence prior to 2009 that the kind of exposure familiar in the US and UK occurred (see Cepernich, 2008). So, can the Berlusconi revelations and other exposés of politicians' extra-marital sex lives that followed in their wake be considered a transformative critical moment? To answer this, we need to examine the various factors that led to the exposure of Berlusconi's personal life in 2009.

The first of these, and perhaps the most important, is Veronica Lario, Berlusconi's second wife. For some time it was known that Berlusconi and his wife lived separate lives, their relationship characterized by the occasional public criticism of each other. In 2002, for example, Berlusconi quipped in a joint press conference with then Danish Prime Minister Anders F. Rasmussen that he would introduce him to his wife as he was better-looking than Cacciari. The comments were widely reported as suggesting his wife was having an affair with Venice Mayor and philosophy professor Massimo Cacciari. Indeed, later that year, when the Berlusconis' daughter enrolled to study philosophy at Cacciari's faculty, Berlusconi told the newspaper *La Libertà di Piacenza* that she was in an ideal situation. Ms Lario was equally vocal about her husband's dalliances with other women. In 2007, having failed to secure a private apology over compliments Berlusconi had paid two women at a television awards ceremony, she was moved to write an open letter demanding a public apology. In the letter published in *La Repubblica*, she said the comments he made – that he would like to marry Miss Amazonia, if he was not married already, and that he would go anywhere with the Miss Smiles winner Mara Carfagna – could not be dismissed as jokes. They

had damaged her dignity. 'To my husband' she wrote '. . . I therefore ask for a public apology not having received one privately'
(see I. Fisher, 2007; Hooper, 2007). The letter gained widespread
media attention, with three evening talk shows devoted to the
affair (I. Fisher, 2007). Berlusconi then apologized in his own open
letter, in which he begged the forgiveness of his wife (2007). In
April 2009, in an email to the Italian news agency ANSA, leaked
to various Italian newspapers, Ms Lario once more voiced her
anger at her husband's relations with young women, this time in
the context of the short-listing of politically inexperienced young
female models as party candidates in the 2009 European parliamentary elections. Berlusconi, in response, publicly complained
that his wife was trying to undermine his campaign. At the same
time, the story surfaced in *La Repubblica* that Berlusconi had
attended the eighteenth birthday of Noemi Letizia, a friend's
daughter, buying her an expensive gold and diamond necklace
(Cepernich, 2010). The liaison was given further credence when
Corriere del Mezzogiorno published an interview with Letizia, in
which she confessed to calling Berlusconi 'Papi'. Lario denounced
this liaison to ANSA, complaining that he (Berlusconi) never
attended his own children's eighteenth birthdays, even though
invited (2010; Owen & Hanley, 2009). A few days later, in early
May 2009, she announced in *La Repubblica* and *La Stampa* that
she intended to divorce Berlusconi. In a detailed statement she laid
out her reasons, the final straw being Berlusconi's attendance of
Noemi Letizia's birthday. She stated she could no longer 'stay with
a man who surrounds himself with minors', and although she had
stood by her husband and tried to help him she could no longer do
so (Cepernich, 2010; Owen & Hanley, 2009).

The second factor we need to consider in combination with
the first is the left/right partisan divide in Italian politics. Italian
media, and the Italian press in particular, are largely divided along
partisan lines (see Hallin & Mancini, 2004). There is a section of
the press that is hostile to Berlusconi. It was no accident that Lario
chose her husband's biggest critic and Italy's largest-circulation
broadsheet, *La Repubblica*, to air her opinions; she knew she
would be guaranteed exposure. Another prominent publisher

of Berlusconi revelations has been the left-of-centre newspaper *Corriere della Sera*. These papers were not just mouthpieces for Veronica Lario but also opponents of her husband. Throughout May 2009, the story of Berlusconi's peccadilloes unfolded as, first, he denied having met Noemi on her own, only to be contradicted by her boyfriend who claimed that they had met the previous year, and then *Corriere della Sera* reported the existence of photographs of Noemi taken at a New Year's Eve party at Berlusconi's villa, a fact confirmed by her mother. By the end of May, Berlusconi was forced to broach the issue once more, issuing a formal statement 'swearing on his children' that he never had 'spicy' relations with Letizia. *La Repubblica* challenged Berlusconi's version of events, demanding that Berlusconi answer eight key questions about his relationship and other issues. In June 2009, the revelations took a new twist when *Corriere della Sera* broke the news that Berlusconi had had a sexual relationship with escort girl Patrizia D'Addario. In July of the same year, *La Repubblica* and Italian news magazine *L'Espresso* posted online secret recordings made by Italian magistrates investigating businessman Giampaolo Tarantini. In one made at the Palazzo Grazioli, Berlusconi could be heard to ask Patrizia D'Addario to wait for him in 'Putin's bed' while he had a shower – the bed being a gift from the former Russian President. In other recordings D'Addario complains to Tarantini about a lack of sleep while with Berlusconi and not having received the pay she was promised (Hooper, 2009). The recordings of Patrizia D'Addario and Berlusconi were made public on the *La Repubblica* website and attracted thousands of hits and comments (see chapter 4). The release of the recordings was condemned by Berlusconi as an attempt to discredit him, but was not legally challenged. We are fortunate enough to have a content analysis of the Italian press coverage of these revelations over seventy-one days, from 29 April when revelations started to 9 July 2009 (see Cepernich, 2010). This shows that the revelations received widespread coverage across all newspapers but that certain papers – namely, left-of-centre critics and right-of-centre Berlusconi supporters – provided the most vociferous coverage, although for very different reasons. In *La Repubblica*, *Corriere della Sera* and *L'Unità*, coverage was hostile, with allegations kept on their front pages nearly every day: *La Repubblica* covered events every day over the period, *Corriere della Sera* covered the allegations every day but one, and *L'Unità* every day but two (Cepernich, 2010).

The revelations continued in 2010; in late October, *La Repubblica* published the strange story of a young woman's release from a Milan police cell (Colaprico & D'Avanzo, 2010). The report suggested that Karima el-Mahroug, a.k.a. Ruby Rubacouri or Ruby Heartbreaker, arrested for theft, had been released without charge on the request of the Prime Minister's office, which claimed that she was the granddaughter of then Egyptian President Hosni Mubarak. In a subsequent interview with prosecutors investigating a vice ring, Ruby claimed to have attended parties at Berlusconi's villa near Milan, where she received numerous gifts from Berlusconi, including money, and had witnessed an after-dinner sex game known euphemistically as 'bunga-bunga' (2010). Having survived a vote of no confidence in January 2011, Berlusconi was placed under official investigation and invited by state prosecutors to appear for questioning in Milan. The news broken by *Corriere della Sera* suggested he was under suspicion of paying for sex with a woman under the official age of consent, 18; Ruby the Heartbreaker was 17 at the time. Further allegations of paying for sex with other young women followed, with the prosecutor's report alleging he had paid for sex with a significant number of women under the official age of consent. While the left-of-centre press seemed determined not to let developments slip from the public's view, the Berlusconi-supporting papers *Il Giornale* and *Libero* were, in contrast, defensive, their copy aimed at refuting allegations and attacking Berlusconi's perceived opponents, such as Veronica Lario, certain judges and influential left-wingers (Cepernich, 2010).

These two factors, a scorned partner and a partisan media hostile towards Berlusconi, were combined with two other ones. The initial revelations were publicized against the backdrop of a European parliamentary election campaign. The campaign added an extra impetus to press coverage as Berlusconi's opponents saw an opportunity to damage him. The other factor, not mentioned so far, is the judiciary, who have played an important political role in the Second Republic in investigating official corruption. Many of these intimate revelations have come to light in judicial investigations. The prosecuting magistrates have been key to investigating the so-called 'bunga-bunga affair'. In January 2011, prosecutors handed a dossier to Parliament containing allegations about Berlusconi paying for sex with under-age women. This is not to say that Berlusconi's personal life was always the focus of such investigations: as the D'Addario tapes show, revelations were also a by-product of investigations focused elsewhere – ones that partisan actors in the press have, though, been keen to exploit for political purposes.

Do the Berlusconi revelations represent a point of change in Italian political communication? Perhaps not on their own, but in the wake of the Berlusconi revelations there was a series of further exposés: in 2009, left-of-centre Governor of Lazio Piero Marrazzo resigned after a blackmail plot, involving a video of him and transgender prostitutes taking drugs, became public (Israely, 2009; Rizzo, 2009). In January 2010, Democratic Party Mayor of Bologna Flavio Delbono was forced to resign after it was revealed that he used public money to fund private trips with his lover while Vice President of the Emilia-Romagna region. In February 2010, Guido Bertolaso, head of the Italian civil protection agency and close friend of Berlusconi, was accused of using the sexual services provided at a spa resort near Rome, and organizing sex parties in return for public contracts. In July, Pier Paolo Zaccai, a councillor in Rome for Berlusconi's PDL (The People of Freedom), was revealed as having an affair with a Brazilian transgender prostitute after he was hospitalized for excessive drug use.

There needs to be some caution in how we interpret these acts, though; their exposure is certainly not driven by media outrage at elite hypocrisy, as is the case in the US and UK, nor do we see the 'politics of mutual destruction' whereby extra-marital dalliances become a weapon designed to cause opponents maximum political damage. Italy still has laws that protect public figures' privacy. In the Delbono case, there was a clear misuse of public funds: it was this, not an issue of character, driving exposure. In the Marrazzo case, it was his admission of a plot to blackmail him that brought the case to public attention, not a kiss-and-tell by one of the prostitutes. In the Zaccai case, it was his hospitalization after shouting at the public from his apartment balcony and the resulting police investigation which led to the discovery of the evidence of the sex-and-drug parties in his flat and of his affairs. In the Bertolaso case, it was an official investigation into construction contracts and bribes that brought his indiscretions to light. In other words, the Italian media are reliant on other actors – spouses, investigating judges – to leak or disclose information but, unlike in the UK, tabloids would not mount their own investigations of politicians' personal lives nor pay for kiss-and-tells. It remains to be seen whether this is a revelatory dynamic that will produce the flows of revelations witnessed in the US and UK – they might well be intermittent and disappear with Berlusconi's replacement Prime Minister, Mario Monti, and the new political climate.

Buntegate

Next I want to consider developments in Germany in light of revelations in 2010 about the lengths the magazine *Bunte* went to to gather information on politicians' sexual relationships. The exposure of politicians' sex lives and extra-marital relationships in Germany has been very rare despite them being known about by journalists (see chapter 2). When exposés have occurred, they have often had a strong public-interest motive. For example, in 1995, married CDU Interior Minister Heinz Eggert was outed by *Der Spiegel*, but only as part of an investigation by the magazine into complaints that he was sexually harassing his male staff. Again, in 2007, revelations emerged in the media of the extra-marital dalliances of SPD MP Hans-Juergen Uhl, but only as part of a wider investigation into corrupt practices at Volkswagen.

They have also been connected to internal party struggles. Much speculation followed revelations in 1993 that Christian Social Union (CSU) politician, and minister in the Kohl government, Theo Waigel, who was standing for leadership of the Bavarian political party the CSU, was living apart from his wife Karin. Although there was never a mention of the woman he was having a relationship with, and would later marry, the Olympic skier Irene Epple, Waigel issued a statement admitting that he and his wife lived separate lives, and appealed for privacy. The rumours damaged his chance of being elected party leader. Some fifteen years later, in 2007, rumours that another challenger for the CSU leadership, Horst Seehofer, was having an extra-marital affair surfaced in German tabloid *Bild* in a story about dirty politics and power struggles in the CSU (Das Gupta, 2007). What these cases share is their link to the internal party struggles for leadership of the Bavarian political party the CSU; Buntegate, though, has different origins.

Buntegate was an outcome of an investigation published in the weekly news magazine *Stern*, in February 2010, alleging that *Bunte* had employed a private research firm, CMK, to spy on politicians over several years. The leaked papers documented CMK's surveillance of the flat of former SPD party chief, Franz Münterfering. The research firm secretly took photographs of him and his new partner Michelle Schumann. Indeed, *Bunte* had broken the news of Münterfering's new romance after the death of his wife in May 2009 with the headline, 'Good to See He Can Laugh Again'. The other tactics revealed included following Schumann, placing a device to intercept her mail, and a motion detector placed under the flat's doormat to signal when the flat was occupied. The documents also showed that *Bunte* was prepared to pay CMK to spy on leader of the Left Party Oskar Lafontaine and party MP Sahra Wagenknecht, his alleged lover. Although the investigation never led to a story, the research firm had planned to install CCTV in the living room of Lafontaine's Berlin home and gain an internship in his party, all to get information on his relationship. *Bunte*'s 2008 revelations about CSU party leader Horst Seehofer's extra-marital affair were also based on information gathered by CMK (Roehrig & Tillack, 2010). *Stern* further alleged that, at the behest of *Bunte*, CMK had followed the CDU premier of Lower Saxony, Christian Wulff, and his new wife on their honeymoon in Pisa; it had spied on the then SPD Transport Minister Wolfgang Tiefensee and his new girlfriend Annette Bender in 2007; and on the former CDU premier of Baden-Württemberg, Günther Oettinger, and his new girlfriend Friederike Beyer in 2008 (*Stern*, 2010). The extent of CMK's alleged activities provoked national debate about the activities of the press. These revelations raise the question whether attitudes are changing in the German media. Is this perhaps a critical moment in the media reportage of German politicians, driven in part by a celebrity-driven media and the need to boost circulation? I would argue that *Bunte*'s activities remain very much an exception. Prior to this, other revelations of infidelity were linked to actual malfeasance or power struggles within the CSU. In addition, as in Italy, the laws which provide public figures with privacy protection, and a strong ethical consensus in the media about when it is appropriate to intrude, mean acts of intrusion such as those witnessed in the Buntegate scandal provoke a strong response which might well lead to a further tightening of the law.

Phone-hacking at News of the World: the return of reticence?

The revelations and wide-spread opprobrium concerning the *News of the World* hacking the phones of celebrities, those in public life and members of the public reached a height in July 2011, and it could be argued they might have spelled the end of the casual exposure of the sex lives of politicians and other public figures. The scandal originated in 2006 with the arrest and trial of *News of the World* journalist Clive Goodman and private investigator Glenn Mulcaire for illegally accessing the voice messages of Princes William and Harry. Over the following four years an investigation by the *Guardian* and the *New York Times*, as well as numerous claims by public figures, including senior politicians, that their phones were hacked, cast doubt on News International's claim that phone hacking was limited to Goodman and Mulcaire (Davies, 2009). Although the *News of the World* was by no means the only newspaper to use private investigators to hack phones (see table 3.2), by July 2011 public outrage reached fever pitch in the wake of revelations about the *News of the World*'s alleged hacking into the phones of murdered schoolgirl Milly Dowler, the families of the 7/7 bombing victims and those of soldiers who had died in Afghanistan. The fallout from these revelations and the public opprobrium were dramatic. Some may argue that we have been here before, the post-war history of the British press is littered with inquiries into press standards, recommendations for reform and some limited reforms (see Koss, 1984). The period saw three Royal Commissions on the Press, the Calcutt review on press standards, and numerous parliamentary investigations. While these altered the regulatory environment, their impact on press behaviour has been limited. The Press Council established in the 1950s, deemed ineffectual, was replaced by the Press Complaints Commission in 1991; it too was seen as lacking the necessary powers to control press excesses. However, I would argue that the current situation, unlike in the past, has the potential to reshape the media environment, for a number of reasons.

First, the hacking scandal comes on top of other important legal developments, which perhaps indicate the attitudes to privacy are changing – most significantly, the inclusion of the European Human Rights Act into UK law (Tambini & Heyward, 2002). This and other laws discussed in chapter 2 have provided a check on the actions of the press. Article 8 of the Human Rights Act, for example, gives individuals privacy rights, which has led to a series of injunctions by high-profile public figures preventing the media from publishing personal information on the grounds that it infringes their privacy. By 2010 the number of injunctions being given had apparently grown (Whittle & Cooper, 2009).

The second reason is the key decision made by Rupert Murdoch to close the *News of the World*. Its closure may not mean the end of exposé journalism, but its disappearance marks an end to one of the most prolific invaders of politicians' privacy. Of the 39 cases of publicized infidelity involving politicians between 1970 and 2009 in the UK, 13 cases (33 per cent) were broken by the *News of the World*. Its absence will make a significant difference to the level of revelations, even if a replacement may emerge. The third reason is the judicial inquiry into events headed by Lord Leveson. In addition to investigating the whole hacking saga, the inquiry was given wide-ranging powers and a remit to examine the culture, practices and ethics of the press and the failure of the current system of self-regulation, and to make recommendations for its reform (see levesoninquiry.org.uk). The final reason is the abolition of the

Table 3.2 The use of private investigators by British newspapers (top five users of private investigators)

Newspaper	Number of transactions positively identified	Number of journalists using services
Daily Mail	952	58
Sunday People	802	50
Daily Mirror	681	45
Mail on Sunday	266	33
News of the World	228	23

Source: compiled by author from Information Commissioner's Office (2006b). See also Leigh & Evans (2006).

Press Complaints Commission and its replacement with a new regulatory body, something perhaps more akin to the Office of Communication (Ofcom), with possible powers to fine newspapers or impose some other credible form of punishment. Although the final look of such a body will be decided at a later date, it is unlikely that it will be as 'ineffective' or 'lacking in rigour' as the current PCC and it will not be one that newspaper owners could decide to opt out of (Sparrow, 2012). These decisions may well have long-lasting implications and, while they are not the first attempt to reform the British press, as noted, it is perhaps less likely that they will be stymied by the press. The press, in the face of the *News of the World* scandal, is perhaps in too weak a position to mount any resistance to reform.

Other newspapers have been implicated in phone hacking and have widely used private investigators to uncover owners of vehicles, ex-directory phone numbers, driving licence details, mobile phone records and the details of any criminal records (Information Commissioner's Office, 2006a). The Leveson inquiry may force further disclosures that may well shame the press into silence.

The hacking scandal, coming on top of the introduction of the Human Rights Act into law, may well come to be seen as a critical moment that reshapes the national privacy culture and marks a return to greater reticence when it comes to reporting politicians' sex lives in the UK.

Conclusion

This chapter used comprehensive time-series data to ascertain the extent to which marital infidelity was publicized across countries over forty years. The data show that there has been a divergence between countries. The key finding is that publicized cases of infidelity were not always at their current levels in the US and UK, but have increased over time and quite dramatically in the 1990s. A gap has opened up between the US and UK and other democracies, especially the continental European states whose levels of exposure have remained quite modest. The chapter has tried to understand this sudden change in the UK and the US by advancing the idea of critical moments as points in time which mark a dramatic change in privacy cultures. The striking increase in the 1990s, this chapter contends, was the result of two critical moments when reticence about reporting the private lives of politicians was fundamentally weakened. The motivation for exposure during these transition points seems to have been a shared sense of outrage at the moral hypocrisy of certain politicians. This led to the exposure of a raft of cases that undermined any remaining consensus about when it is appropriate to expose the sex lives of politicians.

After these critical moments, exposure has continued apace, justified and unjustified, depending on the outlet. All politicians became fair game, and to expose marital infidelity normalized. The secondary historical literature examined here reminds us that revelations about politicians' private lives have been a feature of eighteenth- and nineteenth-century politics in the UK and the US, only to disappear for a good deal of the twentieth century before reappearing once more, if to a greater extent (Summers, 2000). We might, therefore, identify initial events, such as Chappaquiddick and Profumo, and, in the period after, interspersed occurrences, but it was the critical moments in the 1990s which led to an explosion of disclosures in the UK and the US. The *News of the World* hacking scandal may represent another critical moment in the case of the UK, possibly leading to the end of such disclosures, but more time is needed to see whether this is the case. In other words, critical moments may be a key ingredient in understanding the appearance, disappearance and reappearance of exposé journalism and, just as such moments may lead to emergence of such reporting, they may also lead to its demise.

4

Transnational Revelations: Flows, Access and Control in a Global News Environment

News and information flow across borders in ever-increasing volumes and at ever-increasing speeds, and stories about the infidelity of politicians are no exception. In the age of international 24-hour news, the peccadilloes of politicians in one country can become global news. For example, details about Bill Clinton's involvement with Monica Lewinsky were reported not just in the US but around the world, even in countries where the media are reticent about reporting the extra-marital transgressions of their own politicians (see Kumaraswamy, 1999; Merkl, 2001). This transnational news environment is also challenging national political elites' control over the flow of personal information. The legal restraints that have protected politicians' privacy in certain countries are being undermined in some instances by a transnational news environment beyond the control of national laws. In addition, the World Wide Web provides further sources of gossip and rumour about political elites which citizens in any democracy can access. This presents a challenge for politicians keen on keeping their sex lives private.

This chapter examines the degree to which news about politicians' peccadilloes in Australia, the US and the UK is reported in countries with a strong privacy protection, or whether such stories are largely ignored. We do not know to what extent the media in countries with strict privacy laws report the transgressions of the political classes of other countries. It is possible to imagine a scenario in France, Germany, Italy and Spain in which coverage of the extra-marital sex lives of their own politicians is largely absent while those of politicians in Australia, the US and the UK are regularly reported. This chapter also examines attempts by political elites to control the transnational flows of information about themselves. It is important to establish the extent to which this global news environment is challenging these elites and how they respond to the threat of unwanted international publicity. Finally, this chapter examines how the World Wide Web is transforming the flow of news and gossip about politicians' sexual relationships and widening exposure of and access to such information.

Infidelity as foreign spectacle

The global news environment continually recycles the domestic political news of nations; the national news and information from one state become part of the news texts of another (Boyd-Barrett, 2000). Some authors have termed this an 'international media echo' (see Oehlkers, 2000). In simple terms, news about politicians' personal lives in one country is recycled and very often finds its way into media copy in other countries. As mentioned, the Clinton–Lewinsky scandal provides a good example of the international media echo. It was first disclosed in the US press on 21 January 1998 and was picked up by nearly all major news outlets around the world the next day. Over the year, each twist and turn in the Clinton–Lewinsky scandal, from the initial revelations to the impeachment of President Clinton, was followed by international news outlets, with the latest information relayed on almost a daily basis (see Kumaraswamy, 1999, for media coverage in the Middle East, and Merkl, 2001, for media coverage in Western Europe). The example of the Clinton–Lewinsky scandal suggests that some news outlets, while not reporting the sexual transgressions of their own politicians, happily publish those that happen in another country; however, whether such a practice is commonplace or a one-off (as in the Clinton–Lewinsky scandal) is unknown. There has been no systematic examination of the extent to which the extra-marital exploits of Australian, UK and

Table 4.1 The number of cases of politicians' infidelity in Australia, the UK and US reported in French, German, Italian and Spanish newspapers (1992–2009)*

	US		UK		Australia	
Le Monde	28%	(12 of 43 cases)	29%	(10 of 34 cases)	0%	(0 of 10 cases)
Taz	26%	(11 of 43 cases)	26%	(9 of 34 cases)	0%	(0 of 10 cases)
La Stampa	37%	(16 of 43 cases)	38%	(13 of 34 cases)	10%	(1 of 10 cases)
El País	30%	(12 of 40 cases)	22%	(5 of 23 cases)	0%	(0 of 9 cases)

* A total of 87 cases of publicized infidelity were examined between 1992 and 2009 in *Le Monde, Taz* and *La Stampa*. In Spain the time period was 1996 to 2009 and the total number of cases examined for *El País* is 72.

Source: author-compiled from Nexis UK.

US politicians are news in countries with stronger privacy constraints. This section focuses on several issues: first, the extent to which news of infidelity of politicians in Australia, the UK and the US was recycled in the French, German, Italian and Spanish media, or whether the journalistic consensus on private lives of public figures, as outlined in chapter 2, extends to the coverage of politicians in other countries; second, if there *is* news coverage of politicians' infidelity, whether it is mainly US-focused or whether incidents in Australia and the UK are reported as well; and, third, when compared with Australian, UK and US media, do continental European media devote similar or less coverage to specific incidents of infidelity.

Table 4.1 shows the number of publicized cases of infidelity that received coverage in four serious newspapers.[1] What is clear at the start is that politicians' extra-marital sex lives in 'Anglo-American' democracies are not ignored, but neither do they all gain attention. Of the 87 publicized cases of adultery in Australia, the UK and US between 1992 and 2009, fewer than half gained coverage in the French, German, Italian and Spanish press. Of the 43 recorded US cases, 28 per cent of cases received coverage in one or more news items in *Le Monde*, 26 per cent in *Taz*, 37 per cent in *La Stampa*, and 30 per cent in *El País*. When it came to coverage of the UK, of the 34 recorded cases, 29 per cent received coverage in one or more news items in *Le Monde*, 26 per cent in *Taz*, 38 per cent in

La Stampa, and 22 per cent in *El País*. There was no coverage of the 10 cases of politicians' infidelity in Australia, except for in the Italian newspaper *La Stampa* in 2009. The figures also show that there is little difference between the newspapers in the proportion of instances they focused on in the US and the UK. On average over the period, across the newspapers, they covered 30 per cent of identified cases in the US and 29 per cent of possible cases in the UK. So it is clear that not all cases are of interest to the continental European media examined here, although outlets did cover a third of cases. So what cases interested these newspapers and how much coverage did they devote to infidelity? Figures 4.1 to 4.4 show the number of news items from 1992 to 2009 for the same four newspapers. The figures show that not all cases receive the same amount of attention and coverage is focused on certain key cases, with US cases being the subject of more attention than cases in the UK by some margin.

The figures also show coverage focused on cases in certain years. 1998, for instance, is a peak year in the coverage of US sex scandals; this is because of the Clinton–Lewinsky scandal and the subsequent revelations concerning Bob Livingston, Henry Hyde, Helen Chenoweth and Dan Burton, which generated a lot of coverage. There is another peak in 2008 with exposés of the extra-marital sex lives of a raft of politicians: Eliot Spitzer, the New York Governor; his replacement, David Paterson; John McCain, the Republican presidential nominee; John Edwards, a Democrat contender; and Kwame Kilpatrick, Mayor of Detroit. For the UK, the number of mentions peaks in the mid-1990s with the exposure of the extra-marital sex lives of politicians in the John Major government (examined in chapter 3). There is another peak in 2006 with revelations about Deputy Prime Minister John Prescott's affair; the gay affair of Mark Oaten MP, a married Liberal Democrat leadership candidate; and the extra-marital sexual antics of Scottish Socialist MSP Tommy Sheridan.

So why do the extra-marital antics of US and UK politicians attract the level of attention they do in continental European democracies? One possible reason put forward is that such scandals have a cultural significance that transcends national cultural

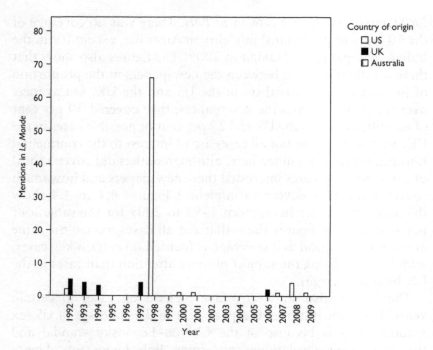

Figure 4.1 The number of news items mentioning politicians' infidelity in Australia, the UK and US in *Le Monde* (1992–2009)*

* Number of mentions for each identified case in a seven-day cycle including the day the story broke and six days after. 1992: Bill Clinton, Paddy Ashdown, David Mellor; 1993: Tim Yeo; 1994: Malcolm Sinclair, David Ashby; 1997: Jerry Hayes, Allan Stewart, Michael Hirst; 1998: Bill Clinton, Bob Livingston, Henry Hyde, Helen Chenoweth, Dan Burton; 2000: Rudy Giuliani; 2001: Gary Condit; 2006: Mark Oaten, John Prescott; 2007: Antonio Villaraigosa; 2008: John McCain, Eliot Spitzer; 2009: Mark Sanford.

Source: author-compiled from Nexis UK.

barriers. Tomlinson (1997) observes that certain scandals are culturally generalizable, and, thus, mobile across borders. They have an immediate relevance to the everyday lives of audiences in different countries. The global scandal is one that can be dis-embedded and re-embedded in a variety of different local contexts (1997). Another reason might be the global spread of market-driven journalism leading to the emergence of a global

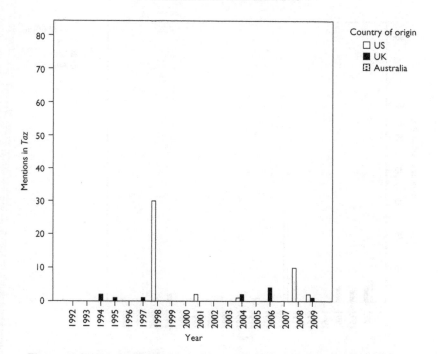

Figure 4.2 The number of news items mentioning politicians' infidelity in Australia, the UK and US in *Taz – die Tageszeitung* (1992–2009)*

*Number of mentions for each identified case in a seven-day cycle including the day the story broke and six days after. 1994: Malcolm Sinclair, Hartley Booth; 1995: Richard Spring; 1997: Michael Hirst; 1998: Bill Clinton, Bob Livingston, Henry Hyde, Helen Chenoweth; 2001: Gary Condit; 2004: Jim McGreevey, David Blunkett; 2006: John Prescott, Mark Oaten, Tommy Sheridan; 2008: David Paterson, John Edwards, John McCain, Eliot Spitzer; 2009: Mark Sanford, David Curry.

Source: author-compiled from Nexis UK.

infotainment culture where news becomes a form of entertainment focusing on sex, scandal, disaster and celebrity (Thussu, 2007, p. 7). However, such explanations, while plausible, do not adequately account for why the indiscretions of some politicians gain coverage while others are ignored, or why the peccadilloes of politicians in the US and the UK gain more attention than those from Australia.

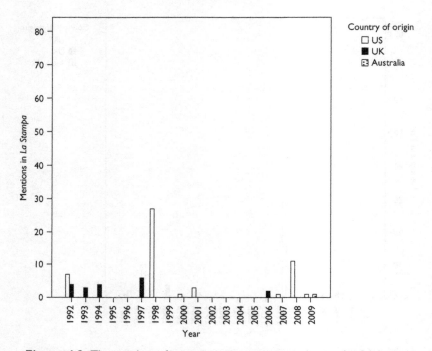

Figure 4.3 The number of news items mentioning politicians' infidelity in Australia, the UK and US in *La Stampa* (1992–2009)*

*Number of mentions for each identified case in a seven-day cycle including the day the story broke and six days after. 1992: Bill Clinton, Paddy Ashdown, David Mellor; 1993: Tim Yeo; 1994: Malcolm Sinclair, David Ashby; 1997: Jerry Hayes, Allan Stewart, Michael Hirst; 1998: Bill Clinton, Bob Livingston, Henry Hyde, Helen Chenoweth, Dan Burton; 2000: Rudy Giuliani; 2001: Gary Condit; 2006: Mark Oaten, John Prescott; 2007: Antonio Villaraigosa; 2008: John McCain, David Paterson, Eliot Spitzer, Kwame Kilpatrick, John Edwards; 2009: Mark Sanford, Mike Rann.

Source: author-compiled from Nexis UK.

There are several other factors that need to be explored in order to explain the patterns found; the first concerns news geography. Existing studies have shown that foreign news tends to be disproportionately focused on so-called 'news centres' – the US and other European countries – while those outside, on the periphery, like Australia, are ignored (see Rössler, 2004). Studies show most foreign news is mainly about the domestic affairs and politics of

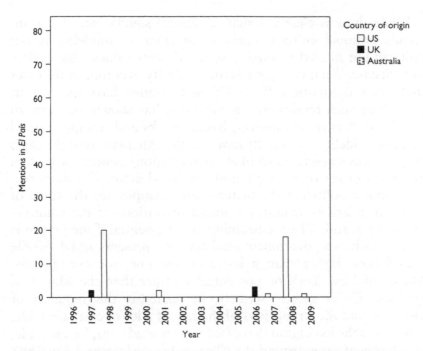

Figure 4.4 The number of news items mentioning politicians' infidelity in Australia, the UK and US in *El País* (1996–2009)*

*Number of mentions for each identified case in a seven-day cycle including the day the story broke and six days after. 1997: Jerry Hayes, Piers Merchant; 1998: Bill Clinton, Bob Livingston, Henry Hyde, Dan Burton; 2001: Gary Condit; 2006: John Prescott, Mark Oaten, Tommy Sheridan; 2007: David Vitter; 2008: John McCain, David Paterson, Eliot Spitzer, Kwame Kilpatrick, John Edwards; 2009: Mark Sanford.

Source: author-compiled from Nexis UK.

rich and powerful nations such as the US (Boyd-Barrett, 2000; Wu, 2000). There was little difference between the four newspapers in this respect. This might help to explain why a similar proportion of cases in the US and the UK were examined while comparable incidents of infidelity in Australia were ignored, and goes some way to account for the amount of coverage that incidents in the US received; it does not account, though, for the clustering of cases.

While there is clearly a shared cultural significance that transcends national cultural barriers, coverage of infidelity is not uniform but filtered through a series of news values which relate to each case. What is striking is the similarity over time in the cases that received attention. While US media outlets have few qualms publishing such revelations, as this book has shown, coverage in non-US outlets is circumspect, having peaks and troughs: not all cases of infidelity are equally newsworthy. An analysis of the cases suggests coverage is more likely if revelations concern a leading politician rather than an unknown political actor. The more recognizable a politician the better – for example, see the spike of newspaper stories around the initial revelations of the Clinton–Lewinsky scandal. Recognizability is not essential if the person is senior, such as a government minister, or represents a high-profile conurbation rather than a lesser-known one, for example the Mayor of New York or Los Angeles rather than the Mayor of Spokane. Coverage also seems to be related to the frequency of instances and the strangeness of the tale. If a lot of cases coincide, this boosts the likelihood that cases are reported – see, for example, the cluster of cases around the Clinton–Lewinsky scandal in 1998 and again in 2008. Coverage is also boosted if the case is bizarre, e.g. someone pretending to be walking in the Appalachians while visiting his lover in Argentina (South Carolina Governor Mark Sanford) (see Sipes, 2011). The final factor concerns the extent to which other media cover events. These incidents are seen as significant if they are also covered by large national news outlets and news agencies or are big news in the country of origin; in such instances the chances of coverage will increase. The research documented whether the instances of infidelity were also covered elsewhere. The 12 US cases covered in *Le Monde*, the 11 in *Taz*, the 16 in *La Stampa*, and the 12 in *El País* were all covered in other news outlets in those countries; the same picture emerged for coverage of the UK. Rarely did any newspaper report a case if it was not covered by other outlets in their own country.

So far, this chapter has shown that the media in continental European democracies are not averse to covering some cases of politicians' infidelity outside their national borders. Freed from the privacy restrictions in their home countries, they seem keen to cover such activities and devote considerable coverage if need be. This focus on the peccadilloes of other countries' politicians raises an interesting question: do continental European newspapers give more, less or the same amount of coverage to incidents and allegations of infidelity, compared to newspapers in the US, the UK and Australia? In other words, do continental European newspapers and those in the US, the UK and Australia exercise similar levels of reticence when reporting politicians playing away? The research examined coverage of two high-profile cases, of alleged infidelity involving Nicolas Sarkozy in 2010 and the other concerning Silvio Berlusconi in 2009.

At the beginning of March 2010 rumours emerged on Twitter that Nicolas Sarkozy and his wife Carla Bruni were having affairs. The claim was that Carla was seeing French singer Benjamin Biolay, while Mr Sarkozy had had a relationship with French Environment Minister Chantal Juanno. Initial reporting of these rumours in the French press was very limited; while they surfaced on Twitter, nearly all French newspapers ignored them – only *Le Journal du Dimanche* posted them on its website, along with TV channel I-Tele, but they soon removed these references (see Campbell, 2010; Kirby, 2010).

By the Wednesday after the rumours first surfaced in France, the media in other countries began to cover the story. An indication of the media's interest could be seen during a press conference held by Nicolas Sarkozy on a trip to London, where he was asked outright by a French journalist whether there was any truth to the rumours. Indignantly, he responded 'he did not have "a second, not even a nano second to lose on such flights of fancy"' (Kirby, 2010, p. 49), but this did not put an end to coverage. What is striking about the data in table 4.2, which shows the number of news items in three 'serious' newspapers per country over four days, is that the newspapers in Germany, Italy and Spain devoted the most number of news items to the allegations, and the Australian, UK and US press the least – the US press had the lowest number of news items.

The news about Silvio Berlusconi's extra-marital dalliances

Table 4.2 The number of newspaper news items mentioning the rumours of Nicolas Sarkozy and Carla Bruni-Sarkozy's extra-marital affairs, in six countries*

Stories in three news-papers from:	10 March, 2010	11 March, 2010	12 March, 2010	13 March, 2010	Total stories
Australia	3	1	3	2	9
Germany	2	6	3	6	17
Italy	3	3	1	3	10
Spain	2	6	1	3	12
UK	3	5	1	0	9
US	2	1	1	0	4

* Three newspapers, tabloid newspapers excluded.

Source: author-compiled from Nexis UK.

Table 4.3 The number of newspaper news items mentioning the Italian Prime Minister Silvio Berlusconi's extra-marital trysts, in six countries*

Stories in three newspapers from:	Mentions of Silvio Berlusconi and Noemi Letizia, May 2009	Mentions of Silvio Berlusconi and Patrizia D'Addario tapes, July 2009	Total stories
Australia	23	15	38
France	13	8	21
Germany	14	6	20
Spain	34	29	63
UK	64	63	127
US	6	6	12

* Three newspapers, tabloid newspapers excluded.

Source: author-compiled from Nexis UK.

unfolds over a longer period of time than the Sarkozy incident, as detailed in chapter 3. Table 4.3 shows international coverage in May and July 2009. The coverage for May was sparked by a public statement from Veronica Lario, Berlusconi's wife, announcing her intention to divorce Silvio after revelations that he had attended the eighteenth birthday party of Noemi Letizia, and was fed by further revelations about his obsession with young women (see chapter 3). The coverage in July followed publication of secret recordings of explicit conversations between Berlusconi and Patrizia D'Addario on the websites of Italian news media, in which Berslusconi could be heard to ask D'Addario to wait for him in bed while he had a shower. The picture presented in table 4.3 is more mixed. The three UK newspapers devoted the most news items in May and July, followed by those in Spain, Australia, France, Germany and the US. Based on these two cases, newspapers in continental European democracies seem equally, if not more, willing to devote attention to cases of infidelity involving high-profile politicians as outlets in the US, UK and Australia.

In sum, if audiences in France, Germany, Italy and Spain do not get to read about the sexual transgressions of their own politicians, they can regularly learn about those in other democracies. The media in countries where a strong privacy culture and other factors limit the exposure of extra-marital sex lives of politicians report the transgressions of the political classes of other countries, especially the US and the UK, and when events happen outside the US and UK they are no less likely to provide coverage than their US and UK counterparts. In addition, this seems to be something that has occurred fairly regularly over the last twenty years. Of course, the recycling process is not straightforward; due to a number of factors, the 'international media echo' amplifies some transgressions more than others. The peccadilloes of politicians in the US and the UK are most likely to receive coverage, while those in Australia are almost totally ignored. Those incidents that attract attention seem to fit a pattern: the subject is a high-profile politician or one whose case coincides with others receiving attention, or is bizarre in some way. This is enhanced by other factors – for example, being covered by other national news outlets and by being big news in the country of origin. Finally, media outlets in continental European democracies seem no less willing than the US, UK and Australian media to devote attention to cases of infidelity involving high-profile non-domestic politicians.

National protection, transnational news

The increasingly globalized news environment which sees news of politicians' peccadilloes flow across borders poses a series of challenges for politicians' attempts to prevent publication. This can be seen clearly in countries where politicians' privacy has generally been respected by national media or the media have been legally constrained from reporting on the personal life of politicians. In these democracies, politicians have been able to use the law to prevent the publishing of such information within national boundaries, in effect stopping the wider citizenry from accessing such information. However, a global information space is opening up beyond the control of any one political actor, which is dominated by numerous news providers and saturated with all kinds of information about politicians' personal lives. For nation states where national reporting of politics is shaped by privacy restrictions, the transnational news sphere represents a significant challenge. Do politicians seek to suppress publication through foreign or transnational courts, without guaranteed success, or do they ignore such disclosures as their attempts to control transnational publication of such information may simply draw further attention to it? This section looks at examples of both strategies.

In January 2003, lawyers acting for Gerhard Schroeder, the then German Chancellor, stopped the German newspapers *Maerkische Oderzeitung* and *Südwestpresse* publishing rumours about his supposed marital difficulties. His attempts to restrain the printing of rumours in the British press failed, though. The *Mail on Sunday*, in the same month, published rumours that Schroeder was having an affair with a television presenter, Sandra Maischberger. Schroeder's lawyers wrote to several newspapers, including the *Mail on Sunday*, to ask them not to repeat these allegations and, in a further attempt to prevent publication, issued an injunction through a court in Hamburg. In 2002, Gerhard Schroeder had successfully obtained an injunction in a German court preventing news agency DDP publishing the story that quoted one of his aides, Sabine Schwind von Egelstein, suggesting he would have greater credibility if he did not dye his hair.

The *Mail on Sunday*'s response to the request on 19 January was a two-page article and an editorial repeating the rumours. Under the headline, 'Sorry, Herr Schroeder but you don't rule Britain . . . at least not yet', the paper noted that 'We do not intend to start taking lessons from German chancellors or German courts about the freedom of the press' (Deacon, 2004; Lister, 2003). This was accompanied by an appeal to the paper's German readers, in German, asking them to call the *Mail on Sunday* with further stories that Mr Schroeder would find embarrassing 'and the German press ought to be publishing' (Deacon, 2004, p. 20). The whole story gained widespread media coverage in Germany. The original *Mail on Sunday* allegations were reprinted in the tabloid *Bild Zeitung* and other newspapers which cited the *Mail on Sunday* as the source; their coverage, though, was 'more cautious in dealing with the substance of the allegations and opted to discuss the questions raised by the involvement of a foreign paper as well as differing journalistic cultures in Germany and the UK' (Holtz-Bacha, 2004, p. 51). In an interview in *Der Spiegel,* in the same month, Schroeder noted that 'there is less and less respect of one's privacy today'. Outside Germany, the allegations and the actions of the Chancellor were subject to further coverage. Table 4.4 shows the initial allegations in the *Mail on Sunday*, published at the beginning of January and, recycled, gaining limited coverage outside Germany. Coverage increased, though, in week 1 and reached a height by week 3, after the German court had issued an injunction and the *Mail on Sunday* had reprinted the allegations.

In June 2009, paparazzi photographs taken of Italian Prime Minister Silvio Berlusconi and semi-dressed guests, including the former Czech Prime Minister Mirek Topolanek, at Berlusconi's Sardinian villa were published in the Spanish newspaper *El País* after Berlusconi's lawyers managed to prevent their publication in the Italian press. Table 4.4 shows that *El País*'s action on 31 May generated a lot of publicity, with a large number of newspapers

Table 4.4 Coverage by country of the *Mail on Sunday* reporting of Gerhard Schroeder's extra-marital affair and of *El País's* publishing of paparazzi photographs of Silvio Berlusconi at the Villa Certosa (number of news items mentioning the event)*

Country	Schroeder revelations in *Mail on Sunday*			Berlusconi Villa Photographs in *El País*		
	7-12 January 2003	13-19 January 2003	20-26 January 2003	1-7 June 2009	8-11 June 2009	12-18 June 2009
Germany	4	7	9	14	5	1
France	0	3	2	8	3	0
Spain	0	0	2	13	1	2
UK	2	1	3	10	3	3
US	1	0	4	4	1	0
Italy	0	0	0	7	2	0
Australia	1	0	0	5	0	0

* Coverage in three newspapers, excludes tabloid newspapers.

Source: author-compiled from Nexis UK.

around Europe covering the story. After a couple of weeks, the number of newspapers reporting the story fell.

Although not able to print the photographs, the website of a leading newspaper opposed to the Berlusconi government, *La Repubblica*, carried a link to the photographs on the *El País* website under the headline 'The *El País* shots reveal the secrets of Berlusconi's Villa Certosa.'[2] In June 2009, the photographs in *El País* were mentioned in sixty articles on *La Repubblica*'s website and in twenty-one on *L'Espresso*'s, another outlet opposed to Berlusconi. In the same month there were also around 40,000 Italian websites and blogs and over 200,000 worldwide that mentioned the photographs, with hundreds linking to the *El País* website where the photos were displayed.[3] The attempts to prevent the photographs becoming visible to Italians and the global public had not only failed but became the story. Berlusconi accused the international media, especially the Murdoch press in the UK, of having a vendetta against him and 'being lackeys of the left', but this was to misunderstand the news values of the global news environment.

While there were rumours in French journalistic circles that the marriage of French Interior Minister and presidential hopeful Nicolas Sarkozy was in trouble, nothing was formally published. It was the Swiss French-language newspaper *Le Matin* that broke the news when it reported, on 25 May 2005, that Cecilia Sarkozy had left him for a French Moroccan businessman, Richard Attias, and the couple were separating (Lechavallier, 2006). Outside the jurisdiction of French privacy law, *Le Matin* felt able to reveal such confidential information to its readers. While Sarkozy filed a lawsuit in France against the paper for violating his privacy – the paper is available in France – he could do nothing to stop the circulation of the story. A month after the *Le Matin* story, five major French newspapers dedicated coverage to his failing marriage (Lechavallier, 2006). In August that year, *Paris Match* finally named Cecilia's lover, putting Richard Attias and her on their front cover. The court case succeeded in generating more publicity outside France and, although Sarkozy won the case, the newspaper's publisher only had to pay a symbolic 1 Euro in damages.

In these cases, attempts to prevent coverage or sue for damages failed and the very attempt became further news. The act of trying to suppress publication further drew attention to the original allegations or photographs. Some politicians, however, have adopted a different strategy when faced with the publication of intrusive information. In 2006, the British newspaper, the *Sun*, under the headline 'I'm big in the Bumdestag', published a paparazzi picture of the German Chancellor Angela Merkel changing out of her swimsuit, her bottom clearly visible. No German newspaper published the paparazzi photos, partly out of respect but also constrained by national laws which prevent publication of such photographs, as outlined in chapter 2. Ms Merkel did not seek to block publication in the UK; rather, she praised the German media for not publishing the pictures. What this highlights is that not trying to prevent publication might often be the least-worst option.

The Web and the global gossip sphere

So far, the focus has been the conventional media; however, the growth of the Web has seen a flourishing of easy-to-access, Internet-only news and gossip outlets (see McNair, 2006). These websites have expanded the flow of revelations and allegations still further. Perhaps the most infamous is the Drudge Report that broke the news of Bill Clinton's affair with Monica Lewinsky in January 1998 (Maltese, 2000). In the February following the initial revelations, the site claimed to have attracted 6.7 million visitors (West, 2001, p. 99). Drudge has since been joined by a host of other news sites and blogs. Among online websites particularly interested in the personal lives of politicians, especially any perceived sexual impropriety, are the partisan blogs on the left and right. One example involves Big Government, a right-wing blog run by Andrew Breitbart before his death in March 2012. Breitbart publicized pictures of Democrat Congressman Anthony Weiner in his Y-fronts that Weiner had sent to a follower on Twitter. The ensuing denials and further revelations led to Weiner's resignation. In addition, there are gossip websites and blogs usually focused on celebrities but that also report on high-profile politicians. In the US, for example, tabloid websites such as Daily Caller and the Daily Beast jostle with celebrity gossip pages such as Gawker, TMZ.com, Radar online, and Perez Hilton. The celebrity gossip website TMZ.com started out focusing on film- and pop-stars but has spread to covering other high-profile public figures including politicians. Two of its early scoops concerned the LA Mayor, Antonio Villaraigosa, photographed out with his mistress, and San Francisco Mayor Gavin Newsom having an argument with his political consultant and lover. TMZ.com opened a Washington, DC office in 2008 dedicated to focusing on Capitol Hill. In the words of the website's editor, politicians, like film-stars, can make 'juicy video and sexy headlines' (Marinucci, 2009). In 2011, Radar was the first outlet to reveal the name of the mother of Arnold Schwarzenegger's illegitimate son, while TMZ.com, not to be outdone, provided a copy of a bank statement showing financial down-payments for his lover's house (Ruttenberg, 2011). In

Table 4.5 The number of posts mentioning Noemi Letizia on Italian blogs and blogs in other languages

Months in 2009	Posts on Italian blogs	Posts on blogs in other languages	Total number of posts
January	7	2	9
February	11	0	11
March	1420	899	2319
April	3139	1524	4663
May	5348	2928	8276
June	2385	960	3345
July	4076	1246	5322
August	3920	1231	5151
September	2136	527	2663

Source: author-compiled from Google Advanced blog and Web search.

2010, Gawker exposed the sex life of US Senate hopeful, Christine O'Donnell, publishing paid-for pictures of her one-night stand (Fallows, 2011). In 2011, Gawker broke the news that married Congressman Chris Lee had described himself as divorced and sent topless pictures of himself to a woman in response to a dating advert on Craigslist (Fahrenthold & Blake, 2011). In the UK, bloggers also feel free to publish gossip. One blogger, Ian Dale, author of the blog Ian Dale's Diary, admitted to playing a role in breaking news about the deputy Prime Minister John Prescott's affair with Tracy Temple in 2006. He published extracts of Temple's story, including Prescott's use of Viagra and the size of his manhood (Whittle & Cooper, 2009, p. 41). The Web also acts as a giant echo chamber. In Italy, while *La Repubblica* broke the news that Berlusconi had attended Noemi Letizia's eighteenth birthday, the information spread rapidly online, with each development of the story generating numerous posts in Italy and around the world (see table 4.5). It could be argued the global echo chamber has been filled by a frenzied real-time cacophony of noise about Berlusconi.

These latter providers may lack the authority of the main news agencies or national news outlets but they are less constrained and accountable for what is published. It is not just websites, blogs and micro blogs that are open to all to use: in the UK, the names of public figures and celebrities who had taken out so-called 'super injunctions' to prevent personal information being published were named by an anonymous user of Twitter (see chapter 2 for more details on injunctions). As mentioned earlier, anonymous rumours emerged on Twitter in France that Nicolas Sarkozy and his wife Carla Bruni were having affairs. Within a short space of time the rumours became international news, published as fact, even though they were completely unsubstantiated, and, even when denied by all actors involved, the stories continued to appear (Kirby, 2010).

Such sites not only further weaken any control that politicians might have had but also place more pressure on conventional news media to publish such allegations or risk missing a major story (see Williams & Delli Carpini, 2000; 2004). To return to the Drudge Report and the Clinton–Lewinsky scandal, Michael Isikoff had been investigating the President's relations with Monica Lewinsky in relation to the ongoing Paula Jones trial; however, *Newsweek* sat on the story, unwilling to publish a piece on presidential extra-marital sex that might not hold up, as the title of Drudge's story, 'Newsweek Kills Story on White House Intern', suggests (Shepard, 1998). Similarly, in the UK, bloggers willingly publish material that the mainstream news outlets might not publish. In 2010, while certain newspapers had hinted that the Foreign Secretary William Hague might be having a relationship with one of his male special advisors, they limited their comment to querying why he needed three special advisors. However, political blogger Guido Fawkes published allegations about Hague's relationship, providing details about him sharing hotel rooms with the special advisor during the 2010 election campaign (Curtis, 2010). Once this disclosure was made public, it was then widely reported by the mainstream media. Gossip about politicians' private lives that might not have received coverage is now subject to online visibility.

What is emerging is a global Internet information sphere consisting of a range of transnational, national and local information providers that are globally accessible and interconnected. International news agencies have been joined by international news channels and the Internet. While the laws remain, politicians cannot prevent their citizens accessing foreign media outlets

Table 4.6 The number of posts mentioning Mara Carfagna on Italian blogs and blogs in other languages

Months in 2008	Posts on Italian blogs	Posts on blogs in other languages	Total number of posts
June	1066	111	1177
July	1210	70	1280

Source: author-compiled from Google Advanced blog and Web search.

via satellite and the Internet and looking at such information and imagery. All the main news organizations in advanced industrial democracies have a Web presence and any information is quickly located via a search engine. Language poses less of a problem than, perhaps, in the past. English, the dominant language of the Internet, is also a predominant second language of most European countries, especially of Internet users, and most search engines now boast translation services. One can imagine a scenario in which national media in one country regularly publish gossip about the sex life of politicians in other democracies which can be accessed by readers in those countries via the Web. For example, in 2008, rumours of a secretly recorded, sexually suggestive conversation between Italian Prime Minister Silvio Berlusconi and his then Minister for Equal Opportunities, former model Mara Carfagna, circulated in the anti-Berlusconi press. While privacy laws meant that publication of the transcripts would be prevented in Italy, the Argentine newspaper *El Clarín* printed extracts of the conversation and made them available online under the headline 'Italian Sexgate: Scandal-tarred Berlusconi and a Minister'.[4] The extracts suggested that Carfagna's appointment was in return for oral sex. Italian Web users could access the transcripts at the newspaper's website. When extracts from the secret recordings were printed in July 2008, 1,210 messages posted on Italian websites and blogs mentioned Mara Carfagna and the *El Clarín* article, with two dozen linking to it directly; there were a further 70 posts on both by non-Italian websites and blogs.[5]

Finally, personal information and rumours now have almost a permanent place in cyberspace. The Web acts as a giant archive which can be searched and where gossip may be retrieved (see Solove, 2007). Prominent political leaders, especially, leave vast digital footprints. There is a more or less permanent record of rumours about aspects of the personal lives of the political class in different democracies. It is a record that citizens can explore, drawing on a range of sources. This information reveals a lot about individual politicians, over which they have little control. The transnational news and information sphere is more than simply an echo chamber; it potentially poses real challenges to national privacy cultures.

Conclusion

News of politicians' infidelity can spread rapidly through the transnational information environment. Media outlets that shy away from covering the extra-marital dalliances of their own politicians eagerly cover those of well-known foreign political actors. The chapter showed that news of politicians' marital infidelity in the US and the UK was considered newsworthy by the media in the four continental European democracies examined. That said, each case did not receive the same amount of coverage. An incident was more likely to receive attention if the actor was well known or if the actor represented a well-known conurbation. In addition, the study showed coverage was more likely if it coincided with other similar acts, or the act was lurid or bizarre or covered by other media. The chapter also showed that continental European news outlets showed no more rectitude in the coverage of extra-marital revelations and rumours than their US and UK counterparts. This is not to argue that continental European outlets seek to investigate and break such stories but that they cover them in a way very similar to US and UK outlets once the influence of privacy restrictions is removed.

The global news environment and growing access to the Web also mean that audiences in continental European democracies can read about the extra-marital antics of their own politicians in the media outlets of other countries. Information and imagery prevented from gaining an airing in France, Germany and Italy have found their way into the media and onto websites based in other countries. The personal lives of politicians in continental European democracies that have traditionally enjoyed a level of privacy protection are now potentially vulnerable to exposure in a way they have not been before. The privacy laws that afford politicians protection in one state do not stretch beyond the boundaries of that state, as the Schroeder example shows. A French court, for example, cannot prevent the publication of personal information, say, about a prominent French politician in the news outlets of other countries – this information can, in turn, be accessed easily online by citizens of France as well as those of other countries. The chance of such exposure may be even higher if that politician has an international profile – such as Nicolas Sarkozy. As a politician becomes a global 'face', there may well be a growing interest in his/her private life which provides more incentives for paparazzi and the tabloid press of other states. In an age of increased transborder information access, politicians have less control over their image; there is always personal information available and search engines have made this information easily accessible. For those in democracies where intrusion is well established, the change may not be that perceptible, but for others, used to the protection of the law, the change might be significant.

5

Drawing Conclusions: Intimization and Democratic Politics

Intimization is clearly an uneven process, impacting on some national political communication environments more than others. This book has demonstrated that the extent to which the personal lives of politicians saturate national mediated public spheres varies, often considerably, between countries. It has also shown that intimization is a process which can strengthen, weaken, or remain fairly static over time due to a number of factors. This chapter starts by summarizing the findings on the exposure of personal lives in different national contexts, and the explanations for these findings, before reflecting on the consequences of the intimization process.

Intimization: trends across countries

Intimization can be seen as a revelatory process which involves the publicizing of information and imagery from what we might understand as a politician's personal life. It is a process that can be consensual but can also involve breaches of politicians' privacy; the information and imagery may be benign or highlight norm transgressions in their personal lives. Figure 5.1 places the democracies examined in this book along two dimensions: the amount of consensual exposure (coverage of certain aspects of national leaders' personal lives) and the amount of non-consensual exposure (the number of publicized cases of marital infidelity). Based on these

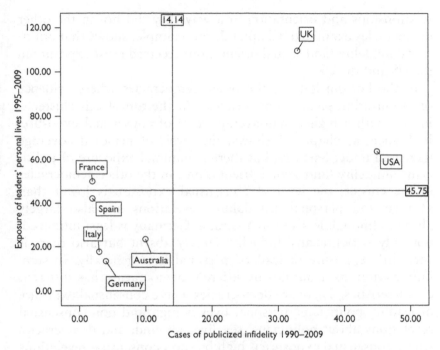

Figure 5.1 Cluster map showing levels of intimization across seven democracies

Note: The y-axis shows yearly average visibility of national leaders' personal lives based on four indicators over the time period – see table 1.8. The x-axis represents the number of cases of publicized infidelity over the time period. The lines in the chart represent the mean level of exposure over the time period.

two dimensions, two clusters emerge. In the top right-hand corner sit the UK and the US. These two democracies stand out in terms of the level of publicity that politicians' personal lives receive. Levels of consensual exposure are higher compared to the other democracies. The media clearly find the personal lives of national leaders newsworthy, and the same elites seem more willing to share their personal lives with the media. Chapter 1 revealed that these media devoted most attention to significant events in the personal lives of their leaders, when compared to the other countries. The levels of intrusion into personal lives were also much higher, with the media regularly exposing politicians' extra-marital sexual relationships and orientation in a way they did not in the other democracies examined. Chapter 2, for example, shows that politicians' infidelity (and sexual orientation) received most exposure in the US and the UK.

In the bottom left are the other democracies where evidence of intimization seems to be weakest. At the top of this cluster is France with a higher-than-average level of consensual exposure. In France, as chapter 1 shows, the levels of personal coverage increased under Sarkozy, but there is minimal exposure of politicians' infidelity (and sexual orientation). In the other democracies in the cluster, the level of consensual exposure is lower than average and personal scandalous revelations are also largely absent, although less so for Australia. Germany is least intimized: not only is politicians' infidelity largely absent but also there is very little exposure of leaders' personal lives generally. In sum, intimization, as it unfolds in different democracies, has different characteristics. There are democracies where consensual exposure of leading politicians' personal lives is high and non-consensual revelations about politicians' sex lives abound; and democracies where consensual exposure is high but non-consensual revelations about sex lives are low or largely absent. In other words, intimization has different characteristics in different democracies. But why is this the case? Rather than a single causal factor, such as new communication technologies, or tabloidization, the solution, as laid out in this book, has to do with the presence of a combination of micro and macro causal conditions, related to the media, political environment and socio-cultural factors. The causal recipes produced in chapters 1 and 2 explain the necessary and sufficient conditions for membership or non-membership of three fuzzy sets. They also clearly show that different causal combinations lead to similar outcomes in different countries and that the presence or absence of an outcome in different countries may be explained by different recipes. In other words, fuzzy set QCA provides a more nuanced account of causation than existing mono-causal explanations.

For a democracy to experience higher-than-average levels of consensual exposure of its leader's personal life, a certain combination of conditions needs to be present (see table 5.1). Chapter 1 showed that there were three causal recipes which combined micro actor-related factors and macro systemic factors. If a country is a presidential democracy with a large tabloid presence in the media environment and falling party membership and a leader that is part of the so-called 'baby boomer' generation – and needs to personally bond with voters – then there will be a high level of consensual exposure. Alternatively, in the second recipe in chapter 1, being a presidential democracy is not necessary; here, having a large tabloid presence in the media environment, with falling party membership and a leader who tries to bond personally with voters and who is a 'baby boomer' but is also on the ideological centre ground, will also lead to higher levels of consensual exposure. In the final recipe, a large tabloid media presence is not necessary; here, being a presidential system with falling party membership and with a leader who tries to bond personally with voters, is a 'baby boomer' and a centrist, will also lead to a high level of consensual exposure. The first recipe helps to explain the high incidence of consensual personal exposure of US leaders, like Bill Clinton, George W. Bush and Barack Obama; the second recipe helps to explain incidences in the UK and Australia – Tony Blair, Gordon Brown and Kevin Rudd could be seen to fit into this. The final recipe helps to explain why leaders such as Nicolas Sarkozy gained personal coverage.

Table 5.1 also provides three possible recipes to explain low levels of exposure. The first suggests that where the country is not a presidential democracy, the leader does not need to bond personally with voters, is more ideologically extreme and not on the centre ground, and is part of the pre-boomer generation, then exposure of the personal life will be absent. The second recipe suggests that if the tabloid presence in the media environment is small or absent, the leader does not need to bond, is more ideologically extreme and is part of the pre-boomer generation, then exposure will also be absent. The final recipe suggests that where the national leader is not directly elected, the tabloid presence in the media environment is small or absent and the leader is more ideologically extreme, then coverage of the leader's personal life

Table 5.1 Causal recipes explaining the visibility of national leaders' personal lives

Causal recipes for high visibility
Presidential system* Large tabloid media*Low party membership*Baby boomer*Need to bond with voters
Large tabloid media*Low party membership*Need to bond with voters*Baby boomer*On centre ground
Presidential system*Low party membership* Need to bond with voters*Baby boomer*On centre ground
Causal recipes for low visibility
Not a presidential system*No need to bond with voters*More ideologically extreme*Pre-boomer
Small tabloid media* No need to bond with voters* More ideologically extreme*Pre-boomer
Not a presidential system* Small tabloid media* More ideologically extreme* Need to bond with voters

will still be absent even if the leader does seek to bond with voters personally. As chapter 1 showed, the first combination of conditions explains the lower levels of exposure of Margaret Thatcher and John Major in the UK and Bob Hawke, Paul Keating and John Howard in Australia. The second combination explains the lack of personal coverage of François Mitterrand in France, Helmut Kohl and Gerhard Schroeder in Germany, Silvio Berlusconi and Romano Prodi in Italy, and Felipe Gonzalez in Spain. The final recipe explains the lower exposure of the personal lives of Angela Merkel in Germany and José Zapatero in Spain.

This book also provides a temporal comparison which reveals an increase of consensual exposure over time in nearly all the countries examined. Chapter 1 shows that exposure had risen fairly steeply in France, the US and the UK, less intensely in Australia, Spain and Italy but had declined slightly in Germany. Those democracies where leading politicians' personal lives are highly visible also seem to be those countries that have seen the greatest increase in consensual exposure over time. Sometimes the comparison between the most recent leaders and their predeces-

Table 5.2 Causal recipes explaining the levels of publicized infidelity

Causal recipes for high levels of publicized infidelity

Presence of the Christian right*Weak privacy culture*Large tabloid media
Politically aligned press*Weak privacy culture*Large tabloid media

Causal recipes for low levels of publicized infidelity

No Christian right*A strong privacy culture*Small tabloid media
No Christian right*Small tabloid media*Politically aligned press

sors in the same democracy is quite stark. In some democracies there seems to be a new generation of leaders whose personal lives are very much lived in the public domain. Nicolas Sarkozy, for example, received a much greater degree of personal coverage, compared to Jacques Chirac and François Mitterrand. His decision to 'sell' himself and his high-profile divorce and relationship with Carla Bruni stands in contrast to previous French Presidents, and it is perhaps not surprising that his actions attracted much coverage (see Dahklia, 2010; Kuhn, 2011). The causal conditions described above also help to explain the within-country variations that have happened over time.

Chapter 2 showed that two recipes explain why a democracy might experience a high level of exposure of infidelity. The first suggests that high levels of publicized infidelity arise where the Christian right and its social conservatism are present in politics, where there is weak privacy protection for political elites and a large tabloid presence in the media environment. This is clearly the case in the US, where the social conservatism of the Christian right has become a key feature of politics, placing personal morality on the political agenda. The second recipe suggests that democracies might also witness high levels of publicized infidelity where the influence of a highly adversarial politically aligned press is strong, where there is a weak privacy culture and a large tabloid presence.

Table 5.2 also shows the two recipes that explain the absence of high levels of publicized infidelity. The first shows that if there is no Christian right, a strong privacy culture that provides protection for political elites, and a small tabloid media sector, then exposure of infidelity will be low or absent. This combination of conditions explains, for example, the lower levels of exposure in Germany and Spain. The second recipe suggests that if there is no Christian right, and the tabloid media sector is small, then there will be an absence of high levels of publicized infidelity, even if there is a politically aligned press. This recipe explains the relative absence of cases in Australia, France and Italy.

Many of the conditions which explained high levels of publicized infidelity go some way to explaining high incidents of outing in the US. The recipe in chapter 2 showed that, where you have the presence of the Christian right, there is weak privacy protection for political elites, a strong tabloid presence in the media environment and a significant presence of gay rights activists, then outing will occur – the key additional ingredient being the presence of gay rights activists.

While these conditions were jointly necessary and sufficient to produce the outcome in the 2000s, this book shows that media exposure of politicians' infidelity has not always been a feature of the US and UK political landscapes. Chapter 3 showed the number of cases of publicized infidelity in the UK and the US increased dramatically in the 1990s. It is difficult to explain such a sudden change in terms of recipes presented above. Most of the conditions in the recipes were present prior to the 1990s; however, one condition visible in both recipes was not – namely, a weak privacy culture. Something fundamentally undermined the journalistic consensus around privacy intrusion in both countries. More specifically, two 'critical moments' can be identified as a tipping point in the non-consensual exposure of infidelity. The impeachment of Clinton and the backlash that followed, and the back-to-basics speech by John Major, mark the start of a greater exposure of politicians' infidelity. This is not to say that all change requires critical moments, but the evidence shows that after these two critical moments reticence has faded and intrusion has become normalized. The type of publication which saw such journalistic practices as abhorrent now publicizes such stories, and even, in some cases, breaks them – see, for example, the *LA Times* breaking the story in 2011 that recently retired California Governor

Arnold Schwarzenegger had an illegitimate child – something unprecedented perhaps in serious political news outlets ten years ago. Thomas Nagel is largely right when he notes that the taboos which 'meant that the sex lives of politicians were rightly treated as irrelevant' no longer have any force (2002, p. 3). The self-imposed rectitude that once characterized reporting in the UK and the US is now much weaker and this, combined with the other conditions identified above, has led to the outcome we see today.

Is there any evidence of potential critical moments elsewhere? It is unclear whether the Berlusconi revelations mark a critical moment in Italian political communication. Prior to these events, media exposure of the extra-marital sex lives of those in political life in Italy was almost entirely absent. It seems such exposure is now present, and has been driven by a range of factors – not least partisan hostility towards Berlusconi. However, it is questionable whether such exposure will continue now Berlusconi has departed the scene. The reticence exercised by the Italian press prior to the Berlusconi era might well and truly be over but factors which retard exposure are still present, privacy laws are still in place and, further, the intrusion has not been on the same scale as in the US and UK. In the UK, the introduction of the European Human Rights Act into law and the revelations about press phone-hacking and the inquiry into it might mean the end to the casual exposure of the sex lives of politicians, but this remains to be seen. In sum, the historical paths taken by democracies can be influenced by critical moments which shape causal processes in ways that may not always be obvious at the time.

While politicians' infidelity receives little attention in France, Germany, Italy and Spain, news outlets in these democracies are connected to a global news environment where information about politicians' peccadilloes freely circulates. Coverage of politicians' infidelity is not absent in these democracies – it is mostly just of cases from the UK and the US, and sometimes other countries (see information on Berlusconi's extra-marital affairs and divorce as an international story in chapter 4). There is a global flow of news about politicians' sexual malfeasance. Extramarital antics are newsworthy, especially when the politicians are from the US and UK, are recognizable or hold an important office, or if the act coincided with other similar acts, or the act was lurid or bizarre. Further, the global spread of the Internet has implications for politicians' privacy in continental European democracies. If citizens in those countries cannot read about the extra-marital affairs of their own politicians locally, they can access material via websites and blogs. Attempts by politicians to prevent such activity only seem to draw attention to it. However, whether this will lead to a change in the privacy cultures of continental European democracies is perhaps unlikely.

In sum, any talk of a transnational trend towards greater intimization of politics across democracies is too simplistic; politicians' personal lives receive publicity in all democracies but to different extents. In the US and the UK the mediated public sphere has been colonized by scandalous and non-scandalous personal information and imagery from the lives of political figures. This has not always been the case though. Chapter 1 showed a clear trend upwards over time in the consensual exposure of leaders' personal lives and a growth in the exposure of politicians' peccadilloes. In terms of non-consensual exposure, there has been a marked divergence between the UK, the US and the other democracies from the 1990s onwards. In France, while personal information and imagery flood the public sphere, revelations about politicians' sexual relations and orientation have remained almost absent. Intimization is a feature but has never gained the same significant intrusive dynamic as in the US and UK. In the other democracies – Germany, Italy, Spain and Australia – the extent to which all types of personal information and imagery enter the public realm is more limited. The exposure of leaders' personal lives has grown in most of these countries, but not all, and not at the same levels as in the UK and US. With the exception of Australia, scandalous revelations have remained almost entirely absent. The levels of exposure in Australia put paid to any suggestion that intimization is present to a greater extent in Anglo-Saxon democracies. Of course, things might always change; intimization is not fixed for all time but can increase and decrease over time, enabled or retarded by a combination of causal conditions and unique events.

The consequences of intimization

The best place to start an examination of the consequences of the intimization process is with the findings of previous studies. Although these studies have not explicitly looked at the impact of intimization in the context of political communication, they have examined and speculated upon the impact of the flow of personal information and imagery in a variety of other contexts. A good place to start is with what Rössler identifies as a 'tradition' in western political thought, most notably seen in the work of Hannah Arendt and Richard Sennett, that 'laments' the incursion of the personal into the public realm (2005, p. 171). Rössler notes these often broad historical studies paint a pessimistic picture in which the 'boundaries between public and private have disappeared' as the 'most intimate of matters are elevated to the level of a media spectacle' (2005, p. 170). The result is a 'demise of the public realm' which leads to a de-politicization of civil society, what has been termed an 'Arendtian nightmare' (Brown, 2004, cited in Rössler, 2005, p. 170). In the context of the intimization of conventional political communication, the Arendtian nightmare, so to speak, can readily be imagined. The flow of information and imagery from politicians' personal lives increases to such an extent that it dominates the public sphere and the nature of political communication itself fundamentally changes, with implications for democracy.

The sense of concern about the consequences of a weakening divide between the public and the private can be seen in studies that have looked at the effects of new technologies on political life. Take the work of Joshua Meyrowitz which focused in part on the impact of television on politicians' spatial privacy (1985). He suggests that television's invasion of politicians' private spaces has undermined their ability to appear differently to different audiences, reduced their time to prepare, and has eroded their image; in his words, the politician is rendered ordinary, hyper-familiar, with a familiarity that 'breeds contempt' (1985, p. 276; see also Hart, 1999). Concerns about the erosion of image and reputation have been raised by others, albeit attributed to different causes. Solove, for example, highlights the challenge that the free circulation of gossip and falsehood on the Internet poses for the reputation of public figures, such as politicians, who are vulnerable to rumours and allegations which remain ever-present on the World Wide Web (Solove, 2007). Neveu talks of a 'desacralisation of politicians and politics' – a result of the exposure of their personal lives on popular talk shows (2005, p. 328; see also Adut, 2004). McNair suggests the large-scale exposure of politicians' personal lives may destabilize political elites (2006). The distance and aloofness of political leaders that helped sustain their aura in the past has been lost in an age of political scandals; the mystique that surrounded political leaders has disappeared (Thompson, 2000). Thompson goes further, suggesting that scandals have the ability to deplete the trust that citizens have in the political system, fuelling suspicion and distrust of political institutions and the political class. For others, the concern is not so much the loss of aura as the costs that scrutiny imposes on office seekers. Sutter (2006) argues one negative side-effect of media scrutiny of candidates is that it discourages from seeking office honest potential public servants who are worried about their privacy being invaded and their reputation being dragged through the mud (see also Lichtenberg, 1989). In sum, for the above studies, the exposure of politicians' personal lives has potential negative consequences, it can undermine the reputation or aura of those who govern and, further, may discourage the honest from entering public office.

However, can the exposure of the personal domain always be said to have negative consequences? The little empirical research that has been conducted paints a less straightforward picture. Take the example of political sex scandals; the actual consequences do not seem as bad for democracy as some might have feared. In the US, a Pew Research Center survey of voters found that only 39 per cent of those sampled said they would be less willing to vote for a candidate who had had an extra-marital affair (Pew Research Center, 2007). Studies of public opinion in the wake of the Clinton–Lewinsky scandal found that it had little negative impact on Clinton's popularity (see Lawrence &

Bennett, 2001; Pew Research Center, 1998; Zaller, 1998). In UK, a Mori poll in 1994, after the revelations about some government ministers' sexual antics, found that 41 per cent of those asked thought that 'they should resign', while 53 per cent of those asked thought 'that as long as they perform their job well they should not be required to resign' (Mortimore, 1995). Also in the UK, Farrell et al. (1998) examined the impact of sleaze allegations on the accused MPs' electoral support during the 1997 general election. They conclude that, while financial misdeeds of MPs were punished by the voter, revelations of sexual impropriety were not, with those accused or guilty polling the same or more votes compared to the previous general election (1998, p. 88). Such exposés may not even lead to politicians resigning. My own research conducted for this book shows that most elected officials between 1970 and 2009 (52 per cent) continued in post and did not resign after the exposure of their extra-marital affairs, and of those that did quit, only 11 per cent left politics altogether, the others preferring either to retire from a ministerial post, to withdraw as a candidate, not to seek re-election or to wait to be deselected.

In what remains of the chapter, I want to shift the focus on to what I see as the consequences for political communication environments rather than politicians' behaviour or public opinion. There is enough empirical evidence presented here and elsewhere to draw some conclusions about the possible effects. I want to suggest that the impact can be most clearly seen in those countries where intimization is most developed, such as the US and the UK, although it is not entirely absent from the others. Looking at the US and the UK, I would argue that the major consequences of intimization are two-fold: first, a politicization of the personal lives of politicians – especially high-profile leading politicians – not a de-politicization, as suggested by others; and, second, the emergence of regular controversies and scandals around privacy intrusion and protection. In other words, the very act of exposure and what is revealed can be the site of intense struggle. These are by no means the only developments, but are significant and connected to the process of intimization.

Politicization of the personal domain

Once personal information enters the public sphere, what a politician, especially a leading politician, does in his or her personal life has the potential to be criticized by opponents and to become a topic for wider public debate. In short, it has the potential to become politicized (see also Langer, 2012). What I mean by politicization is not so much that personal lives are shaped by public factors, although they clearly are – Williams (2004), for example, shows women's personal lives are clearly ordered by public policies – as, rather, that what a politician does in his or her personal life is subsumed into the political fray, becoming another issue about which political opponents can attack and political struggle can ensue (see also Holmes, 2000). In other words, politicization is different from exposure – the two are often connected but are not the same. The extent to which an aspect of a politician's personal life is politicized depends on numerous factors, not least the presence of actors who want to criticize these aspects and attack the politician in question.

This not to say that all personal information, once public, attracts criticism, but if there is a high flow of such personal information, then a politician's actions and behaviour in their personal domain – and, it should be noted, the actions and behaviour of those close to them – have greater potential to be criticized by opponents in the way their actions in public office are. In other words, the larger the flow of personal information into the mediated public sphere, the greater the chance it will be subsumed into the political fray by opponents. The politicization of personal lives, I want to suggest, can be seen mainly, although not exclusively, in countries where the revelatory dynamic is most evident, and especially around personal scandals. Take the example of the revelations in the Clinton–Lewinsky scandal. Here, extremely personal information about the US President's extra-marital affair was drip-fed into the media, with each disclosure being used by his opponents to attack him and, in turn, provoking reactions (Davis, 2006; Hayden, 2002; Lowi, 2004). In this scenario, political opponents and supporters mobilized around the President's personal life, condemning and defending the President in relation to each development. In the UK, revelations about the marital infidelity of a string of Conservative government ministers and MPs were used by John Major's opponents to attack him and brand his government as 'sleazy' (Jones, 1995). In France, as revelations of infidelity have largely been absent, so have such debates, but this does not mean they do not occur when such exposés arise. The alleged rape of a hotel chambermaid by presidential hopeful and former IMF chief Dominique Strauss-Kahn in New York, in 2011, led to a widespread debate about the sexual behaviour of the French political class, and initiated a discussion of rape and sexual harassment in the workplace (Davies, 2011; Lehrer, 2011). In Italy, revelations about Silvio Berlusconi's personal behaviour became a central issue in Italian politics around which his opponents and supporters rallied, as chapter 3 showed. Scandalous revelations about the personal lives of leading politicians, including national leaders, have become a terrain upon which existing political and ideological differences collide, with political opponents willing to use the personal information and imagery for advantage.

These are not everyday situations, but politicization does occur in other scenarios, if sometimes less dramatically. Events and actions in each dimension of the personal domain have the potential to become the source of controversy generated by a growing army of commentators in the news media and online. Take, for example, national leaders' families. Their actions are closely scrutinized; allegations of favouritism or special treatment are often levelled by opponents, regardless of evidence. Thérèse Rein's business career, Cherie Blair's legal career and Jean Sarkozy's political career have all been said to have benefited from their family connections. Events in the national leader's family life also have the potential to be used to criticize the leader. For example, in the UK, the Blairs' luxury holidays abroad became the subject of criticism by Blair's opponents, especially in the conservative press. During his term in office, there was coverage of the fact that Blair and his family often vacationed for free at various venues, the guests of rich friends, or used an Air Force jet to travel. In 1999, the closing of public access to a local beach where they were staying in Tuscany and the putting in place of an exclusion zone to stop paparazzi gained widespread attention; in 2002, it was the Egyptian authorities' closing of an airport for the Blairs, leading to the stranding of other holidaymakers. Other concerns aired included: the size of the Blair family's carbon footprint from their foreign holidays and whether the UK tax-payers were picking up the cost of his security. Information about a supposed personal getaway became an issue about which opponents could attack, and public debates emerged. Similarly in the US, the length of George W. Bush's holidays attracted criticism, and no more so than in 2005, when his slowness to break from his vacation and respond to Hurricane Katrina provoked widespread criticism.

In this political landscape, the actions of leading politicians are subject to criticisms, claims and counter-claims, concerning personal judgement about using their families or, more substantially, charges of hypocrisy. Actions in politicians' personal lives are inevitably compared to their public actions and pronouncements. In the US and UK, amongst the media, there is an almost complete intolerance of hypocrisy. The extra-marital dalliances of politicians who espouse family values attract widespread opprobrium in the media. News that some of the leading Republican politicians involved in the impeachment of President Clinton had also committed adultery provoked widespread condemnation, as did the news that numerous Conservative government ministers had engaged in extra-marital affairs, having called for a return to family values. While disjunctures between the personal domain and public life are not new, as more personal information and imagery flood into the public sphere, there is greater potential for disjunctures to generate claims of hypocrisy, which may be damaging to a politician's career or may undermine public trust in politicians, as others have noted (see Thompson, 2000).

Intrusion controversies and scandals

It is not just actions in personal lives that are the subject of scrutiny, debate and criticism but also the intrusive acts by which information and images enter into the public realm. These transgressions of journalistic norms of disclosure provoke outbursts of criticism or, in some instances, full-blown scandals. The criticism of the intrusive tactics of the UK tabloid press has been particularly shrill. The post-war history of the British press is one characterized by excesses in press behaviour which have been accompanied by widespread opprobrium. The criticism has prompted commissions of inquiry, which have condemned the practices of the tabloid press, called for tighter regulation and revamped the regulatory system (see chapter 3). The Press Complaints Commission (PCC) was formed in 1991 in the wake of recommendations of the Calcutt Report, which also led to a new code of press conduct. The death of Princess Diana a few years later in 1997 and the ensuing anger at tabloids' use of paparazzi photographs led to a further tightening of the PCC code of conduct. Since then the House of Commons Culture, Media and Sport Committee has produced three reports on press standards (2003, 2007, 2009). In 2011, revelations about systematic phone-hacking by private investigators employed by the *News of the World* led to massive public opprobrium, the closure of the paper, discussions about press standards, further investigations, the closure of the PCC and promises of further regulatory reform. The activities of the popular media do provoke debates in other democracies too, but not on the same scale or as frequently, it could be argued.

The outing of public figures is an act that also generates controversy (see chapter 2). Activists make a series of justifications for exposing the sexual orientation of politicians without their consent. For activists, while sex is private, sexuality is not. As noted, activists focus on closeted homosexuals in public life who, they argue, are hypocrites and, as such, forfeit their right to keep their sexual identity private. The actions of Mike Rogers in the US have attracted criticism. What right do activists have to decide that someone's sexuality should be a matter of public record? Is hypocrisy really sufficient justification? Many would argue that the wishes of the public figure deserve to be respected; in democracies without statutory privacy protection, such decisions are left to civil society actors and the courts to solve (see Mayo & Gunderson, 1994).

Attempting to reassert control

Public figures in the US and the UK, in particular, have attempted to reassert control over access to and disclosures about their personal lives. As outlined in chapter 2, the civil law is used to protect their personal privacy from what they see as unwarranted intrusion. In the UK, public figures have been able to complain to the PCC about the intrusive actions of the press but often, unsatisfied with the response, have also turned to a range of laws, in addition to libel, to protect their privacy (Lauterbach, 2005; Rozenberg, 2004; Scott, 2009). Perhaps the most frequently used since 2000 is the European Human Rights Act. Article 8 of the Act gives individuals privacy rights for the first time (Tambini & Heyward, 2002). The number of privacy injunctions and 'super injunctions' (where the presence of the injunction cannot be mentioned publicly) being granted has apparently been growing since the late 2000s, and these remain an option for politicians wanting to protect their personal lives. The attempts by public figures to protect their privacy by using injunctions have, in turn, generated concern that press freedom might be under threat. The tabloid press in the UK, the outlets most often cited as intruding into public figures' private lives, have mounted a sustained campaign against the emergence of what they term 'judge-made privacy law'.

In the US, there have been regular calls for a privacy tort, and attempts to restrain paparazzi activity (McNamara, 2009). In 1998, in the wake of the death of Princess Diana, numerous celebrities championed a bill to create civil and criminal penalties for the invasion of privacy; although this was unsuccessful, some states have passed laws to limit privacy intrusion (2009, p. 17). The state of California, for example, passed a law designed to constrain the activities of the paparazzi. The law, which came into force in 2005, means that paparazzi photographers can be fined, even imprisoned, for a range of actions in pursuit of photographs (2009). In the US, divorcing public figures keen to ensure that any details of the divorce remain out of the public domain vigorously contest applications to have their divorce files unsealed. In 2004, presidential candidate John Kerry successfully prevented details of his divorce entering the public domain. However, those in public life are increasingly turning to private judges to ensure such details are not published. These divorce settlements are more likely to remain sealed than those made in a public court, which remain vulnerable to applications to have them unsealed (Kasindorf, 2005).

Controversial intrusive acts and attempts by public figures to reinforce their control over access to their personal life become subject to continuous discussion in which a perennial conflict of rights can be observed. Do those exercising power deserve a private life? In what circumstances are intrusive acts into the personal lives of politicians justified? If they are justified in the public interest, what constitutes the public interest? In continental European democracies these issues seem more settled. The law and journalistic norms afford political elites more control over their personal lives and determine the extent of possible personal exposure. This does not mean that controversies are absent – as this book has shown, Buntegate in Germany is an example of how the transgressions of societal norms about privacy generate much opprobrium – but they are much less frequent.

Certain political communication environments, for a variety of reasons, afford politicians more control over the extent of intimization than others. However, even though public figures in continental European democracies may have greater privacy protection at home, a global media environment means their ability to maintain their privacy can in some instances be difficult to protect. The struggle over privacy is increasingly transnational as information flows across borders. Leaders on holiday abroad with their families step outside the controlled national spaces and may be subject to intrusive paparazzi. External media publish rumours, which are easily accessible via the Web. Laws in European states cannot prevent publication of personal details in the US for instance.

This book has identified and examined the development of intimization in different democracies and explained why it has happened. While there remains more to investigate, the book has moved discussion beyond naive universalist assumptions to reveal the varied nature of intimate politics, shedding light on the extent to which politicians' personal lives are a recognized feature of different democratic political communication environments in late modernity.

Appendix Research Notes

The appendix provides further information on the selection of indicators and the gathering of data, and details about the calibration of the underlying causal conditions used in fuzzy set analyses in chapters 1 and 2.

Selecting suitable indicators of intimization

With no ready-made database, it was important that the various indicators captured the different dimensions of personal life as much as possible, as well as reflecting the different means of exposure. What follows is a detailed description of the selection of the indicators and the challenges that arose in that process.

Measuring the exposure of national leaders' personal lives (chapter 1)

Most studies of the personalization of political communication have looked for presence of indicators in newspapers, which is perhaps not surprising given the practicalities of examining large amounts of television footage. This research also focused on newspapers but complemented this with an examination of books about national leaders, and recorded appearances of leaders on entertainment talk shows. Newspaper coverage was examined via Nexis UK, which provides access to papers from a range of countries. The problems associated with the Nexis database have been widely discussed elsewhere (see Deacon, 2007; Weaver & Bimber, 2008), but this study encountered a number of specific challenges relating to comparative research. First, the earliest newspaper records started in the mid-1980s for some countries, while for others they started later. After an initial interrogation of the database, it was found that it was not possible to offer an analysis before 1990 for Germany, 1995 for Italy and 1996 for Spain. Second, the number of newspapers varied according to country. For some countries, such as the US, the database has a large number of newspapers, while for others, such as Italy, it has relatively few. Third, the newspapers available in some countries also varied over time and it was not always possible to access the same newspapers over the selected period. In order to ensure equivalence between countries, it was decided to limit research to a fixed number of broadsheet or serious newspapers with the most news items over each selected period – tabloid newspapers were excluded from the sample as they were not ubiquitous across all the countries and years in the study (see Wirth & Kolb, 2004).

Existing studies use a range of indicators to measure newspapers' exposure of politicians' personal lives. For example, Langer's study of coverage of leaders' private lives focuses on coverage of five elements of Prime Ministers' personal lives in the *Times* newspaper: family, personal appearance, lifestyle (i.e. hobbies, likes/dislikes and recreational activities), upbringing and religion (Langer, 2007, p. 381). Errera's examination of the coverage of politicians' private lives in celebrity magazines in France looked at coverage of six areas: love life, health, the home, family life, past life and personal finance (Errera, 2006). Although these studies examine different media in different countries, some common indicators are used, such as family and early life (see also Rawlins, 1998, p. 370; Van Aelst et al., 2012). I chose birthdays, holidays and leaders' families as the three indicators I looked for, in the main due to their ease of capture – dates and times could be clearly identified – and because of their universality: every leader has a birthday and goes on holiday, but not all have poor health, get divorced or discuss their hobbies.

The research consisted of a series of name searches. For coverage of birthdays, these name searches consisted of name of the politician within a three-day period, the day of the birthday and a day either side for each year in office. For coverage of holidays, these name searches consisted of name of the politician together with the word 'holiday'/'vacation' in each relevant language. This search was conducted over two one-month periods for each year in office, one for summer and one for winter. For coverage of leaders' families, the name of each spouse and child was entered into the database search facility; leaders' siblings were not examined. For research on birthdays and holidays, results represent the three national newspapers with the most stories mentioning the birthday or holiday. For research on leaders' spouses and children – conducted later and with Emily Harmer – one national newspaper was chosen.

Nexis UK shows the number of times a word is mentioned in different newspapers, displaying the results as 'mentions'. Mentions are literally the number of times the search term appeared, which is not the same as the number of news items; that said, there is a very close correspondence between the figures. In each case the author checked to ensure that the number of mentions was the same as the number of news items; items with more than one mention were counted once. The number of news items mentioning each search term were recorded. As some actors had somewhat common names, a simple name search would not always suffice. The problem was resolved by adding further terms to the search criteria. For example, Sarah Brown was searched along with the phrase 'Prime Minister' to ensure that the results were not skewed by other women called Sarah Brown. Every effort was made to exclude names that were not relevant. A similar challenge was posed by certain letters and accents used in one language but not another, such as 'ö' in German. For example, Schröder or Schröder-Köpf, was often spelt either Schroder or Kopf or Schroeder or Koepf by newspapers. All spellings were used when searching non-German newspapers. Furthermore, the nature of the database meant that the Australian press was grouped together with other countries in an 'Asia-Pacific' category, meaning that the mentions from newspapers in Japan, Singapore and New Zealand had to be removed before the number could be recorded.

The study was only concerned with those mentions that occurred during the leader's period in office; this was partly to place a limit on the scope of the study. The start and end of each leader's period in office was noted but, as leaders took office on different dates in a year, to ensure ease of capture the period in office was measured from 1 January of the year that the leader took office and until 31 December of the year he or she vacated it. The same procedure was adopted for leaders' spouses and children. It should be noted that, to ensure equivalence, the charts only show the mentions for two children who were dependent or living at home, and exclude leaders' children who were fully independent adults, such as Jean Sarkozy, Claude Chirac, Pier Silvio and Marina Berlusconi.

Tracking the appearances of politicians on entertainment talk shows was not straightforward; as Bastien (2008) notes, politicians' appearances on such shows are intermittent and there are no national records. The study drew on several available sources to establish the appearance of national leaders on entertainment talk shows. First, the Internet Movie Data Base (IMDB) logged many high-profile leaders' appearances in a variety of media. This was combined with a Nexis search to document any other mentioned appearances. The credibility of sources was of vital importance. IMDB examples were double-checked and only where an appearance was confirmed by an independent source was it included. Each show could not, however, be content-analysed. It was assumed, based on other empirical studies of entertainment talk shows, that the majority of show content was highly personal (see Bastien, 2008; Baum, 2005; Ericson, 2010; Holtz-Bacha, 2004; Just et al., 1996).

Books are an important but under-examined source of personal information about political leaders. There was an exhaustive search for all books published on each leader over their period in office, back to 1980, using several search facilities. The most productive sources were the catalogues of the Library of Congress and the British Library; AbeBooks, a website consisting of hundreds of second-hand book sellers from around the world; and Google Books. I was aided in the search by research assistants conversant in the relevant languages. The search term was the leader's name and the search was conducted for each year he or she was in office.

With hundreds of books identified, it was not possible to read them cover to cover. The classification of books was based on title, short description provided by book seller or library, additional search of reviews and other descriptive sources. This was not ideal but sufficient to build up a clear picture of the book's focus. Each book was then allocated to one of seventeen categories. The categories were devised after an exploratory study of books on the US President, back to 1900. This study found a series of recurring themes present in books: life and career; life pre-politics; photographic record; religion; psychological profile; secret life and conspiracies; relationships; comedy/humour; family; views, values, policies; record and policies in office; campaign for office; published public papers, speeches and quotations; scandal in office; insider account of office; correspondence; other activities in office. These categories formed the basis of the content analysis for the other democracies. A sample of ten books was double-coded to assess coding reliability. A coding based on a book title and short description was cross-checked with a lengthier reading of the original. In those books examined there was 90 per cent agreement on allocation of books to category. Further, to ensure that books were allocated to the correct category, coders were trained on a sample of five book titles and short descriptions. Throughout the coding process, the coders were in constant contact with each other. Any queries that arose were discussed by the coders and final decisions were made. At a later stage of analysis, these codes were then collapsed by the author to show whether the focus was mainly on personal life or public life.

Measuring marital infidelity and outing (chapters 2 and 3)

To gauge the extent of non-consensual exposure of sexual relations, the study documented all publicized cases of politicians' marital infidelity and any gay revelations publicized between 1970 and 2009. All cases that feature in this book were sourced over a three-year period. The cases were gleaned from a number of sources. First, newspaper and magazine articles from the seven countries accessible via the Nexis UK database were used. A range of specially selected words were used in combination for numbers searches. These words included: 'politicians', 'politics', 'sex scandal', 'affair', 'divorce'. The words were translated into the relevant language, where appropriate. The articles were then read by the author and a research assistant fluent in these languages to see whether the identified cases matched the definition mentioned earlier. Second, special features in newspapers, magazines and news websites concerned with political scandals were used – see, for example, Blenkin (2002), Connolly (2009), Dubecki (2007), Rudin (1998), Vest (1998) and Wolcott (2007), the *Independent's* sleaze list (1995), the *Spectator's* Top 50 Political Scandals, parts one and two (2009a, b). Despite searches, no newspaper supplements documenting sex and other scandals were found in Germany, France, Italy or Spain. Third, books and articles about political scandals were a fruitful source of cases, especially Adut (2008), Bingham (2009), Cepernich (2008), Dagnes (2011), Esser & Hartnung (2004), Holtz-Bacha (2004), Kohn (2000), Kuhn (2004), Parris & Maguire (2005), Ross (1988). Sabato et al. (2000), Summers (2000), Thompson (2000) and Tiffin (1999). Fourth, in order to ensure that I was not overlooking cases, I turned to country experts, namely political scientists / communication scientists who have published on this topic or are interested in it: their knowledge of politics was particularly important, and I used them both to confirm what I had found and to source new examples, especially for non-English-speaking countries.

The credibility of sources was of vital importance. Less credible Internet-only sources were double-checked as a matter of routine and only where an example of marital infidelity was confirmed by two or more independent sources was it included. If no confirmation was available, the example was not included. In addition, all cases had to have been publicized in some media outlet while the subject was in office, between 1970 and 2009. So, for example, the US Congressman Mark Souder was not included as his affair was publicized in 2010; neither was former Speaker Newt Gingrich, whose affair only came to light in 2001 after he left office. In addition, research only focused on office holders in national or state/regional-level assemblies and/or Mayors of large cities (populations of 100,000 or higher). For each case I sought to establish: whether the office holder was elected to an individual post or what type of assembly they belonged to, national or regional; what year the case was publicized; who initiated the disclosure; and whether the protagonist resigned. The cases are available on request.

International coverage of publicized infidelity (chapter 4)

To get a sense of the extent of infidelity in international news, chapter 4 examined coverage in France, Germany, Italy and Spain of 87 cases of adultery, committed in Australia, the UK and the US between 1992 and 2009. In Spain the time period was 1996 to 2009 (total number of cases examined was 72). The examination of coverage of publicized cases of infidelity focused on four newspapers, due to time and resource constraints. The papers chosen were *Le Monde, Taz – die Tageszeitung, La Stampa* and *El País.* The choice of papers was determined by availability of titles on Nexis UK. The study searched coverage of all 87 cases of infidelity in Australia, the UK and the US. The search used name of person and lover and was time-limited to the day the story broke and six days after. The examination of coverage of rumours of Nicolas Sarkozy's and Carla Bruni's infidelity and the extra-marital antics of Berlusconi, focused on three serious or broadsheet newspapers in each country. The time-scales for each varied. The exploration of the Sarkozy/Bruni rumours was over a four-day period and a two-month period was used for Berlusconi.

While some of these sources are not conventional, it is important to note that the nature of the research on intimization required the author to seek out information which was not available from more orthodox sources, which meant using previously untapped sources.

Explaining why

To elucidate the causes underlying intimization, this book employed two case-oriented methods, a cross-case analysis using fuzzy set qualitative comparative analysis (fsQCA) (Ragin, 2000, 2008) and a within-case qualitative analysis (Bennett, 2010). Fuzzy set QCA is a set-theoretic approach to causation developed by Charles Ragin, which identifies set-theoretic relationships between causes and outcomes. FsQCA from the outset assumes causation is 'configurationally complex' and is interested in discovering how causal conditions work together to produce an outcome (Ragin 2008, p. 155). Rather than trying to identify which out of a list of variables are most influential, based on statistical estimates of the net effect of each variable, fsQCA sees conditions as mutually reinforcing, the aim being to find which causal 'recipes' produce which outcomes (see Ragin, 2008). In addition, fsQCA assumes that different recipes may produce the same outcome (equifinality) and that the presence or absence of an outcome may be explained by different recipes (asymmetry). A full explanation of fsQCA can be found in Ragin (2000, 2008) or, in relation to the personalization of political communication, see Downey and Stanyer (2010). In simple terms, the first step in fsQCA is to turn the outcome (the result one wants to explain) into set membership scores via calibration. Due to the nature of the data available, I adopted an indirect method of calibration (Ragin, 2008, pp. 94–7). This approach involved an initial sorting of cases, and the assignment of preliminary set membership scores to each case (see Ragin, 2008). The first step in calibrating membership scores is to establish the divide between membership and non-membership, before allocating each country or person a membership score. The researcher determines set membership based on theoretical and substantive knowledge. This act is, of course, fundamentally interpretive, but this is one of its strengths (see Ragin, 2000, p. 166). In this book I used a combination of six-value, four-value fuzzy sets, and crisp sets where necessary. In a six-value fuzzy set, each case is allocated one of the following membership scores: 1 = full membership of the set, 0 = full non-membership, 0.8 = mostly but not fully in, 0.6 = more or less in, 0.4 = more or less out, 0.2 = mostly but not fully out. In a four-value set, the scores are: 1 = full membership of the set, 0 = full non-membership, 0.7 = more in than out, and 0.3 = more out than in. With crisp sets, membership scores are limited to: 1 = full membership of the set, and 0 = full non-membership.

Having allocated membership scores for the first fuzzy set (the outcome we want to explain), membership of each causal subset also needs to be calibrated and scores allocated to each case. Membership of each causal subset was calibrated drawing on general resource books, as well as a range of nationally focused articles and book chapters. Once this process is complete and all relevant causal conditions are calibrated, a truth table can be produced and the data can be analysed using freely available software downloadable from Charles Ragin's website (www.u.arizona. edu/~cragin/fsQCA/). The software engages in a process of systematic simplification with the aim of producing more parsimonious configurations by using counterfactuals – logically possible combinations with no empirical instances (see Ragin, 2000, 2008 and Mahoney, 2007 for a wider discussion of Mill's methods of agreement and disagreement). While the limited diversity of the social world hinders any simplification of causal recipes, the inclusion of counterfactuals allows such a simplification, with conditions that make no difference to the generation of an outcome being identified and removed. The software produces three types of solution or causal recipe: complex, intermediate and simple (see Ragin, 2008). The intermediate solution is the preferred solution for Ragin, as it 'strike[s] a balance between parsimony and complexity, based on the substantive and theoretical knowledge of the investigator' (2008, p. 175). What follows is detailed information about the calibration processes for the causal recipes discussed in chapters 1 and 2.

To explain the average visibility of national leaders (see table 1.10), the study used a six-value fuzzy set with each leader being allocated a membership score according to their degree of exposure. The cross-over point for membership of the fuzzy set '*leaders whose personal lives are highly visible*' was set at 101, the mean score. The score for full membership was 200 or almost twice the mean. The scores for mostly but not fully in were 150 to 199; for more or less in, 102 to 149. The threshold for full non-membership was set at 25. For more or less out, scores were set at 51 to 100 and for mostly but not fully out, between 26 and 49. The calibration of each causal condition is discussed below.

The first causal condition '*member of the baby boomer generation*' was calibrated using the birth date of each leader. It was a crisp set: those born in 1946 or after were considered to be 'baby boomers' and full members; those born before were full non-members. Membership of the second causal condition '*centrist political leaders*' was based on each leader's position on the ideological continuum derived from Comparative Manifestos Project data (http://manifestoproject.wzb.eu/). This comparative content analysis of party manifestos places each one on a right–left continuum from –100 (extreme right) to +100 (extreme left). Using these scores, membership was set at +20 to –20. The score for full membership was +5 to –5. For mostly but not fully in, scores were set at between +6 to +12 and –6 to –12; for more or less in, scores were set at between +13 to +20 and –13 to –20. For more or less out scores were set at +21 to +35 and –21 to –35 and for mostly but not fully out, between +36 and +50 and –36 and –50. The threshold for full non-membership was set at +51 and –51.

The third causal condition '*bonding with voters*' is a 'higher-order construct', a combination of pre-existing causal conditions to form a third condition (Ragin, 2000). Ragin notes that causal conditions can be regrouped into 'meaningful sets' and reconceptualized (2000, p. 321). There are various ways of joining two fuzzy sets; in this instance I used the process of 'logical or', namely, taking the maximum value in either condition (2000). Leaders needing to bond with voters could be members of the set '*short time spent in politics before election*' or '*democracies where leaders are selected by an open primary*'. Membership of the set '*short time spent in politics before election*' was based on an examination of number of years an actor held political office before being elected President or Prime Minister. The cross-over point for membership was 9 years. Full membership was set at 2 years or less. The threshold for full non-membership was set at 20 years. For mostly but not fully in, scores were set at between 3 and 5 years; for more or less in, scores were between 6 and 8 years. For more or less out, scores were set at 9 to 13 years, and for mostly but not fully out, between 14 and 19 years. The set '*democracies where leaders are selected by an open primary*' was calibrated with evidence from Scarrow et al. (2000). Leaders selected in primaries where non-party members voted were given a score of 1. Where only party members could vote, 0.7. If only parliamentary party members could vote, the score was 0.3, and if selection was by a non-transparent other process, the score was 0.

The causal condition '*low party membership*' was calibrated using Green (2002), Magone (2009), Scarrow (2000), Schmitt & Holmberg (1995), Wattenberg (1996), Webb et al. (2002). The cross-over point for membership was 9 per cent. Leaders were considered full members of the set if party membership as a percentage of the electorate, during their term in office, stood at less than 2 per cent. They were considered mostly but not full members at 3–5 per cent; more or less in with scores of 6 to 8 per cent. The threshold for full non-membership was set at 20 per cent. For more or less out, scores were set at 9 to 13 per cent, and for mostly but not fully out, between 14 and 19 per cent (see table 6.2).

To gauge membership to the condition '*large tabloid media presence*' the study used data from World Press Trends (www.wan-press.org) and World Magazine Trends (www.fipp.com), supplemented with data drawn from national case studies (see Hallin, 2000; Schoenbach, 1998; Seib, 2002; Sparks & Tulloch, 2000; Weaver, 1998). It looked at three measures to gauge the size of the tabloid media sector while each leader was in office: first, the number of tabloids in the top 10 circulating newspapers; second, the number of 'celebrity' magazines in circulation up to a maximum of five; and, finally, the presence of high-profile celebrity gossip websites in the national media environment (McNamara, 2011). A score of 5 was awarded where celebrity gossip websites were deemed to have a high presence, down to 0 if there was no presence. The scores for each three parts were added together to form an overall score. The cross-over point was set at 10. Actors with scores of 20 or more were considered full members. For mostly but not fully in, scores were set at between 14 and 19; for more or less in, scores were between 10 and 12.

For more or less out, scores were set at 8 to 9, and for mostly but not fully out, at 3 to 7. The threshold for full non-membership was set at 2.

The final condition selected was the degree of membership of the set of presidential democracies. It is often argued that a more personalized style of politics is evident in democracies where the national leader is directly elected, as opposed to in a parliamentary system where voters choose a party or parties to govern. Studies of the US, for example, show that the issue of personality often surfaces in presidential campaigns and in their media coverage (see Hacker, 1995). Membership of the set '*Presidential democracies*' was established with data from Blais and Massicotte (2002: 42) and Plasser with Plasser (2002). Countries which were Presidential democracies were considered full members; countries where Presidents were not directly elected or which were parliamentary democracies were considered full non-members. Due to the crisp nature of these data there was no point of maximum ambiguity (see table 6.1 for membership scores).

Membership of the fuzzy set '*democracies with high levels of publicized infidelity*' was established by drawing from sources mentioned above. The cross-over point was established by the author at 10, or 1 publicized case every year between 2000 and 2009. For anything less than 10 cases of publicized infidelity, it was not deemed to be a significant feature of national political life. The author set the threshold for full membership at 20, at least 2 cases per year, or more; for mostly but not fully in, between 16 and 19 instances; for more or less in, a minimum of 10 cases but no more than 15. The threshold for full non-membership was set at 0, that is, no cases at all over the period; for more or less out, at 5 to 9 cases; and for mostly but not fully out, at 1 to 4 cases (see table 6.2).

Drawing on the literature on political sex scandals, the author examined a range of possible causal conditions, drawing up a long-list before reducing them down to a final list of five. These included a combination of what were perceived as the most relevant political, media, legal and cultural conditions, and not necessarily ones identical to those examined in the literature.

Table 6.1 Causal conditions for membership of fuzzy set 'leaders with highly visible personal lives'

National leader	Personal Lives visible*	Baby boomer	Centrist	Fewest years in politics[1]	Leader selected by primary[1]	Need to build close bond[2]	Party membership levels	Presidential System	Tabloid media presence
Obama	1.00	1.00	.80	.40	1.00	1.00	.40	1.00	.80
Clinton	1.00	1.00	.60	.20	1.00	1.00	.20	1.00	.60
Sarkozy	1.00	1.00	.80	.40	.70	.70	.40	1.00	.40
Bush Snr	1.00	.00	.40	.60	1.00	1.00	.60	1.00	.40
Blair	1.00	1.00	.80	.40	.70	.70	.40	.00	.80
Bush Jnr	.80	1.00	.40	.20	1.00	1.00	.20	1.00	.80
Aznar	.80	1.00	.60	.20	.30	.30	.20	.00	.20
Rudd	.80	1.00	.80	.60	.30	.60	.60	.00	.60
Chirac	.60	.00	1.00	.00	.70	.70	.00	1.00	.20
Brown	.60	1.00	1.00	.00	.70	.70	.00	.00	.80
Reagan	.60	.00	.40	.20	1.00	1.00	.20	1.00	.40
Zapatero	.40	1.00	.80	.20	.30	.30	.20	.00	.20
Berlusconi	.40	.00	.20	1.00	.30	1.00	1.00	.00	.20
Howard	.40	.00	.40	.00	.30	.30	.00	.00	.60
Major	.40	.00	.40	.40	.30	.40	.40	.00	.40

Table 6.1 (continued)

National leader	Personal Lives visible*	Baby boomer	Centrist	Fewest years in politics[1]	Leader selected by primary[1]	Need to build close bond[2]	Party membership levels	Presidential System	Tabloid media presence
Kohl	.20	.00	.40	.00	.30	.30	.00	.00	.20
Keating	.20	.00	.60	.00	.30	.30	.00	.00	.20
Schroeder	.20	.00	.60	.20	.30	.30	.20	.00	.20
Gonzalez	.20	.00	.80	.80	.30	.80	.80	.00	.00
D'Alema	.00	1.00	.60	.40	.30	.40	.40	.00	.20
Hawke	.00	.00	.60	.40	.30	.40	.40	.00	.20
Prodi	.00	.00	.60	1.00	.30	1.00	1.00	.00	.20
Merkel	.00	1.00	.40	.80	.30	.80	.80	.00	.20
Dini	.00	.00	.20	1.00	.30	1.00	1.00	.00	.20
Amato	.00	.00	.60	1.00	.30	1.00	1.00	.00	.20
Thatcher	.00	.00	.40	.20	.30	.30	.20	.00	.20
Mitterrand	.00	.00	.40	.00	.30	.30	.00	1.00	.20

* *Outcome*. [1] Indicates sets that were combined by 'logical or' to form a higher-order construct. [2] Indicates higher-order construct.

184

Appendix

To measure membership of the first causal condition *'democracies with an intensely adversarial partisan press'*, the study drew on research from Hallin and Mancini (2004) and Jones and Pusey (2010) on press–party parallelism. Drawing on this evidence, the author gave each country the following scores. It considered Italy a full member; Australia, the UK and France more in than out, with a score of 0.7; and Germany, Spain and the US more out than in, with a score of 0.3. The second causal condition, *'weak privacy culture'*, was a higher-order construct derived from merging two conditions: *'weak statutory protection of private lives'* and *'weak consensus about when exposure is in the public interest'*. I also used the process of 'logical or' – namely, taking the maximum value in either condition (Ragin, 2000). Membership of the set *'weak statutory protection of private lives'*, was established with data from Bueno et al. (2007), Holtz-Bacha (2004), Klein (2000), Morrison et al. (2007), Shackelford (2011), Trouille (2000) and Whitman (2004). Countries were full members if public figures had no statutory protection of privacy or recourse to the law; mostly but not fully in if they had no statutory protection of privacy and/or more limited recourse to the law; and more or less in if they had no statutory protection but could use other legal avenues. They were full non-members if public figures had statutory protection and recourse to other legal means. They were more or less out if they had full statutory protection of privacy but the recourse to other legal means was more limited, and mostly but not fully out if they had some statutory protection of privacy but the recourse to other legal means was more limited. Membership of the set *'weak consensus about when exposure is in the public interest'* was established with data from a range of sources. While there are no data specifically showing the level of consensus about when exposure is in the public interest, a survey of journalists' views on ethical issues provides some insight into levels of consensus in different countries (see Weaver, 1996; 1998). Based on Weaver (1998), the US and the UK were considered full members of the set, Australia more or less in, and France, Germany, Italy and Spain mostly but not fully out.

To gauge membership of the fourth condition '*large tabloid media sector*', the study used data sources mentioned above. As above, it looked at three elements of the media but only for a ten-year period: first, the number of tabloids in the top ten circulating newspapers; second, the number of celebrity magazines in circulation up to a maximum of five; and, finally, the presence of high-profile celebrity gossip websites. A score of 5 was awarded where celebrity gossip websites were deemed to have a high presence, down to 0 if there was no presence. The scores for each part were added together to form an overall score. The cross-over point was set at 10. Actors with scores of 20 or more were considered full members. For mostly but not fully in, scores were set at between 14 and 19; for more or less in, scores were between 10 and 12. For more or less out, scores were set at 8 to 9, and for mostly but not fully out, 3 to 7. The threshold for full non-membership was set at 2.

The author drew on a range of nationally focused articles and book chapters to calibrate membership of the set '*democracies where the Christian right has a large presence in politics*' (see Eisenstein, 1982; Marks, 1986; Petchesky, 1981; Wilcox & Robinson, 2010; Williams, 2010). The criteria for membership was whether a country had a government that adopted socially conservative Christian right policies in the last ten years. France, Germany, Italy and Spain were considered full non-members, as none had experienced a government with Christian right social conservative policies. This is not to suggest that certain political parties are not socially conservative in outlook in these countries, but that the Christian right was not a political force and personal morality not the contentious political issue. The US was considered a full member, in part because it had conservative Republican presidential administrations for eight of the years between 2000 and 2009, but also because of the broad grouping of activists and politicians at the state and national level who espouse a conservative stance on social issues as part of their political platform. The socially conservative agenda can be seen in the policies of George W. Bush and the stance of Republican politicians in Congress on the liberalization of abortion laws and same-sex marriage. The UK was considered mostly out. It had Conservative governments that adopted a fairly socially conservative agenda in the 1980s; however, I argue that, while social conservatism has remained an important force in US politics, it has always been weaker in the UK, and weakened further with the election of the Blair government in 1997. Australia was considered more or less out, in part because, while the Howard government adopted a socially conservative stance on many social issues while in office, such as on euthanasia and same-sex marriage, his social conservatism was perhaps not as overt as in the US and his government tended not to interfere in these policy areas, which were the responsibility of individual states (Hollander, 2008).

To calibrate the final causal condition, *'democracies with high presence of gay rights activists'*, the author drew on a range of nationally focused studies (see Adam et al., 1999; Malagreca, 2007; Rimmerman et al. 2000; Tremblay & Paternotte, 2011). Drawing on this evidence, the author gave each country the following scores. The US was considered mostly but not a full member (0.8). Australia, France, Germany and the UK more or less out (0.4), and Italy and Spain mostly but not fully out (0.2). The truth tables are shown below.

Table 6.2 Causal conditions for membership of fuzzy set *'democracies with high levels of publicized infidelity 2000–2009'*

	Publicized infidelity*	Tabloid media presence	Weak privacy protection[1]	Weak privacy consensus[1]	Weak privacy culture[2]	Politically aligned press	New Christian right
Australia	.40	.40	.80	.60	.80	.70	.40
France	.0	.20	.00	.20	.20	.70	.00
Germany	.20	.20	.00	.20	.20	.30	.00
Italy	.20	.20	.20	.20	.20	1.00	.00
Spain	.20	.20	.00	.20	.20	.30	.00
UK	.60	.80	.80	1.00	1.00	.70	.20
US	1.00	.80	1.00	1.00	1.00	.0	.80

Outcome. [1] Indicates sets that were combined by 'logical or' to form a higher-order construct. [2] Indicates higher-order construct.

Table 6.3 Causal conditions for membership of the fuzzy set *'democracies with high levels of outing 2000–2009'*

	Outing*	Activist	Tabloid media presence	Weak privacy culture[1]	Politically aligned press	New Christian right
Australia	.20	.40	.40	.80	.70	.40
France	.00	.40	.20	.20	.70	.00
Germany	.20	.40	.20	.20	.30	.00
Italy	.00	.20	.20	.20	1.00	.00
Spain	.00	.20	.20	.20	.30	.00
UK	.40	.40	.80	1.00	.70	.20
US	.60	.80	.80	1.00	.00	.80

* *Outcome.* [1] Indicates higher-order construct – see table 6.2

Finally, chapter 3 presented a specific challenge, namely how to explain the sudden rise in the exposure of politicians' infidelity in the UK and the US in the 1990s. Having systematically discounted the influence of the various conditions explored in chapter 2, I drew on a range of secondary sources for alternative potential explanations (Berke, 1998; Davis, 2006; Franklin, 1997; Jones, 1995; Kurtz, 1998; Robertson, 1998; Sabato et al., 2000; Schudson, 2004; Thompson, 2000; Tunstall, 1996). Through this literature, two key events were identified. The first was the 'back-to-basics' speech delivered by the then UK Prime Minister John Major in October 1993, and the second, the 1998 push for the impeachment of President Clinton by Republican Congressmen in the wake of the Clinton–Lewinsky scandal. A closer examination of these events and the number of cases of publicized infidelity after them indicated their importance to any understanding of the sudden change that occurred.

Notes

Introduction: Politicians' Personal Lives in the Media Spotlight

1 This book does not examine the large literature on the projection and effect of politicians' characteristics. While it can be argued that a politician's characteristics are personal they are not specifically related to the flow of information about the personal life of politicians with which this book is concerned (see Van Aelst et al., 2012).

I Soft Focus: Leaders' Personal Lives Close-up

1 The two one-month periods were 15 December–15 January and 15 July–15 August. In Australia the two one-month periods were 15 December–15 January and 1–31 July. Excludes tabloid newspapers.

2 Digging for Dirt: Publicizing Politicians' Sex Lives

1 Sabato et al. define family values as 'the collection of images and policies that conservative groups see as underpinning the traditional American family' (2000, p. 62).

3 Changing Exposure: Critical Moments and the Uncovering of Politicians' Infidelity

1 My use of the term 'critical moment' differs from 'critical juncture', widely used in political science and elsewhere; while both contain a choice point, critical moments do not 'close off important future outcomes' as Mahoney suggests critical junctures do (2001, p. 113). Critical moments in this context were unforeseen events in response to which journalists in the US and UK made a series of choices, but these events did not close off future possible outcomes – instead, they changed the game, in that certain coverage became,

if not permissible, then normalized, due to a change in the normative environment.

4 Transnational Revelations: Flows, Access and Control in a Global News Environment

1 The papers chosen were *Le Monde, Taz – die Tageszeitung, La Stampa, El País*. The study looked for coverage of all 87 cases of infidelity in Australia, the UK and the US. The search used name of person and of their lover. It was time-limited to the day the story broke and for six days after (see appendix for more details).

2 'Gli scatti segreti di Berlusconi El País svela Villa Certosa': www.repubblica. it/2009/06/sezioni/politica/berlusconi-divorzio-6/pais-villa-certosa/pais-villa-cer tosa.html.

3 Data from Google Advanced blog and Web search collated by the author.

4 'Sexgate a la Italiana: el escandalo salpica a Berlusconi y una Ministra': www. clarin.com/diario/2008/07/05/elmundo/i-01708762.htm.

5 Data from Google Advanced blog and Web search collated by the author.

References

Adam, B. D., Duyvendak, J. W. and Krouwel, A. (eds.) 1999: *The Global Emergence of Gay and Lesbian Politics: National Imprints of a Worldwide Movement*. Philadelphia, PA: Temple University Press.

Adam, S. and Maier, M. 2010: Personalization of Politics: A Critical Review and Agenda for Research. In C. T. Salmon (ed.) *Communication Year Book 34*. New York: Routledge.

Adut, A. 2004: The Desacralization of Politics and the Escalation of Political Scandals in the West. Paper presented at the annual meeting of the American Sociological Association, San Francisco, CA, Aug 14. www.allacademic.com/meta/p109172_index.html (accessed 27.04.09).

Adut, A. 2008: *On Scandal: Moral Disturbances in Society, Politics and Art*. Cambridge: Cambridge University Press.

Allern, S., Kantolu, A., Pollack, E. and Balch-Orsten, M. 2012: Increased Scandalization: Nordic Political Scandals, 1980–2010. In S. Allern and E. Pollack (eds.) *Scandalous! The Mediated Construction of Political Scandals in Four Nordic Countries*. Gothenberg: Nordicom.

Allum, F. and Cilento, M. 2001: Parties and Personalities: The Case of Antonio Bassolino, Former Mayor of Naples. *Regional and Federal Studies*, 11 (1): 1–26.

Astier, H. 2003: Reticent French Media under Fire, *BBC News Online*, 4 September. www.bbc.co.uk/news (accessed 10.05.07).

Baecque, A. 1989: Pamphlets, Libel and Political Mythology. In R. Darton and J. D. Popkin (eds.) *Revolution in Print: The Press in France 1775–1800*. Berkeley, CA: University of California Press.

Barker, A. 1994: The Upturned Stone: Political Scandals and Their Investigation Processes in Twenty Democracies. *Crime, Law and Social Change*, 21 (4): 337–73.

Barnett, S. and Gaber, I. 2001: *Westminster Tales: Twenty-First-Century Crisis in Political Journalism*. London: Continuum.

References

Bastien, F. 2008: Let Me Talk! Politicians and Televised Interviews in Information, Infotainment and Entertainment Programmes. Paper presented at the annual meeting of the Midwest Political Science Association, Chicago, 3–6 April.

Bauer, S. W. 2008: *The Art of the Public Grovel: Sexual Sin and Public Confession in America*. Princeton, NJ: Princeton University Press.

Baum, M. 2005: Talking the Vote: Why Presidential Candidates Hit the Talk Show Circuit. *American Journal of Political Science*, 49 (2): 213–34.

Bauman, Z. 2011: Privacy, Secrecy, Intimacy, Human Bonds and Other Collateral Casualties of Liquid Modernity. *The Hedgehog Review*, 13 (2): 20–9. www.iasc.-culture.org.

Benn, S. I. and Gaus, G. F. 1983: The Public and the Private: Concepts and Action. In S. I. Benn and G. F. Gaus (eds.) *Public and Private in Social Life*. London: Croom Helm.

Bennett, A. 2010: Process Tracing and Causal Inference. In H. E. Brady and D. Collier (eds.) *Rethinking Social Inquiry: Diverse Tools, Shared Standards*. Lanham, MD: Rowman and Littlefield (2nd edition).

Benoit, K. and Laver, W. 2006: *Party Policy in Modern Democracies*. London: Routledge.

Berke, R. L. 1998: The 1998 Campaign: Commercials; Gleeful Democrats Assail Ads by GOP on Clinton Scandal. *New York Times*, 29 October. www.nytimes.com/ (accessed 01.07.10).

Bilger-Street, H. 2010: The Private Lives of French Politicians, A Matter for Political Scandal or for Entertainment? Paper delivered at Political Studies Association Annual Conference, Edinburgh, 30 March – 1 April.

Bingham, A. 2007: 'Drinking in the Last Chance Saloon': The British Press and the Crisis of Self-regulation, 1989–95. *Media History*, 13 (1): 79–92.

Bingham, A. 2009: *Family Newspapers? Sex, Private Life, and the British Popular Press, 1918–1978*. Oxford: Oxford University Press.

Blais, A. and Massicotte, L. 2002: Electoral Systems. In L. Le Duc, R. G. Niemi and N. Norris (eds.) *Comparing Democracies 2*. London: Sage.

Blenkin, M. 2002: Australian Political Sex Scandals. *Sydney Morning Herald*, 4 July. www.smh.com.au/ (accessed 05.04.10).

Boling, P. 1996: *Privacy and the Politics of Intimate Life*. Ithaca, NY: Cornell University Press.

Bonner, F. and McKay, S. 2007: Personalizing Current Affairs Without Becoming Tabloid: The Case of *Australian Story*. *Journalism Studies*, 8 (6): 640–56.

Bourne, B. 2004: Coe Fails to Stop News of His Ten-Year Affair Emerging. *Sunday Times*, 30 May. www.timesonline.co.uk/ (accessed 13.09.07).

Boyd-Barrett, O. 2000: Constructing the Global, Constructing the Local: News Agencies Re-present the World. In A. Malek and A. P. Kavoori (eds.) *The Global Dynamics of News: Studies in International News Coverage and News Agenda*. Stamford, CT: Ablex.

References

Brady, H. E., Collier, D. and Seawright, J. 2010: Refocusing the Discussion of Methodology. In H. E. Brady and D. Collier (eds.) *Rethinking Social Inquiry: Diverse Tools, Shared Standards.* Lanham, MD: Rowman and Littlefield (2nd edition).

Breit, R., Harrison, J., Hirst, M., McLellan, T. and Bartlett, D. 2002: Ethics in Journalism and Cheryl Kernot: A Colloquium. *Australian Studies in Journalism*, 10–11: 33–57.

Bueno, M., Cardenas, M.L. and Esquivias, L. 2007: The Rise of the Gossip Press in Spain. *Journalism Studies*, 8 (4): 621–33.

Bystrom, D. D. 2004: Women as Political Communication Sources and Audiences. In L. L. Kaid (ed.) *Handbook of Political Communication Research.* London: Sage.

Calabrese, A. 2000: Political Space and the Trade in Television News. In C. Sparks and J. Tulloch (eds.) *Tabloid Tales: Global Debates over Media Standards.* Lanham, MD: Rowman and Littlefield.

Calvert, C. 2000: *Voyeur Nation: Media, Privacy and Peering in Modern Culture.* Boulder, CO: Westview Press.

Campbell, M. 2010: Carla Bruni and Nicolas Sarkozy: L'affaire Twitter. *The Times*, 14 March. www.timesonline.co.uk/ (accessed 02.04.10).

Campus, D. 2002: Leaders, Dreams and Journeys: Italy's New Political Communication. *Journal of Modern Italian Studies*, 7 (2): 171–91.

Campus, D. 2006: The 2006 Election: More than Ever, a Berlusconi-centred Campaign. *Journal of Modern Italian Studies*, 11 (4): 516–31.

Campus, D. 2010a: The Mediatization and Personalization of Politics in Italy and France: The Cases of Berlusconi and Sarkozy. *International Journal of Press Politics*, 15 (2): 219–35.

Campus, D. 2010b: *Antipolitics in Power: Populist Language as a Tool for Power.* Cresskill, NJ: Hampton Press.

Carlson, M. 1989: A Skeleton in Barney's Closet. *Time*, 25 September. www.time.com/ (accessed 02.11.07).

Caroli, B. B. 2003: *First Ladies: From Martha Washington to Laura Bush.* New York: Oxford University Press.

Castells, M. 2004: *The Information Age: Economy, Society and Culture.* Volume 2: *The Power of Identity.* Oxford: Blackwell (2nd edition).

Castles, F. G. and Obinger, H. 2008: Worlds, Families and Regimes: Country Clusters in European and OECD Area Public Policy. *West European Politics*, 31 (1–2): 321–44.

Cepernich, C. 2008: Landscapes of Immorality: Scandals in the Italian Press (1998–2006). *Perspectives on European Politics and Society*, 9 (1): 95–109.

Cepernich, C. 2010: Opposite Hysterics: Veronica, Noemi, Patrizia and the Italian Media System on the Verge of a Nervous Breakdown. Paper presented at XXIV Convegno SISP, Venice, 16–18 September.

References

Chalaby, J. K. 2004: Scandal and the Rise of Investigative Reporting in France. *American Behavioral Scientist*, 47 (9): 1194–207.

Chase, J. and Ford, L. 2004: Ryan File a Bombshell: Ex-Wife Alleges GOP Candidate Took Her to Sex Clubs. *Chicago Tribune*, 22 June. www.chicago tribune.com/ (accessed 12.01.10).

Chekola, M. 1994: Outing, Truth Telling and the Shame of the Closet. *Journal of Homosexuality*, 27 (3–4): 67–90.

Chenu, A. 2008: From Paths of Glory to Celebrity Boulevards: Sociology of *Paris Match* Covers. Notes and Documents, 2008–05, Paris OSC Sciences, Po / CNRS. Published as: Des sentiers de la gloire aux boulevards de la célébrité: Sociologie des couvertures de *Paris Match*, 1949–2005. *Revue Française de Sociologie*, 49 (1): 3–52.

Chrisafis, A. 2007: A Very Public Affair. *The Guardian*, G2, 24 October, pp. 10–13.

Clark, A. 2003: *Scandal: The Sexual Politics of the British Constitution*. Princeton, NJ: Princeton University Press.

Clarke, D. H., Sanders, D., Stewart, M. and Whiteley, P. 2004: *Political Choice in Britain*. Oxford: Oxford University Press.

Clayman, S. and Heritage, J. 2002: *The News Interview: Journalists and Public Figures on the Air*. New York: Cambridge University Press.

Cockerell, M. 1989: *Live From Number Ten*. London: Faber and Faber.

Cogan, B. and Kelso, T. 2009: *Encyclopedia of Politics, the Media and Popular Culture*. Santa Barbara, CA: Greenwood Press.

Cogan, J. K. 1996: The Reynolds Affair and the Politics of Character. *Journal of the Early Republic*, 16 (3): 389–418.

Colaprico, P. and D'Avanzo, G. 2010: Ruby and Berlusconi, 'My Nights in Arcore'. *La Repubblica*, 28 October. www.repubblica.it/ (accessed 13.01.11).

Collier, D., Brady, H. E. and Seawright, J. 2010: Introduction to the Second Edition: A Sea Change in Political Methodology. In H. E. Brady and D. Collier (eds.) *Rethinking Social Inquiry: Diverse Tools, Shared Standards*. Lanham, MD: Rowman and Littlefield (2nd edition).

Connolly, K. 2009: Sex Scandals Through the Years: Both Parties Even. *Newsweek*, 25 June. http://blog.newsweek.com/blogs/thegaggle/ (accessed 09.07.09).

Corner, J. 2003: Mediated Persona and Political Culture. In J. Corner and D. Pels (eds.) *Media and the Restyling of Politics*. London: Sage.

Corner, J. and Pels, D. 2003: Introduction: The Re-Styling of Politics. In J. Corner and D. Pels (eds.) *Media and the Restyling of Politics*. London: Sage.

Curtis, P. 2010: Speculation, Lurid Sex Claims and William Hague's Very Public Outpouring. *The Guardian*, 1 September. http://media.guardian.co.uk (accessed 12.05.11).

References

Dagnes, A. (ed.) 2011: *Sex Scandals in American Politics: A Multi-disciplinary approach to the Construction and Aftermath of Contemporary Political Sex Scandals*. London: Continuum.

Dakhlia, J. 2008: *Politique People*. Paris: Edition Breal.

Dakhlia, J. 2010: Une chute du 'mur français de la vie privée'? La peopolisation politique des années 2000. *The Web Journal of French Media Studies*, 8. http://wjfms.ncl.ac.uk/.

Dalton, R. J. and Wattenberg, M. P. (eds.) 2000: *Parties Without Partisans: Political Change in Advanced Industrial Democracies*. Oxford: Oxford University Press.

Das Gupta, O. 2007: Liebe, Sex und Öffentlichkeit. *Süddeutsche Zeitung*, 16 January. www.sueddeutsche.de (accessed 28.06.10).

Davies, L. 2011: How Dominique Strauss-Kahn's Arrest Awoke a Dormant Anger in the Heart of France's Women. *The Guardian*, 22 May. http://media.guardian.co.uk (accessed 23.05.11).

Davies, N. 2009: Murdoch Papers Paid £1m to Gag Phone-hacking Victims. *The Guardian*, 8 July. http://media.guardian.co.uk (accessed 12.08.09).

Davis, A. 2010: *Political Communication and Social Theory*. London: Routledge.

Davis, L. 2006: *Scandal: How Gotcha Politics is Destroying America*. New York: Palgrave.

Deacon, D. 2004: Politicians, Privacy and Media Intrusion in Britain. *Parliamentary Affairs*, 57 (1): 9–23.

Deacon, D. 2007: Yesterday's Papers and Today's Technology: Digital Newspaper Archives and 'Push Button' Content Analysis. *European Journal of Communication*, 22 (1): 2–25.

Diamond, M. 2004: *Victorian Sensation: On the Spectacular, the Shocking and the Scandalous in Nineteenth-Century Britain*. London: Anthem Press.

Diamond, E. and Silverman, R. A. 1997: *White House to Your House: Media and Politics in Virtual America*. Cambridge, MA: MIT Press.

Domeier, N. 2007: A Global Scandal? Eulenburg Affair in Germany, 1906–1909. Paper delivered at the Collective Memory and Collective Knowledge in a Global Age Interdisciplinary Workshop, 17–18 June. www.lse.ac.uk/Depts/global/EventsPDFs/MemoryWorkshop/AGlobalScandal_Domeier.pdf (accessed 14.02.10).

Donsbach, W. and Klett, B. 1993: Subjective Objectivity: How Journalists in Four Countries Define a Key Term of Their Profession. *International Communication Gazette*, 51 (1): 53–83.

Downey, J. and Stanyer, J. 2010: Comparative Media Analysis: Why Some Fuzzy Thinking Might Help. *European Journal of Communication*, 25: 331–47.

Dubecki, L. 2007: Dirty Politics. *The Age*, August 21. www.theage.com.au/ (accessed 14.12.10).

Eisenstein, Z. R. 1982: The Sexual Politics of the New Right: Understanding the 'Crisis of Liberalism' for the 1980s. *Signs*, 7 (3): 567–88.

References

Entman, R. M. 2012: *Scandal and Silence: Media Responses to Presidential Misconduct*. Cambridge, UK: Polity Press.

Ericson, G. 2010: Politicians in Celebrity Talk Show Interviews: The Narrativization of Personal Experience. *Text and Talk*, 30 (5): 529–51.

Errera, C. 2006: La vie privée des politiques, un tabou de la politique française. *Communication et Langages*, 148 (1): 81–102.

Esser, F. 1999: Tabloidization of News: A Comparative Analysis of Anglo-American and German Press Journalism. *European Journal of Communication*, 14 (3): 291–324.

Esser, F. and Hartung, U. 2004: Nazis, Pollution, and No Sex: Political Scandals as a Reflection of Political Culture in Germany. *American Behavioral Scientist*, 47 (8): 1040–71.

Fahrenthold, D. A. and Blake, A. 2011: Rep. Chris Lee Resigns after Reports of Craigslist Flirtation. *Washington Post*, 10 February. www.washingtonpost.com (accessed 14.07.11).

Fallows, J. 2011: Learning to Love the (Shallow, Divisive, Unreliable) New Media. *The Atlantic*, April. www.theatlantic.com (accessed 14.10.11).

Farrell, D., McAllister, I. and Studlar, T. 1998: Sex, Money and Politics: Sleaze and the Conservative Party in the 1997 Election. In D. Denver, J. Fisher, P. Cowley and P. Pattie (eds.) *British Elections and Parties Review*. Volume VIII: *The 1997 General Election*. London: Frank Cass.

Fielden, L. 2012: *Regulating the Press: A Comparative Study of International Press Councils*. Oxford: Reuters Institute for the Study of Journalism.

Fisher, I. 2007: Berlusconi Flirts. Wife Fed Up. Read All About It. *New York Times*, 1 February. www.nytimes.com/ (accessed 06.04.08).

Fisher, M. 2007: Who Among Us Would Cast the First Stone? This Guy. *Washington Post*, 6 September.

Flemming, J. 2006: 'Keeping the Bastards Honest': Australia and the Investigation of Political Scandal. In J. Garrard and J. Newell (eds.) *Scandals in Past and Contemporary Politics*. Manchester: Manchester University Press.

Foley, M. 2000: *The British Presidency*. Manchester: Manchester University Press.

Franklin, B. 1997: *Newszak and News Media*. London: Arnold.

Frost, C. 2000: *Media Ethics and Self-Regulation*. Harlow: Longman.

Furedi, F. 2004: *Therapy Culture: Cultivating Vulnerability in an Uncertain Age*. London: Routledge.

Gamson, J. 1994: *Claims to Fame: Celebrity in Contemporary America*. Berkeley, CA: University of California Press.

Gamson, J. 2001: Normal Sins: Sex Scandal Narratives as Institutional Morality Tales. *Social Problems*, 48 (2): 185–205.

George, A. L. and Bennett, A. 2005: *Case Studies and Theory Development in the Social Sciences*. Cambridge, MA: MIT Press.

Gibran, B. 2006: Books as a Political Communication Medium in the United States. *Publishing Research Quarterly*, 22 (2): 38–48.

References

Giddens, A. 1991: *Modernity and Self-Identity: Self and Society in the Late Modern Age*. Cambridge: Polity.

Gimson, A. 2001: Married to a Monster. *The Spectator*, 28 July. www.spectator.co.uk (accessed 05.05.09).

Glover, J. 2008: Tittle-Tattle, They Wrote. *The Guardian*, 13 May. www.guardian.co.uk/ (accessed 20.05.08).

Goertz, G. 2005: *Social Science Concepts: A User's Guide*. Princeton, NJ: Princeton University Press.

Goffman, E. 1971[1959]: *The Presentation of Self in Everyday Life*. London: Pelican.

Goldenberg, S. 2007: Porn King Offers $1m for US Political Scandal. *The Guardian*, 4 June, p. 17.

Goot, M. 2012: Stripped Bare: A Short History of the Australian Tabloid. *Australian Journal of Communication*, 38 (2).

Green, J. C. 2002: Still Functional after All These Years: Parties in the United States 1960–2000. In P. Webb, D. Farrell and I. Holliday (eds.) *Political Parties in Advanced Industrial Democracies*. Oxford: Oxford University Press.

Gronbeck, B. E. 1997: Character, Celebrity, and Sexual Innuendo. In J. Lull and S. Hinerman (eds.) *Media Scandals: Morality and Desire in the Popular Culture Marketplace*. Cambridge: Polity.

Gross, L. P. 2003: Privacy and Spectacle: The Reversible Panopticon and Media-Saturated Society. In L. P.Gross, J. S. Katz and J. Ruby (eds.) *Image Ethics in the Digital Age*. Minneapolis, MI: University of Minnesota Press.

Gurevitch, M. and Blumler, J. G. 2004: State of the Art of Comparative Political Communication Research: Poised for Maturity? In F. Esser and B. Pfetsch (eds.) *Comparing Political Communication: Theories, Cases and Challenges*. Cambridge: Cambridge University Press.

Hacker, K. L. 1995: Introduction: The Importance of Candidate Images in Presidential Elections, in K. L. Hacker (ed.) *Candidate Images in Presidential Elections*. Westport, CT: Praeger.

Hall, A. 1977: *Scandal, Sensation and Social Democracy: The SPD Press and Wilhelmine Germany 1890–1914*. Cambridge: Cambridge University Press.

Hallin, D. C. 2000: Commercialism and Professionalism in the American News Media. In J. Curran and M. Gurevitch (eds.) *Mass Media and Society*. London: Arnold.

Hallin, D. C. and Mancini, P. 2004: *Comparing Media Systems: Three Models of Media and Politics*. Cambridge: Cambridge University Press.

Hart, R. P. 1999: *Seducing America: How Television Charms the Modern Voter*. London: Sage.

Hayden, J. 2002: *Covering Clinton: The President and the Press in the 1990s*. Westport, CT: Praeger.

Heffernan, R. A. and Webb, P. 2004: The British Prime Minister: Much More than First Amongst Equals. In T. Poguntke and P. Webb (eds.) *The*

References

Presidentialization of Politics: A Comparative Study of Democracies. Oxford: Oxford University Press.

Henningham, J. 1998: Australian Journalists. In D. H. Weaver (ed.) *The Global Journalist: News People around the World.* Cresskill, NJ: Hampton Press.

Hirdman, A., Kleberg, M. and Widestedt, K. 2005: Intimization of Journalism: Transformations of Medialized Public Spheres from 1880s to Current Times. *Nordicom Review*, 2: 109–17.

Hogan, J. and Doyle, D. 2007. The Importance of Ideas: An *A Priori* Critical Juncture Framework. *Canadian Journal of Political Science*, 40 (4): 883–910.

Holbert, R. L. 2005: A Typology for the Study of Entertainment Television and Politics. *American Behavioural Scientist*, 49 (3): 436–53.

Hollander, J. 2008: John Howard, Economic Liberalism, Social Conservatism, and Australian Federalism. *Australian Journal of Politics and History*, 54 (1): 85–103.

Holmes, M. 2000: When is the Personal Political? The President's Penis and Other Stories. *Sociology*, 34 (2): 305–21.

Holtz-Bacha, C. 2004: Germany: How the Private Life of Politicians Got into the Media. *Parliamentary Affairs*, 57 (1): 41–52.

Hooper, J. 2007: Scusi is the Hardest Word: Berlusconi's Wife Forces Him into a Public Apology. *The Guardian*, 1 February. www.guardian.co.uk/ (accessed 07.04.08).

Hooper, J. 2009: We Didn't Sleep a Wink: Escort Releases Her Recording of Her Night with Berlusconi. *The Guardian*, 20 July. www.guardian.co.uk/ (accessed 07.08.09).

Horton, D. and Wohl, R. 1956: Mass Communication and Para-social Interaction: Observations on Intimacy at a Distance. *Psychiatry*, 19: 215–29.

House of Commons Culture, Media and Sport Committee 2003: *Privacy and Media Intrusion.* Volume I. Fifth Report of Session 2002–03. London: The Stationery Office.

House of Commons Culture, Media and Sport Committee 2007: *Self-Regulation of the Press.* Seventh Report of Session 2006–07. London: The Stationery Office.

House of Commons Culture, Media and Sport Committee 2009: *Press Standards, Privacy and Libel.* Report of Session 2009–10. London: The Stationery Office.

The Independent (1995) Sleaze: the List. *The Independent*, 23 July. www.Independent.co.uk/ (accessed 04.02.10).

Information Commissioner's Office (ICO) 2006a: *What Price Privacy? The Unlawful Trade in Confidential Personal Information.* London: The Stationery Office.

Information Commissioner's Office (ICO) 2006b: *What Price Privacy Now? The First Six Months Progress in Halting the Unlawful Trade in Confidential Personal Information.* London: The Stationery Office.

References

Inglehart, R. 2000: Culture and Democracy. In L. E. Harrison and S. P. Huntingdon (eds.) *Culture Matters: How Values Shape Human Progress*. New York: Basic Books.

Israely, J. 2009: In Italy a Sex Scandal to Rival Berlusconi's. *Time* Magazine, 26 November. www.time.com/ (accessed 23.04.10).

Jamieson, K. H. 1992: *Dirty Politics: Deception, Distraction and Democracy*. New York: Oxford University Press.

Jiménez, F. 2004: The Politics of Scandal in Spain: Morality Plays, Social Trust, and the Battle for Public Opinion. *American Behavioral Scientist*, 47 (8): 1099–121.

Jones, N. 1995: *Soundbites and Spin Doctors: How Politicians Manipulate the Media and Vice Versa*. London: Cassell.

Jones, P. K. and Pusey, M. 2010: Political Communication and 'Media System': The Australian Canary. *Media, Culture and Society*, 32 (3): 451–71.

Jones, S. 2008: Clegg Tots Up Sex Encounters in GQ Interview. *The Guardian*, 1 April. www.guardian.co.uk (accessed 15.06.10).

Juntunen, L. and Valiverronen, E. 2010: Politics of Sexting: Renegotiating the Boundaries of Private and Public in Political Journalism. *Journalism Studies*, 11 (6): 817–31.

Just, M., Crigler, A. N., Alger, D. E., Cook, T. E., Kern, M. and West, D. M. 1996: *Crosstalk: Citizens, Candidates and the Media in Presidential Campaigns*. Chicago, IL: University of Chicago Press.

Kane, P. and Murray, S. 2007: GOP Senator Pleaded Guilty After Restroom Arrest. *Washington Post*, 28 August. www.washingtonpost.com/ (accessed 25.09.07).

Karvonen, E. 2009: Entertainmentization of the European Public Sphere and Politics. In J. Harrison and B. Wessels (eds.) *Mediating Europe: New Media, Mass Communications and the European Public Sphere*. Oxford: Berghahn Books.

Karvonen, L. 2010: *The Personalization of Politics: A Study of Parliamentary Democracies*. Colchester: ECPR Press.

Kasindorf, M. 2005: Rich and Famous Push For Secrecy in Divorce. *USA Today*, 12 August. www.usatoday.com/ (accessed 27.07.09).

Keane, J. 2009: Monitory Democracy and Media-Saturated Societies. *Griffith Review*, 24, Participation Society. www.griffithreview.com/ (accessed 25.10.10).

King, A. 1986: Sex, Money and Power. In R. Hodder-Williams and J. Ceaser (eds.) *Politics in Britain and the United States: Comparative Perspectives*. Durham, NC: Duke University Press.

Kirby, E. J. 2010: *The Presidential Influence on the French Media under Nicolas Sarkozy*. Reuters Institute Fellowship Paper. Oxford: Reuters Institute for the Study of Journalism.

Klein, U. 2000: Tabloidized Political Coverage in the German *Bild-Zeitung*. In C. Sparks and J. Tulloch (eds.) *Tabloid Tales: Global Debates over Media Standards*. Lanham, MD: Rowman and Littlefield.

References

Kohn, G. C. 2000: *The New Encyclopedia of American Scandal*. New York: Facts on File.

Koss, S. 1984: *The Rise and Fall of the Political Press in Britain*. Volume II: *The Twentieth Century*. London: Hamish Hamilton.

Kraus, S. and Davis, D. with Lang, G. and Lang, K. 1975: Critical Events Analysis. In S. H. Chaffee (ed.) *Political Communications: Issues and Strategies for Research*. Beverly Hills, CA: Sage.

Kriesi, H. P. 2010: Personalization of National Election Campaigns. Paper presented at Political Studies Association Annual Conference, Edinburgh, UK, 29 March – 1 April.

Kuhn, R. 2004: Vive la différence? The Mediation of Politicians' Public Images and Private Lives in France. *Parliamentary Affairs*, 57 (1): 24–40.

Kuhn, R. 2007: The Public and the Private in Contemporary French Politics. *French Cultural Studies*, 18 (2): 185–200.

Kuhn, R. 2010: 'Les médias, c'est moi.' President Sarkozy and News Management. *French Politics*, 8 (4): 355–76.

Kuhn, R. 2011: *The Media in Contemporary France*. Maidenhead: Open University Press.

Kumaraswamy, P. R. 1999: Monica Lewinsky in Middle Eastern Eyes. *Middle East Quarterly*, 6 (1) March. www.meforum.org (accessed 03.05.10).

Kurtz, H. 1998: Others Fair Game for Scandal in Wake of Affair. *The Washington Post*, 11 September. www.washingtonpost.com/ (accessed 05.10.08).

Kurtz, H. 2009: The Hills? No, TMZ Now Hits the Hill. *The Washington Post*, March 19. www.washingtonpost.com/ (accessed 05.05.09).

Laine, T. 2010: SMS Scandals: Sex, Media and Politics in Finland. *Media, Culture and Society*, 32 (1): 151–60.

Lang, K. and Lang, G. E. 1956: The Television Personality in Politics: Some Considerations. *Public Opinion Quarterly*, 20 (1): 103–12.

Langer, A. I. 2007: A Historical Exploration of the Personalization of Politics in the Print Media: The British Prime Minister, 1945–1999. *Parliamentary Affairs*, 60 (3): 371–87.

Langer, A. I. 2010: Politicization of the Private Persona: Exceptional Leaders or the New Rule? The Case of the United Kingdom and the Blair Effect. *International Journal of Press/Politics*, 15 (1): 60–76.

Langer, A. I. 2012: *The Personalisation of Politics in the UK: Mediated Leadership from Attlee to Cameron*. Manchester: Manchester University Press.

Lauterbach, T. 2005: A Celebrity Fight-Back Par Excellence. *Computer Law and Security Report*, 21 (1): 74–7.

Lawrence, R. G. and Bennett, W. L. 2001: Rethinking Media Politics and Public Opinion: Reactions to the Clinton-Lewinsky Scandal. *Political Science Quarterly*, 116 (3): 425–46.

Lechavallier, A. S. 2006: French Roast Served up American Style. *Global Journalist*, 1 January. www.globaljournalist.org/ (accessed 13.12.09).

References

Lehrer, N. 2011: D'Artagnan's Tune. *Index on Censorship*, 40 (2): 56–66.

Leigh, D. and Evans, R. 2006: Newspapers that Used Illegal Information Listed. *The Guardian*, 14 December. http://media.guardian.co.uk (accessed 15.12.07).

Lichtenberg, J. 1989: *The Politics of Character and the Character of Journalism.* The Joan Shorenstein Barone Center, Harvard University – Discussion Paper D-2.

Lindsay, D. and Ricketson, S. 2006: Copyright, Privacy and Digital Rights Management. In A. T. Kenyon and M. Richardson (ed.) *New Dimensions in Privacy Law: International and Comparative Perspectives.* Cambridge: Cambridge University Press.

Lister, D. 2003: Schroeder Steps Up War over Press Allegations. *The Independent*, 20 January. www.independent.co.uk/ (accessed 23.01.10).

Lowenthal, L. 1961: *Literature, Popular Culture, and Society.* Palo Alto, CA: Pacific Books.

Lowi, T. J. 2004: Power and Corruption: Political Competition and the Scandal Market. In P. Apostolidis and J. A. Williams (eds.) *Public Affairs: Politics in the Age of Sex Scandals.* Durham, NC: Duke University Press.

Maarek, P. J. 2011: *Campaign Communication and Political Marketing.* New York: Wiley.

McAllister, I. 2007: The Personalization of Politics. In R. J. Dalton and H. D. Klingemann (eds.) *Oxford Handbook of Political Behavior.* New York: Oxford University Press.

McCormick, N. 2005: The Politics of Privacy. *Legal Week*, 5 May. www.legal-week.com (accessed 05.10.07).

McNair, B. 2000: *Journalism and Democracy: An Evaluation of the Political Public Sphere.* London: Routledge.

McNair, B. 2006: *Cultural Chaos: Journalism, News and Power in a Globalised World.* London: Routledge.

McNamara, K. 2009: Publicising Private Lives: Celebrities, Image Control and the Reconfiguration of Public Space. *Social and Cultural Geography*, 10 (1): 9–23.

McNamara, K. 2011: The Paparazzi Industry and New Media: The Evolving Production and Consumption of Celebrity News and Gossip Websites. *International Journal of Cultural Studies*, 14 (5): 516–630. (Published online first, 8 April.)

Magone, J. M. 2009: *Contemporary Spanish Politics.* London: Routledge.

Mahoney, J. 2001: Path-Dependent Explanations of Regime Change in Central America: A Comparative Perspective. *Comparative International Development*, 36 (1): 111–41.

Mahoney, J. 2007: Qualitative Methodology and Comparative Politics. *Comparative Political Studies*, 40 (2):122–44.

Malagreca, M. A. 2007: *Queer Italy: Contexts, Antecedents and Representation.* New York: Peter Lang.

References

Maltese, J. A. 2000: The Media: The New Media and the Lure of the Clinton Scandal. In M. J. Rozell and C. Wilcox (eds.) *The Clinton Scandal and the Future of American Government*. Washington, DC: Georgetown University Press.

Mancini, P. 2008: The Berlusconi Case: Mass Media and Politics in Italy. In I. Bondebjerg and P. Madsen (eds.) *Media, Democracy and European Culture*. Bristol: Intellect.

Mancini, P. 2011: *Between Commodification and Lifestyle Politics: Does Silvio Berlusconi Provide a New Model of Politics for the Twenty-First Century?* Oxford: Reuters Institute for the Study of Journalism.

Marinucci, C. 2009: Paparazzi Turning Lenses on Politicians. 2 March, *San Francisco Chronicle*. http://articles.sfgate.com/ (Accessed 5.8.10)

Marks, G. 1986: The Revival of Laissez-Faire. In R. Hodder-Williams and J. Ceaser (eds.) *Politics in Britain and the United States: Comparative Perspectives*. Durham, NC: Duke University Press.

Marrin, M. 2005: Used and Abused by Mr Five Times Nightly. *The Sunday Times*, 8 May. www.timesonline.co.uk/ (aqccessed 05.11.10).

Mayo, D. J. and Gunderson, M. 1994: Privacy and the Ethics of Outing. *Journal of Homosexuality*, 27 (3–4): 47–65.

Maza, S. C. 1993: *Private Lives and Public Affairs: The Causes Célèbres of Pre-Revolutionary France*. Berkeley, CA: University of California Press.

Merkl, P. H. 2001: *A Coup Attempt in Washington: A European Mirror on the 1998–1999 Constitutional Crisis*. New York: Palgrave.

Meyrowitz, J. 1985: *No Sense of Place: The Impact of Electronic Media on Social Behaviour*. New York: Oxford University Press.

Morrison, D. E. and Svennevig, M. 2002: The Public Interest, the Media and Privacy. Unpublished Report.

Morrison, D. E. and Svennevig, M. 2007: The Defence of Public Interest and Intrusion of Privacy: Journalists and the Public. *Journalism*, 8 (1): 44–65.

Morrison, D. E., Kieran, M., Svennevig, M. and Ventress, S. 2007: *Media and Values: Intimate Transgressions in a Changing Moral Landscape*. Bristol: Intellect.

Mortimore, R. 1995: Public Perceptions of Sleaze in Britain. *Parliamentary Affairs*, 48 (4): 579–89.

Mughan, A. 2000: *Media and the Presidentialization of Parliamentary Elections*. Basingstoke, UK: Palgrave.

Muir, K. 2005: Media Darlings and Falling Stars: Celebrity and the Reporting of Political Leaders. *Westminster Papers in Communication and Culture*, 2 (2): 54–71.

Muir, K. 2005b: Political Cares: Gendered Reporting of Work and Family Issues in Relation to Australian Politicians. *Australian Feminist Studies*, 20 (46): 77–90.

Murdock, G. 2010: Celebrity Culture and the Public Sphere: The Tabloidization

References

of Power. In J. Gripsrud and L. Weibull (eds.) *Media, Markets and Public Spheres: European Media at the Crossroads*. Bristol: Intellect.

Nagel, T. 2002: *Concealment and Exposure and Other Essays*. New York: Oxford University Press.

Neiwert, D. 1998: Secret Lives of Republicans Part Two. *Salon.com*, 16 September. www.salon.com/news/1998/09/16news.html (accessed 13.10.10).

Neveu, E. 2005: Politicians Without Politics, a Polity Without Citizens: the Politics of the Chat Show in Contemporary France. *Modern and Contemporary France*, 13 (3): 323–35.

Nolan, J. L. 1998: *The Therapeutic State: Justifying Government at Century's End*. New York: New York University Press.

Norris, P. 2009: Comparative Political Communications: Common Frameworks or Babelian Confusion? *Government and Opposition*, 44 (3): 321–40.

Norris, P. and Inglehart, R. 2004: *Sacred and the Secular: Religion and Politics Worldwide*. Cambridge: Cambridge University Press.

Nye, J. S. 1997: In Government We Don't Trust. *Foreign Policy*, 108 (Autumn): 99–111.

Oehlkers, P. W. 2000: Mediating News: The International Media Echo and Symbolic International Relations. In A. Malek and A. P. Kavoori (eds.) *The Global Dynamics of News: Studies in International News Coverage and News Agenda*. Stamford, CT: Ablex.

Owen, R. and Hanley, A. 2009: Wife of the Italian Prime Minister Silvio Berlusconi Sues for Divorce. *The Times*, 4 May. www.timesonline.co.uk/ (accessed 31.05.09).

Page, R. E. 2003: Cherie: Lawyer, Wife, Mum: The Contradictory Patterns of Representation in Media Reports of Cherie Booth/Blair. *Discourse and Society*, 14 (5): 599–679.

Paolucci, C. 2002: Campaign Strategies and Tactics: Leaders, Experts and the Media. In J. L. Newell (ed.) *The Italian General Election of 2001: Berlusconi's Victory*. Manchester: Manchester University Press.

Parris, M. and Maguire, K. 2005: *Great Parliamentary Scandals: Five Centuries of Calumny, Smear and Innuendo*. London: Robson Books.

Parry-Giles, S. and Parry-Giles, T. 2002: *Constructing Clinton*. New York: Peter Lang Publishing.

Paterno, S. 1997: An Affair to Ignore: Why Did a Story about Bob Dole's Dalliance Get So Little Play? *American Journalism Review*, 19 (January–February). www.ajr.org/ (accessed 23.3.10).

Perloff, R. M. 1998: *Political Communication: Politics, Press and Public in America*. New York: Routledge.

Petchesky, R. P. 1981: Antiabortion, Antifeminism, and the Rise of the New Right. *Feminist Studies*, 7 (2): 206–46.

Pew Research Center for People and the Press 1998: *Scandal Reporting Faulted for Bias and Inaccuracy*. http://people-press.org/ (accessed 21.01.12).

References

Pew Research Center for People and the Press 2007: *Voters Remain in Neutral as Presidential Campaign Moves into Higher Gear*. http://people-press.org/ (accessed 21.01.12).

Phillips, A., Couldry, N. and Freedman, D. 2009: Accountability, Norms and the Material Conditions of Contemporary Journalism. In N. Fenton (ed.) *New Media, Old News: Journalism and Democracy in the Digital Age*. London: Sage.

Plasser, F. and Lengauer, G. 2008: Television Campaigning Worldwide. In D. W. Johnson (ed.) *Handbook of Political Management*. London: Routledge.

Plasser, F. with Plasser, G. 2002: *Global Political Campaigning: A Worldwide Analysis of Campaign Professionals and their Practices*. Westport, CT: Praeger.

Ponce de Leon, C. L. 2003: *Self-Exposure: Human Interest Journalism and the Emergence of Celebrity in America, 1890–1940*. Chapel Hill, NC: University of North Carolina Press.

Ponder, S. 1999: *Managing the Press: Origins of the Media Presidency, 1897–1933*. Basingstoke, UK: Palgrave.

Popkin, J. D. 1990: *Revolutionary News in France, 1789–1799*. Durham, NC: Duke University Press.

Quinn-Musgrove, S. L. and Kanter, S. 1995: *America's Royalty: All the President's Children*. Westport, CT: Praeger.

Ragin, C. 2000: *Fuzzy Set Social Science*. Chicago: University of Chicago Press.

Ragin, C. 2008: *Redesigning Social Inquiry: Fuzzy Sets and Beyond*. Chicago: University of Chicago Press.

Rahat, G. and Sheafer, T. 2007: The Personalization(s) of Politics: Israel, 1949–2003. *Political Communication*, 24: 65–80.

Rawlins, W. K. 1998: Theorizing Public and Private Domains and Practices of Communication: Introductory Concerns. *Communication Theory*, 8 (4): 369–80.

Reinemann, C. and Wilke, J. 2007: It's the Debates, Stupid: How the Introduction of Televised Debates Changed the Portrayal of Chancellor Candidates in the German Press, 1949–2005. *The International Journal of Press/Politics*, 12 (4): 92–111.

Riffe, D. 2003: Public Opinion about News Coverage of Leaders' Private Lives. *Journal of Mass Media Ethics*, 18 (2): 98–110.

Rimmerman, C. R., Wald, K. D. and Wilcox, C. (eds.) 2000: *The Politics of Gay Rights*. Chicago: University of Chicago Press.

Rizzo, A. 2009: Transsexual Blackmail Plot Forces Governor of Lazio to Step Down. *The Independent*, 25 October. www.independent.co.uk/ (accessed 23.03.10).

Roberts, B. K. 2002: *Drinking in the Last Chance Saloon: Individual Privacy, Media Intrusion and the Press Complaints Commission*. Manchester Papers in Politics: EPRU Series 1/2003.

Roberts, C. M. 1997: An Easy Call. *American Journalism Review*, January/February. www.ajr.org/ (accessed 04.04.08).

References

Robertson, L. 1998: The Politics of Sex at Salon. *American Journalism Review*, November. www.ajr.org/ (accessed 04.04.08).

Robinson, S. 2009: The Cyber-Newsroom: A Case Study of the Journalistic Paradigm in a News Narratives Journey from Newspaper to Cyberspace. *Mass Communication and Society*, 14 (4): 403–22.

Roehrig, J. and Tillack, H. M. 2010: Müntefering und Lafontaine – verfolgt und ausgespäht. *Stern*, 24 February. www.stern.de (accessed 10.05.10).

Roncarolo, F. 2004: Mediation of Italian Politics and the Marketing of Leaders' Private Lives. *Parliamentary Affairs*, 57 (1): 108–17.

Ross, C. 2008: *Media and the Making of Modern Germany: Mass Communications, Society and Politics from the Empire to the Third Reich.* Oxford: Oxford University Press.

Ross, S. 1988: *Fall From Grace: Sex, Scandal and Corruption in American Politics from 1702 to the Present.* New York: Ballantine Books.

Rössler, B. 2005: *The Value of Privacy.* Cambridge: Polity.

Rössler, P. 2004: Political Communication Messages: Pictures of Our World on Television News. In F. Esser and B. Pfetsch (eds.) *Comparing Political Communication: Theories, Cases and Challenges.* Cambridge: Cambridge University Press.

Rozenberg, J. 2004: *Privacy and the Press.* Oxford: Oxford University Press.

Ruddock, A. 2010: 'I'd Rather be a Cat than a Poodle': What Do Celebrity Politicians Say about Political Communication? In L. Baruh and J. H. Park (eds.) *Reel Politics: Reading Television as a Platform for Political Discourse.* Cambridge: Cambridge Scholars Publishing.

Rudin, K. 1998: Congressional Sex Scandals in History. *The Washington Post.* www.washingtonpost.com/ (accessed 15.05.09).

Ruttenberg, J. 2011: Gossip Machine, Churning Out Cash. *New York Times*, 22 May. www.nytimes.com (accessed 22.05.11).

Sabato, L. J., Stencel, M. and Lichter, S. R. 2000: *Peepshow: Media and Politics in an Age of Scandal.* Lanham, MD: Rowman and Littlefield.

Sachleben, M. 2011: A Framework for Understanding: Sex Scandals in Comparison. In A. Dagnes (ed.) 2011: *Sex Scandals in American Politics: A Multidisciplinary Approach to the Construction and Aftermath of Contemporary Political Sex Scandals.* London: Continuum.

Sanders, K. and Canel, M. J. 2004: Spanish Politicians and the Media: Controlled Visibility and Soap Opera Politics. *Parliamentary Affairs*, 57 (1): 196–208.

Sanders, K. and Canel, M. J. 2006: A Scribbling Tribe: Reporting Political Scandal in Britain and Spain. *Journalism*, 7 (4): 453–76.

Sartori, G. 1970: Concept Misinformation in Comparative Politics. *The American Political Science Review*, 64 (4): 1033–53.

Sartori, G. (ed.) 1984: *Social Science Concepts: A Systematic Analysis.* London: Sage.

References

Scarrow, S. E. 2000: Parties without Members? Party Organization in a Changing Electoral Environment. In R. J. Dalton and M. P. Wattenberg (eds.) *Parties without Partisans: Political Change in Advanced Industrial Democracies.* Oxford: Oxford University Press.

Scarrow, S. E., Webb, P. and Farrell, D. 2000: From Social Integration to Electoral Contestation: The Changing Distribution of Power within Political Parties. In R. J. Dalton and M. P. Wattenberg (eds.) *Parties without Partisans: Political Change in Advanced Industrial Democracies.* Oxford: Oxford University Press.

Schickel, R. 2000: *Intimate Strangers: The Culture of Celebrity in America.* Chicago: Ivan R. Dee.

Schmitt, H. and Holmberg, S. 1995: Political Parties in Decline? In H.-D. Klingemann and D. Fuchs (eds.) *Citizens and the State.* Oxford: Oxford University Press.

Schoenbach, K., Stuerzebecher, D. and Schneider, B. 1998: German Journalists in the Early 1990s. In D. H. Weaver (ed.) *The Global Journalist: News People around the World.* Cresskill, NJ: Hampton Press.

Schroeder, A. 2004: *Celebrity-in-Chief: How Show Business Took Over the White House.* Boulder, CO: Westview Press.

Schudson, M. 1995: *The Power of News.* Cambridge, MA: Harvard University Press.

Schudson, M. 2004: Notes on Scandal and the Watergate Legacy. *American Behavioural Scientist,* 47 (9): 1231–8.

Scott, A. 2009: Flash Flood or Slow Burn? Celebrities, Photographers and Protection from Harassment. *LSE Law, Society and Economy Working Papers,* 13/2009. www.lse.ac.uk (accessed 0-.05.10).

Seaton, J. 2003: Public, Private and the Media. *Political Quarterly,* 74 (2): 174–83.

Seib, P. M. 2002: *Going Live: Getting the News Right in a Real-Time, Online World.* Lanham, MD: Rowman and Littlefield.

Sennett, R. 2002[1974]: *The Fall of Public Man.* London: Penguin.

Seymour-Ure, C. 2003: *Prime Ministers and the Media: Issues of Power and Control.* Oxford: Blackwell.

Shackelford, S. J. 2011: *Fragile Merchandise: A Comparative Analysis of the Privacy Rights for Public Figures.* ExpressO. http://works.bepress.com/scott_shackelford/9 (accessed 04.10.11).

Shepard, A. C. 1998: A Scandal Unfolds. *American Journalism Review,* March. www.ajr.org/ (accessed 04.05.11).

Shepard, A. C. 1999: Gatekeepers without Gates. *American Journalism Review,* March. www.ajr.org/ (accessed 04.04.08).

Sipes, C. 2011: Men, Mistresses and Media Framing: Examining Political Sex Scandals. In A. Dagnes (ed.) *Sex Scandals in American Politics: A Multi-disciplinary approach to the Construction and Aftermath of Contemporary Political Sex Scandals.* London: Continuum.

References

Smith, A. 2008: New Man or Son of the Manse? Gordon Brown as a Reluctant Celebrity Father. *British Politics*, 3 (4): 556–75.

Solove, D. J. 2007: *The Future of Reputation: Gossip, Rumour and Privacy on the Internet*. New Haven, CT: Yale University Press.

Sparks, C. 2000: Introduction: The Panic over Tabloid News. In C. Sparks and J. Tulloch (eds.) *Tabloid Tales: Global Debates over Media Standards*. Lanham, MD: Rowman and Littlefield .

Sparks, C. and Tulloch, J. (eds.) 2000: *Tabloid Tales: Global Debates over Media Standards*. Lanham, MD: Rowman and Littlefield.

Sparrow, A. 2012: Hunt Hails Greater than Expected Agreement on Newspaper Regulation. *The Guardian*, 12 February. www.guardian.co.uk/ (accessed 17.02.12).

Spectator 2009a: Top 50 Political Scandals: Part One. *The Spectator*, 8 July. www.spectator.co.uk (accessed 05.02.10).

Spectator 2009b: Top 50 Political Scandals: Part Two. *The Spectator*, 16 July. www.spectator.co.uk (accessed 05.02.10).

Splichal, S. and Garrison, B. 2000: Covering Public Officials: Gender and Privacy Issue Differences. *Journal of Mass Media Ethics*, 15 (3): 167–79.

Stanyer, J. 2007: *Modern Political Communication: Mediated Politics in Uncertain Times*. Cambridge: Polity.

Stanyer, J. 2008: Elected Representatives, Online Self-Presentation and the Personal Vote: Party, Personality and Webstyles in the United States and United Kingdom. *Information, Communication and Society*, 11 (3): 414–31.

Stanyer, J. and Wring, D. 2004: Public Images, Private Lives: An Introduction. *Parliamentary Affairs*, 57 (1): 1–8.

Stephanopoulos, G. 1997: White House Confidential. *Newsweek*, 5 May: 34.

Stern, 2010: Weitere Politiker im Visier von CMK. *Stern*, 3 March. www.stern.de (accessed 10.05.10).

Street, J. 2004: Celebrity Politicians: Popular Culture and Political Representation. *The British Journal of Politics and International Relations*, 6 (4): 435–52.

Street, J. 2011: *Mass Media, Politics and Democracy*. Basingstoke: Palgrave (2nd edition).

Strudwick, P. 2010: Outrageous and Proud: Why Peter Tatchell Will Never Stop Fighting. *The Independent*, 7 May. www.independent.co.uk (accessed 10.05.10).

Summers, J. H. 2007[2000]: What Happened to Sex Scandals? Politics and Peccadilloes, Jefferson to Kennedy. In N. Negrine and J. Stanyer (eds.) *The Political Communication Reader*. London: Routledge.

Sutter, D. 2006: Media Scrutiny and the Quality of Public Officials. *Public Choice*, 129 (1/2): 25–40.

Sweney, M. 2008: Sarkozy and Bruni Win Ryanair Payout. *The Guardian*, 5 February. www.guardian.co.uk/ (accessed 07.07.09).

References

Tambini, D. and Heyward, C. 2002: Introduction. In D. Tambini and C. Heyward (eds.) *Ruled by Recluses? Privacy, Journalism and the Media after the Human Rights Act*. London: IPPR.

Tebbel, J. and Watts, S. M. 1985: *The Press and the Presidency: From George Washington to Ronald Reagan*. New York: Oxford University Press.

Thompson, J. B. 1995: *The Media and Modernity*. Cambridge: Polity.

Thompson, J. B. 2000: *Political Scandal*. Cambridge: Polity.

Thompson, J. B. 2011: Shifting Boundaries of Public and Private Life. *Theory, Culture and Society*, 28 (4): 49–70.

Thussu, D. K. 2007: *News as Entertainment: The Rise of Global Infotainment*. London: Sage.

Tiffen, R. 1999: *Scandals: Media, Politics and Corruption in Contemporary Australia*. Sydney: University of New South Wales Press.

Tilly, C. and Goodin, R. E. 2006: It Depends. In R. E. Goodin and C. Tilly (eds.) *The Oxford Handbook of Contextual Political Analysis*. Oxford: Oxford University Press.

Timberg, T. and Erler, B. 2002: *Television Talk: A History of the Talk Show*. Austin, TX: University of Texas Press.

Tomlinson, J. 1997: 'And Besides, the Wench is Dead': Media Scandals and the Globalization of Communication. In J. Lull and S. Hinerman (eds.) *Media Scandals: Morality and Desire in the Popular Culture Marketplace*. Cambridge: Polity.

Tremblay, M. and Paternotte, D. (eds.) 2011: *The Lesbian and Gay Movement and the State: Comparative Insight into a Transformed Relationship*. Farnham: Ashgate.

Trouille, H. 2000: Private Life and Public Image: Privacy Legislation in France. *International Comparative Law*, 49 (1): 199–208.

Tumber, H. 2004: Scandal and the Media in the United Kingdom. *American Behavioral Scientist*, 47 (8): 1122–37.

Tumber, H. and Waisbord, S. R. 2004a: Introduction: Political Scandals and Media across Democracies, Part 1. *American Behavioral Scientist*, 47 (8): 1031–9.

Tumber, H. and Waisbord, S. R. 2004b: Introduction: Political Scandals and Media across Democracies, Part 2. *American Behavioral Scientist*, 47 (9): 1143–52.

Tunstall, J. 1996: *Newspaper Power*. Oxford: Oxford University Press.

Turner, G., Bonner, F. and Marshall, P. D. 2000: *Fame Games: The Production of Celebrity in Australia*. Cambridge: Cambridge University Press.

Van Aelst, P., Sheafer, T. and Stanyer, J. 2012: The Personalization of Mediated Political Communication: Operationalizing Key Concepts for the Analysis of News Content. *Journalism*, 13 (2): 203–30.

Van Zoonen, L. 1991: A Tyranny of Intimacy? Women, Femininity and Television News. In P. Dahlgren and C. Sparks (eds.) *Communication and Citizenship: Journalism and the Public Sphere*. London: Routledge.

References

Van Zoonen, L. 1998: The Ethics of Making Private Life Public. In K. Brants, J. Hermes and L. Van Zoonen (eds.) *The Media in Question: Popular Cultures and Public Interests*. London: Sage.

Van Zoonen, L. 2005: *Entertaining the Citizen: When Politics and Popular Culture Converge*. Lanham, MD: Rowman and Littlefield.

Van Zoonen, L. 2006: The Personal, the Political and the Popular: A Woman's Guide to Celebrity Politics. *European Journal of Cultural Studies*, 9 (3): 287–301.

Van Zoonen, L. and Holtz-Bacha, C. 2000: Personalisation in Dutch and German Politics: The Case of the TalkShow. *Javnost: The Public*, 7 (2): 45–56.

Van Zoonen, L., Muller, F., Alinejad, D., Dekker, M., Duits, L., Van Romondot Vis, P. and Wittenberg, W. 2007: Dr Phil Meets the Candidates: How Family Life and Personal Experience Produce Political Discussions. *Critical Studies in Media Communication* 24 (4): 323–38.

Vargo, M. E. 2003: *Scandal: Infamous Gay Controversies of the 20th Century*. New York: Hartington Park Press.

Vest, J. 1998: Secret Lives of Republicans Part One. *Salon.com*, 11 September. www.salon.com/news/1998/09/11newsb.html (accessed 17.02.10).

Walker, K. 2007: Gordon Bean's holiday: Premier heads for the beach but he keeps his jacket on. *Daily Mail*, 4 August. www.dailymail.co.uk/ (accessed 31.11.10).

Watson, R. P. 2000: *Presidents' Wives Reassessing the Office of the First Lady*. New York: Lynne Rienner.

Wattenberg, M. P. 1996: *The Decline of American Political Parties 1952–1994*. Cambridge, MA: Harvard University Press.

Wayne, S. J. 2000: Presidential Personality: The Clinton Legacy. In M. J. Rozell and C. Wilcox (eds.) *The Clinton Scandal*. Washington, DC: Georgetown University Press.

Wead, D. (2003) *All the President's Children: Triumph and Tragedy in the Lives of America's First Families*. New York: Atria Books.

Weaver, D. H. 1996: Journalists in Comparative Perspective: Background and Professionalism. *Javnost: The Public*, 3 (4): 83–91.

Weaver, D. H. 1998: Journalists around the World: Commonalities and Differences. In D. H. Weaver (ed.) *The Global Journalist: News People around the World*. Cresskill, NJ: Hampton Press.

Weaver, D. H. and Bimber, B. 2008: Finding News Stories: A Comparison of Searches Using LexisNexis and Google News. *Journalism and Mass Communication Quarterly*, 85 (3): 515–31.

Webb, P., Farrell, D. and Holliday, I. (eds.) 2002: *Political Parties in Advanced Industrial Democracies*. Oxford: Oxford University Press.

Weintraub, J. and Kumar, K. (eds.) 1997: *Public and Private in Thought and Practice: Perspectives on a Grand Dichotomy*. Chicago: University of Chicago Press.

References

West, D. M. 2001: *The Rise and Fall of the Media Establishment*. New York: Bedford / St Martin's.

West, D. M. and Orman, J. 2003: *Celebrity Politics*. Upper Saddle River, NJ: Prentice Hall.

White, M. 2007: Why Gordon Brown Needs More than a Four Hour Holiday. *The Guardian*, G2 Section, 15 August, p. 2.

White, M. 2008: Say Cheese! *The Guardian*, G2 Section, 29 July, p. 7.

Whitman, J. Q. 2004: Two Western Cultures of Privacy: Dignity versus Liberty. *Yale Law Journal*, 113 (April): 1153–96.

Whittle, S. and Cooper, G. 2009: *Privacy, Probity and Public Interest*. Oxford: Reuters Institute for the Study of Journalism.

Wilby, P. 2005: Private Moments and Public Motives: Leisure Interests of Public Figures. *The Independent*, 17 August. www.independent.co.uk (accessed 01.03.10).

Wilcox, C. and Robinson, C. 2010: *Onward Christian Soldiers? The Religious Right in American Politics*. Boulder, CO: Westview Press (4th edition).

Williams, B. A. and Delli Carpini, M. X. 2000: Unchained Reaction: The Collapse of Media Gatekeeping and the Clinton–Lewinsky Scandal. *Journalism*, 1 (1): 61–85.

Williams, B. A. and Delli Carpini, M. X. 2004: Monica and Bill All the Time and Everywhere. *American Behavioural Scientist*, 47 (9): 1208–30.

Williams, D. K. 2010: *God's Own Party: The Making of the Christian Right*. New York: Oxford University Press.

Williams, J. A. 2004: Privacy, Publicity, and the Conditions of Democratic Citizenship. In P. Apostolidis and J. A. Williams (eds.) *Public Affairs: Politics in the Age of Sex Scandals*. Durham, NC: Duke University Press.

Wilson, J. 2011: Sunrise to Sunset: Kevin Rudd as Celebrity in Australia's Post-Broadcast Democracy. *Celebrity Studies*, 2 (1): 97–9.

Winfield, B. H. and Friedman, B. 2003: Gender Politics: News Coverage of the Candidates' Wives in Campaign 2000. *Journalism and Mass Communication Quarterly*, 80 (3): 548–66.

Winnet, R. and Prince, R. 2008: Public Should Know What Makes Me Tick, Says Cameron. *Daily Telegraph*, 15 March, p. 10.

Wirth, W. and Kolb, S. 2004: Designs and Methods of Comparative Political Communication Research. In F. Esser and B. Pfetsch (eds.) *Comparing Political Communication: Theories, Cases and Challenges*. Cambridge: Cambridge University Press.

Wolcott, J. 2007: Why Are British Sex Scandals So Much Better than Ours? *Vanity Fair*, February. www.vanityfair.com (accessed 02.11.07).

Wouters, C. 1986: Formalization and Informalization: Changing Tension Balances in Civilizing Processes. *Theory, Culture and Society*, 3 (2): 1–18.

Wright, T. 2009: Forget Staid: Adelaide has Randygate. *The Age*, 23 November. www.theage.com.au/ (accessed 26.04.10).

References

Wu, H. D. 2000: Systematic Determinants of International News Coverage: A Comparison of 38 Countries. *Journal of Communication*, Spring: 110–30.

Zaller, J. 1998: Monica Lewinsky's Contribution to Political Science. *PS: Political Science and Politics*, 31 (2): 182–9.

Zaller, J. 1999: Market Competition and News Quality. Paper presented at the American Political Science Association annual meeting, Atlanta, GA, August–September.

Index

Numbers shown in italics refer to figures.

Abbott, Tony, 80
Adam, S., 25
adultery: measuring, 175–7
Adut, A., 20, 77, 111
Affleck, Ben, 47
Allason, Rupert, 107
Amato, Giuliano, 58, 64, 184
Anderson, Robin, 19
Archer, Jeffrey, 80
Arendt, Hannah, 161
Ashby, David, 99, 134, 136
Ashdown, Paddy, 134, 136
Attias, Richard, 145
Australia
    attitude to privacy intrusion, 85–6, 185
    Christian right in, 91, 187
    intimization levels summarized, 153, 154–60
    measuring outing, 187–8
    media partisanship, 90
    privacy protection, 79–80, 81
    reporting of other countries' sex scandals, 139–41
    tabloid media, 66, 89, 185
Australian politicians

birthdays, 46, 47, 48, 49
books about, 55, 56
families, 36, 37
holidays, 39, 40, 41
homes, 42–4
personal lives' visibility, 56, 57–9, 60, 62, 69–70, 71
private lives, 3–4
sex lives, 73, 74, 76, 85–6, 89, 93, 94
    changing exposure, 102, 103, 104
    reported abroad, 131–8
on talk shows, 53, 54
Australian Story (TV programme), 42–4
Aznar, José María
    family, 35
    holidays, 39
    personal life's visibility, 57, 58, 59, 63, 183

Barker, Greg, 89
Barr, Bob, 108
Bartlett, D., 85–6
Bastien, F., 51, 174
Bauman, Z., 13
BBC, 86–7
Beazley, Kim, 4, 43, 44

Belafonte, Harry, 45
Bender, Annette, 124
Berlusconi, Barbara, 36
Berlusconi, Marina, 174
Berlusconi, Pier Silvio, 174
Berlusconi, Silvio
  holidays, 40
  personal life's visibility, 56, 58,
    59–60, 64, 70, 183
  politicization of his scandals, 165
  researching, 177
  self-exposure, 3
  sex life, 74, 118–22, 139–41,
    143–5, 147, 149
  on talk shows, 3, 53
Bertolaso, Guido, 122, 123
Beust, Ole von, 95
Beyer, Friederike, 124
Big Government, 146
Bilger-Street, H., 81
Bingham, A., 102
Biolay, Benjamin, 139
birthdays, 44–9, 173
Bisek, Callista, 88, 110
Black, Cilla, 46
Blair, Cherie
  birthdays, 49
  holidays, 38–9
  intimization's consequences for, 165
  personal life's visibility, 34–5, 36
  and privacy protection, 80–1
  self-exposure, 2
Blair, Euan, 35, 36
Blair, Tony
  birthdays, 46, 48
  books about, 55, 56
  family, 21
  and growth in UK intimization, 25
  holidays, 38–9, 40–1, 165–6
  home, 42
  personal life's visibility, 57, 58, 59,
    61, 69, 183
  and privacy protection, 21

  self-exposure, 2
  on talk shows, 52
blogactive.com, 97
Blunkett, David, 135
Boling, P., 96–7
Bon Jovi, Jon, 45
Bonner, F., 42–3
books, 55–6, 174–5
Booth, Hartley, 106, 135
Boothby, Lord, 108
Bourne, B., 81
Brady, H. E., 25
Breit, R., 85–6
Breitbart, Andrew, 146
Britton, Nan, 111–12
Brown, Fraser, 52
Brown, Gordon
  holidays, 39
  personal life's visibility, 57, 58, 59,
    61, 69, 183
  on talk shows, 52–3
Brown, Jennifer, 52
Brown, Michael, 99
Brown, Nick, 99
Brown, Sarah, 35, 47, 49, 52, 80, 173
Bruni, Carla
  birthday party for Sarkozy, 46
  personal life's visibility, 36
  and privacy protection, 82
  researching, 177
  self-exposure, 2, 35, 40
  sex life, 6, 85, 139–40
Buntegate scandal, 117, 123–5, 169
Burton, Dan, 108, 133, 134, 136,
  137
Bush, Barbara, 47
Bush, George Snr, 38, 51, 58, 60, 183
Bush, George W.
  birthday presents for Laura, 47
  birthdays, 45
  books about, 55
  Christian right policies, 186–7
  holidays, 38, 40, 166

Index

personal life's visibility, 57, 58, 60, 69, 183
on talk shows, 3, 51
Bush, Laura, 3, 34, 47, 49, 51
Bute, Lord, 113

Cacciari, Massimo, 118
Cairns, Jim, 102
Caithness, Earl, 106
calibration, 67, 178–9
Callaghan, Audrey, 42
Callaghan, Jim, 38
Calvert, C., 19
Cameron, David, 1, 2, 39, 52
Canada, 51
Canel, M. J., 35, 82
Carfagna, Mara, 118, 149
Carter, Jimmy, 50
Castells, M., 73
Chantelois, Michelle, 86
Chappaquiddick incident, 22, 101–2, 108
Chase, Chevy, 47
Chenoweth, Helen, 108, 133, 134, 135, 136
Cher, 47
Chifley, Ben, 102
children
privacy protection, 83
see also families and family life
Chirac, Claude, 174
Chirac, Jacques, 40, 57, 58, 59, 84, 183
Clarín, El (newspaper), 149
Clark, A., 112
Clegg, Nick, 50
Clinton, Bill
birthdays, 45, 48
books about, 55, 56
family life, 41
and growth in US intimization, 22
impeachment attempt and effects, 105, 107–10, 188

personal life's visibility, 58, 60, 69, 183
politicization of Lewinsky scandal, 164–5
public reaction to Lewinsky scandal, 162–3
self-exposure, 3
sex life, 4, 21, 87, 88, 131
reported abroad, 24, 134, 135, 136, 137, 138
reported on Internet, 146, 148
on talk shows, 51
Clinton, Chelsea, 36
Clinton, Hillary, 34, 36, 37–8, 46–7, 49
Coe, Sebastian, Lord, 81
Collier, D., 25
Condit, Gary, 80, 134, 135, 136, 137
confidentiality agreements, 80–1
Coolidge, Grace, 34
Corner, J., 12–14
Corriere della Sera (newspaper), 120–1
Costello, Peter, 80
Coty, René, 42
Craig, Larry, 95, 97
Craxi, Bettino, 118
Crean, Simon, 43
critical junctures and moments
definition, 22, 104–5, 189
effect on intimization, 22–3
examples, 105–10, 117–29, 158–9, 188
Curry, David, 135
Curtis, Richard, 91

D'Addario, Patrizia, 120, 122, 140–1
Daily Mail, 127
Daily Mirror, 127
Dakhlia, J., 1, 6
Dale, Ian, 147
D'Alema, Massimo, 40, 58, 64, 184
Davies, Ron, 99

Index

Davis, D., 104
deference, 76
Delbono, Flavio, 122
Della Bosca, John, 86, 89
Delli Carpini, M. X., 66
Despoja, Natasha Stott, 4, 43
Deviers-Joncour, Christine, 84
Diana, Princess of Wales, 167, 168
Diaz, Cameron, 47
Dick, Kirby, 97
Dilke, Charles, 113
Dini, Lamberto, 58, 64, 184
divorce settlements, 5, 168–9
Dole, Bob, 88, 110
Douglas, Helen Gahagan, 112
Douglas Home, Alec, 38
Dowler, Milly, 125
Downer, Alexander, 43
Doyle, D., 22
Drudge, Matt, 24
Drudge Report, 24, 146, 148
Dumas, Alexandre, 116
Dumas, Roland, 84

Edwards, John, 88, 133, 135, 136, 137
Eggert, Heinz, 95, 123
Eisenhower, Dwight D., 111–12
el-Maroug, Karima see Rubacouri,
    Ruby
Elio, Donna Marie, 45
Ensign, John, 91
Epple, Irene, 124
Errera, C., 2, 172
Espinosa, Sonsoles, 85
Espresso, L' (newspaper), 144
Esser, F., 78
Eulenburg-Hertefeld, Prince Philipp
    zu, 115
European Human Rights Act, 126, 168
Evans, Gareth, 85–6

families and family life, 33–44, 165–6,
    173, 174

family values, 90–1, 105–7
Farrell, D., 163
Faure, Félix, 116
Fay, Laura, 88
Finland, 5–6
Fitzgerald, Ella, 45
Flemming, J., 85
Flower, Gennifer, 88
Flynt, Larry, 107–8
Fossella, Vito, 88
France
    attitude to privacy intrusion, 83–4,
        185
    and Christian right, 186
    intimization levels summarized,
        153, 154–60
    measuring outing, 187–8
    media partisanship, 90
    politicization of scandals, 165
    privacy protection, 81–2, 116
    reporting of other countries' sex
        scandals, 132–41
    tabloid press, 66, 185
Frank, Barney, 95
Franklin, Aretha, 45
Franklin, Benjamin, 111
Franklin, Bob, 5
French politicians
    birthdays, 46, 47, 48, 49
    books about, 55, 56
    families, 35, 36, 37
    holidays, 40, 41
    homes, 42, 44
    other studies, 172
    personal lives' visibility, 56, 57–9,
        65–6, 69, 70, 71
    private lives, 1–2, 6
    sex lives, 73, 74–5, 76, 77–8, 79,
        84–5, 93, 94, 95, 103,
        115–16
    reported abroad, 139–40, 145,
        151
    on talk shows, 50, 53, 54

fsQCA, 28–9, 67–71, 91–4, 154,
   178–88
Furedi, F., 19, 23

Garrison, B., 23, 109–10
Gawker, 146–7
gay rights activists, 96–7, 98–9, 100,
   158, 187
George III, King, 112–13
German politicians
   birthdays, 46, 47, 48, 49
   books about, 55, 56
   families, 36, 37
   holidays, 39–40, 41
   homes, 44
   intrusive reporting overseas, 145
   personal lives' visibility, 56, 57–8,
      60, 64–5, 70, 71
   private lives, 3, 6
   sex lives, 6, 73, 74–5, 78, 79, 84,
      93, 94, 95, 142–4
      changing exposure, 103, 114–15,
         117, 123–5
   on talk shows, 50, 51, 54
Germany
   attitude to privacy intrusion, 83,
      84, 185
   and Christian right, 186
   intimization levels summarized,
      153, 154–60
   measuring outing, 187–8
   media partisanship, 90
   press intrusion scandals, 117,
      123–5, 169
   privacy protection, 82, 115
   research constraints, 172
   reporting of other countries' sex
      scandals, 132–41
   tabloid press, 66, 185
Gillard, Julia, 43
Gingrich, Marianne, 110
Gingrich, Newt, 88, 110, 176
Giscard d'Estaing, Mme, 42

Giscard d'Estaing, Valéry, 42
Giuliani, Rudy, 134, 136
Goffman, E., 14
González, Felipe, 58, 63, 70, 184
Goodin, R. E., 28
Goodman, Clive, 125
Gore, Al, 3, 34, 51
Gorton, John, 102
Gray, James, 88
Grenville, George, 113
Guido Fawkes, 148

Hague, William, 5, 148
Hall, A., 114, 115
Hallin, D. C., 90
Hamlish, Marvin, 45
Harden, Maximilian, 115
Harding, Florence, 33–4
Harding, Warren, 101, 111–12
Harmer, Emily, 173
Harrison, J., 85–6
Harry, Prince, 125
Hart, Gary, 23, 108
Hartung, U., 78
Hatfield, Mark, 97
Hawke, Bob, 46, 58, 62, 69–70, 184
Hayes, Jerry, 99, 134, 136, 137
Heath, Edward, 38
Heffernan, R. A., 34–5
Hirdman, A., 11, 12
Hirst, Michael, 107, 134, 135, 136
Hogan, J., 22
holidays, 37–41, 165–6, 173
Holtz-Bacha, C., 51, 64–5, 143
homosexuality
   gay rights activists, 96–7, 98–9,
      100, 158, 187
   measuring outing, 175–7, 187–8
   reporting, 94–100, 115, 158, 167
Horton, D., 10
House of Commons Culture, Media
      and Sport Committee, 167
houses and homes, 41–4

Howard, John
  birthdays, 48
  holidays, 39
  home, 4, 43–4
  personal life's visibility, 58, 62,
      69–70, 183
  and social conservatism, 187
  and talk shows, 53
Hughes, Robert, 107
Huhne, Chris, 5
Hunter, Rielle, 88
Hyde, Henry, 108, 133, 134, 135,
      136, 137

Ian Dale's Diary, 147
IMDB *see* Internet Movie Data Base
Inglehart, R., 75–6
injunctions, 81, 126, 148, 168
Internet
  checking of sources, 176
  impact on politicians' image, 162
  role in intimization, 24, 131,
      146–51, 160
Internet Movie Data Base (IMDB), 174
interviews, 18, 49–54
intimization
  causation analysis methods, 178–88
  causation summary, 154–60
  consequences, 161–7
  definition, 12–17
  drivers, 17–22
  growth trend summary, 156–7,
      158–60
  introduction to concept, 9–12
  national differences, 23–4
  study analysis methods, 28–9,
      66–71, 171–88
  study selection criteria, 24–8
Iseman, Vicki, 110
Isikoff, Michael, 148
Italian politicians
  birthdays, 47, 48, 49
  books about, 55, 56

families, 36, 37
holidays, 40, 41
homes, 44
personal lives' visibility, 56, 57–60,
      64, 70, 71
private lives, 3
sex lives, 73, 74–5, 93, 94, 103,
      117–23, 139–41, 143–5, 149
on talk shows, 53, 54
Italy
  attitude to privacy intrusion, 83,
      84, 185
  blogs, 147, 149
  and Christian right, 186
  intimization levels summarized,
      153–60
  measuring outing, 187–8
  media partisanship, 90, 119–21
  politicization of scandals, 165
  privacy protection, 82
  reporting of other countries' sex
      scandals, 132–41
  research constraints, 172
  tabloid press, 66, 185

Jellicoe, Earl, 102
Johnson, Boris, 88
Johnson, Lyndon B., 101, 112
Jones, Nick, 106
Jones, Paula, 87, 148
journalism and journalists *see* media
Joyce, Barnaby, 43
Juanno, Chantal, 139

Kasich, John, 96
Keating, Paul, 39, 58, 62, 69–70, 184
Keetch, Paul, 88
Kennedy, Jacqueline, 34, 41
Kennedy, John F., 45, 51, 101, 112
Kennedy, Ted, 22, 101–2
Kennedy family, 22–3, 101–2
Kernot, Cheryl, 4, 85–6
Kerry, John, 169

Kilpatrick, Kwame, 133, 136, 137
Kleberg, M., 11, 12
Kluttz, Jerry, 112
Kohl, Hannelore, 84
Kohl, Helmut
  birthdays, 46
  holidays, 39–40
  personal life's visibility, 58, 65, 70,
    184
  sex life, 84
Kopechne, Mary Jo, 22, 101–2
Kraus, S., 104
Kuhn, R., 2, 6, 77–8
Kuronen, Susan, 5–6

Lafontaine, Oskar, 124
Lambton, Lord, 102
Lang, G., 104
Lang, G. E., 10
Lang, K., 10, 104
Langer, A. I., 2, 64–5, 172
Lario, Veronica, 118–20, 140–1
Latham, Mark, 4
Laws, David, 5
Lee, Chris, 147
Lee, Peggy, 45
LeHand, Missy, 111–12
Lengauer, G., 8
Leno, Jay, 51
Letizia, Noemi, 119, 120, 140–1, 147
Leveson inquiry, 126
Lewinsky, Monica
  affair with Clinton, 4, 24, 87, 131,
    138
  impact of scandal, 21, 22
  Internet coverage, 146, 148
  politicization of scandal, 164–5
  public reaction to scandal, 162–3
libel law, 80
Lichter, S. R., 87, 88, 189
Lindsay, D., 116
Livingston, Bob, 108, 133, 134, 135,
  136, 137

Lloyd George, David, 113
Lowenthal, L., 11

McAllister, I., 66, 163
McCain, John, 110, 133, 134, 135,
  136, 137
McCormick, N., 80
McGraw, Phil, 51
McGreevey, James, 95, 135
McKay, S., 42–3
McLellan, T., 85–6
Macmillan, Dorothy, 113
Macmillan, Harold, 38
McNair, B., 162
Mahoney, J., 189
Maier, M., 25
Mail on Sunday, 127, 142–4
Maischberger, Sandra, 142
Major, James, 35
Major, John
  'back-to-basics' speech and effects,
    105–7, 109–10, 188
  birthdays, 46
  holidays, 38
  personal life's visibility, 58, 61,
    69–70, 183
  politicization of scandals during
    leadership, 165
  sex life, 80
Mancini, P., 90
Marks, Rosalind, 80–1
Marrazzo, Piero, 122–3
Matin, Le (newspaper), 145
MDSD, 29
media
  adversarial partisanship, 90, 93–4
  attitude to adultery, 76–8, 78–9
  checking sources, 175–7
  ethical codes, 83–8, 95, 109–10
  globalization's effects, 130–51,
    159–60
  growth in tabloid style, 66
  see also Internet; press; television

Index

Mellor, David, 5, 106, 134, 136
Merchant, Piers, 107, 137
Merkel, Angela
  birthdays, 46
  holidays, 40
  intrusive reporting by overseas
    press, 145
  personal life's visibility, 56, 58, 60,
    65, 70, 184
Messner, Reinhold, 40
Meyer, Eugene, 112
Meyrowitz, Joshua, 10, 17, 161
Milligan, Steven, 107
Mitterand, François, 58, 59, 70, 76,
  184
Mitterand, Frédéric, 95
Moltke, General Graf von, 115
Monde, Le (newspaper), 132–3, 134
Monroe, Marilyn, 45, 112
Monti, Mario, 123
Morgan, Piers, 52–3
Morris, Dick, 37–8
Morrison, D. E., 83, 86
Mortimore, R., 163
MSSD, 29
Mulcaire, Glenn, 125
Münterfering, Franz, 124
Murdoch, Rupert, 126, 144–5

Nader, Ralph, 51
Nagel, Thomas, 21, 159
Neal, Belinda, 43
Netherlands, 3
Neveu, E., 50, 53, 162
News of the World, 117, 125–7, 128,
  167
Newsom, Gavin, 146
newspapers see press
Nexis UK, 171–2, 173, 176
Nixon, Richard, 41, 51
Norman, Greg, 46
Norris, P., 75–6
Norris, Steven, 106

Oaten, Mark, 133, 134, 135, 136,
  137
Obama, Barack
  birthdays, 45–6, 47, 48
  books about, 56
  holidays, 38, 40
  personal life's visibility, 58, 59, 69,
    183
  on privacy intrusion, 1
  on talk shows, 51–2
Obama, Michelle, 34, 36, 47, 49
O'Donnell, Christine, 147
O'Donnell, Rosie, 47
Oehlkers, P. W., 131
Oettinger, Günther, 124
O'Shea, Kitty, 113
outing, 94–100, 158, 167, 175–7,
  187–8
Outrage (documentary), 97
Outrage! (activist group), 99

Paar, Jack, 51
País, El (newspaper), 132–3, 137,
  143–4
Paris Match (magazine), 42
Parnell, Charles, 113
Parry-Giles, S., 19
Parry-Giles, T., 19
Paterno, S., 110
Paterson, David, 133, 135, 136,
  137
Paxon, Bill, 96
PCC see Press Complaints
  Commission
Perloff, R. M., 2–3
Perot, Ross, 51
Perry, Rick, 96
personal life
  disclosure types, 15–17
  domain mapping, 13–15, 15
  modern obsession with disclosure,
    19–20
  politicization, 163–6

personalization concept and literature, 7–8

Phillips, Carrie, 111–12

Pickering, Chip, 91

Pingeot, Anne, 76

Plasser, F., 8

politicians
  deference to, 76
  inclusion criteria, 176–7
  measuring average visibility, 179–84
  operation spheres, 12–14, *13*
  personal sphere, 13–15, *15*
  politicization of personal lives, 163–6
  reasons for non-consensual exposure, 20–1
  reasons for self-disclosure, 17–20

Politician's Wife, The (TV programme), 5

Ponce de Leon, C. L., 11

Pozzi, Moana, 118

Prescott, John, 89, 133, 134, 135, 136, 137, 147

presidents, and intimization, 18–19, 25, 68–71, 182

press
  adversarial partisanship, 90, 93, 100, 185
  checking of sources, 175–7
  coverage of sex scandals abroad, 131–45
  intrusion scandals, 117, 123–7, 166–7, 169
  measuring size of tabloid, 181–2
  regulatory bodies, 81, 126–7, 167, 168
  researching, 171–3
  tabloid campaign against greater privacy protection, 168
  tabloid press and intimization, 66, 68–9, 70, 77, 88–9, 92–3, 95–6, 98, 100, 155–8, 186

  see also media

Press Complaints Commission (PCC), 81, 126–7, 167, 168

privacy protection
  effect on levels of exposure, 92–3, 95, 98, 100
  and European Human Rights Act, 126, 168
  history of, 115, 116–17
  measuring, 185
  overview, 79–83
  recent increases, 168–9
  transnational, 24, 142–5

privatization concept and literature, 8–9

Prodi, Romano
  holidays, 40
  personal life's visibility, 58, 64, 70, 184
  self-exposure, 3
  on talk shows, 3, 53

Profumo, John, 102

Radar, 146

Ragin, Charles, 29, 67, 68, 92, 178, 179, 180

Rahat, G., 8, 12

Rann, Mike, 86, 136

Rasmussen, Anders F., 118

Rawlins, W. K., 14

Reagan, Nancy, 45, 47

Reagan, Ronald, 38, 45, 57, 58, 60, 183

Rein, Thérèse, 165

religion
  Christian right and outing, 96, 98–9, 100, 158
  Christian right and sexual fidelity, 90–1, 92, 93, 100, 157–8
  measuring Christian right's presence, 185–6
  Protestant and Catholic attitudes to sexual fidelity, 75–6

Index

Repubblica, La (newspaper), 119–20, 120–1, 144
research methods, 28–9, 66–71, 171–88
Richards, Rod, 107
Ricketson, S., 116
Roberts, B. K., 81
Roberts, C. M., 112
Robinson, Geoffrey, 38
Robinson, Smokey, 45
Rogers, Mike, 97, 167
Roosevelt, Alice, 34
Roosevelt, Eleanor, 34
Roosevelt, Franklin D., 45, 101, 111–12
Roosevelt, Theodore, 111
Ross, S., 22, 101–2
Rössler, B., 7, 161
Royal, Ségolène, 2
Royer-Collard, Pierre Paul, 116
Rubacouri, Ruby (Karima el-Mahroug), 121
Rudd, Kevin
    holidays, 39
    personal life's visibility, 57, 58, 59, 62, 69, 183
    on talk shows, 53
Ruddock, Philip, 43
Rutherford, Lucy Mercer, 111–12
Ryan, Jack, 5
Ryan, Jeri, 5
Ryanair, 82

Sabato, L. J., 87, 88, 189
Sancha, Antonia de, 106
Sanders, K., 35, 82
Sanford, Mark, 91, 134, 135, 136, 137, 138
Sarkozy, Cécilia, 2, 145
Sarkozy, Jean, 165, 174
Sarkozy, Nicolas
    birthdays, 46
    books about, 56
    holidays, 40
    personal life's visibility, 57, 58–9, 69, 157, 183
    and privacy protection, 82
    researching, 177
    self-exposure, 2, 35, 40
    sex life, 6, 74–5, 84–5, 139–40, 145, 151
Sarpong, June, 42
Scharping, Rudolf, 3
Schickel, R., 10, 17
Schrock, Edward, 97
Schroeder, A., 45
Schroeder, Gerhard
    birthdays, 46
    holidays, 40
    personal life's visibility, 56, 58, 65, 70, 184
    researching, 173
    sex life, 6, 142–3, 144
Schumann, Michelle, 124
Schwarzenegger, Arnold, 146, 158–9
Schwind von Egelstein, Sabine, 142–3
Seawright, J., 25
Seehofer, Horst, 124
Sennett, Richard, 9, 161
Seymour-Ure, C., 35
Sheafer, T., 8, 12
Sheridan, Tommy, 133, 135, 137
Signorile, Michelangelo, 97
Sinclair, Malcolm, 134, 135, 136
Solove, D. J., 162
Sonder, Mark, 176
Spain
    attitude to privacy intrusion, 83, 85, 185
    and Christian right, 186
    intimization levels summarized, 153–60
    measuring outing, 187–8
    media partisanship, 90
    privacy protection, 82–3
    research constraints, 172

Index

reporting of other countries' sex
    scandals, 132–41, 143–5
tabloid press, 66, 185
Spanish politicians
    birthdays, 47, 48, 49
    books about, 55, 56
    families, 35, 36, 37
    holidays, 39, 40–1
    homes, 44
    personal lives' visibility, 56, 57–9,
        63, 70, 71
    sex lives, 73, 74–5, 79, 93, 94, 103
    on talk shows, 53, 54
Spitzer, Eliot, 133, 134, 135, 136, 137
Splichal, S., 23, 109–10
Spring, Richard, 106–7, 135
Stampa, La (newspaper), 132–3, 136
Stencel, M., 87, 88, 189
Stern (news magazine), 124
Stevenson, Frances, 113
Stewart, Allan, 107, 134, 136
Strauss-Kahn, Dominique, 165
Streisand, Barbra, 47
Studler, T., 163
Summers, J. H., 22–3
Summers, John, 111, 112, 117
Summersby, Kay, 111–12
Sun (newspaper), 106, 145
Sunday People (newspaper), 127
super injunctions *see* injunctions
Sutter, D., 162
Svennevig, M., 83, 86
Sweden, 11, 12
Switzerland, 145

talk shows, 3, 49–54, 162, 174
Tarantini, Giampaolo, 120
Tatchell, Peter, 99
Taz (newspaper), 132–3, 135
television
    impact on politicians' image, 161,
        162
    role in intimization, 9–10, 17

talk shows, 3, 49–54, 162, 174
    see also media
Temple, Tracey, 89, 147
Thatcher, Margaret
    holidays, 38
    home, 42
    personal life's visibility, 58, 61,
        69–70, 184
    on talk shows, 52
Thatcher, Mark, 35
Thompson, J. B., 13, 74, 76–7, 113,
    114, 162
Tiefensee, Wolfgang, 124
Tiffen, R., 73
Tilly, C., 28
TMZ.com, 146
Tomlinson, J., 134
Topolanek, Mirek, 143
Tumber, H., 77
Turnbull, Malcolm, 43
Twain, Shania, 45
Twitter, 148

Uhl, Hans-Juergen, 123
UK
    attitude to privacy intrusion,
        86–8, 104–7, 108–10, 116–17,
        158–9, 185
    blogs, 147–8
    Christian right in, 91, 187
    history of press, 113
    intimization levels, 25, 153–60
    measuring outing, 187–8
    media partisanship, 90
    politicization of scandals, 165–6
    press intrusion scandals, 125–7,
        167
    privacy protection, 79–81, 116–17,
        126–7, 167, 168
    public reaction to sex scandals, 163
    reporting of other countries' sex
        scandals, 139–41, 142–4
    tabloid press, 66, 88–9, 185

UK politicians
  birthdays, 46, 47, 48, 49
  books about, 55, 56
  families, 11, 34–5, 36, 37
  holidays, 38–9, 40–1
  homes, 41–2, 44
  other studies, 172
  personal lives' visibility, 56–9, 61,
    64–5, 66, 69–70, 71, 72
  private lives, 2, 5
  sex lives, 73, 74–5, 77, 78, 88–9,
    93, 94, 99, 100
    changing exposure, 102, 103,
      104–7, 108–10, 112–14, 117,
      125–7, 128–9
    reported abroad, 131–9
  on talk shows, 52–3, 54
Unità, L' (newspaper), 120–1
US politicians
  birthdays, 44–6, 46–7, 48–9
  books about, 55, 56
  ethical standards, 77
  families, 11, 33–4, 36, 37
  holidays, 37–8, 40–1
  homes, 41, 44
  importance of personal morality for,
    20
  personal lives' visibility, 56, 57–60,
    65–6, 69, 71, 72
  private lives, 2–3, 4–5
  sex lives, 73, 74–5, 76–7, 78–9, 88,
    90–1, 92, 93–8, 99, 100
    changing exposure, 101–2, 103,
      104–5, 107–10, 111–12, 117,
      128
    reported abroad, 131–9
  on talk shows, 51–2, 54
USA
  attitude to privacy intrusion,
    86–8, 104–5, 107–10, 116–17,
    158–9, 185
  attitude to sexual fidelity, 75, 91
  blogs, 146–7, 148

  Christian right in, 90–1, 186–7
  intimization levels, 153–60
  measuring outing, 187–8
  media partisanship, 90, 117
  politicization of scandals, 164–5,
    166
  privacy protection, 79–80, 116–17,
    168–9
  public reaction to sex scandals,
    162–3
  reporting of other countries' sex
    scandals, 139–41
  tabloid press, 66, 88–9, 185

Van Zoonen, L., 11, 14
Vanhanen, Matti, 5–6
Vietnam War, 23
Villaraigosa, Antonio, 134, 136, 146
Vitter, David, 91, 137

Wagenknecht, Sahra, 124
Waigel, Theo, 123–4
Waller, Gary, 106
Washington Post, 110, 112
Webb, P., 34–5
Weber, Juliane, 84
Weiner, Anthony, 146
Weinstein, Harvey, 47
West, Jim E., 95
Widestedt, K., 11, 12
Wilhelm II, Kaiser, 115
Wilkes, John, 112–13
William, Prince, Duke of Cambridge,
  125
Williams, B. A., 66
Williams, J. A., 164
Winfrey, Oprah, 46, 51, 52
Wohl, R., 10
women politicians: personal lives'
  visibility, 62–3
World Wide Web *see* Internet
Wouters, C., 63
Wulff, Christian, 124